D1013657

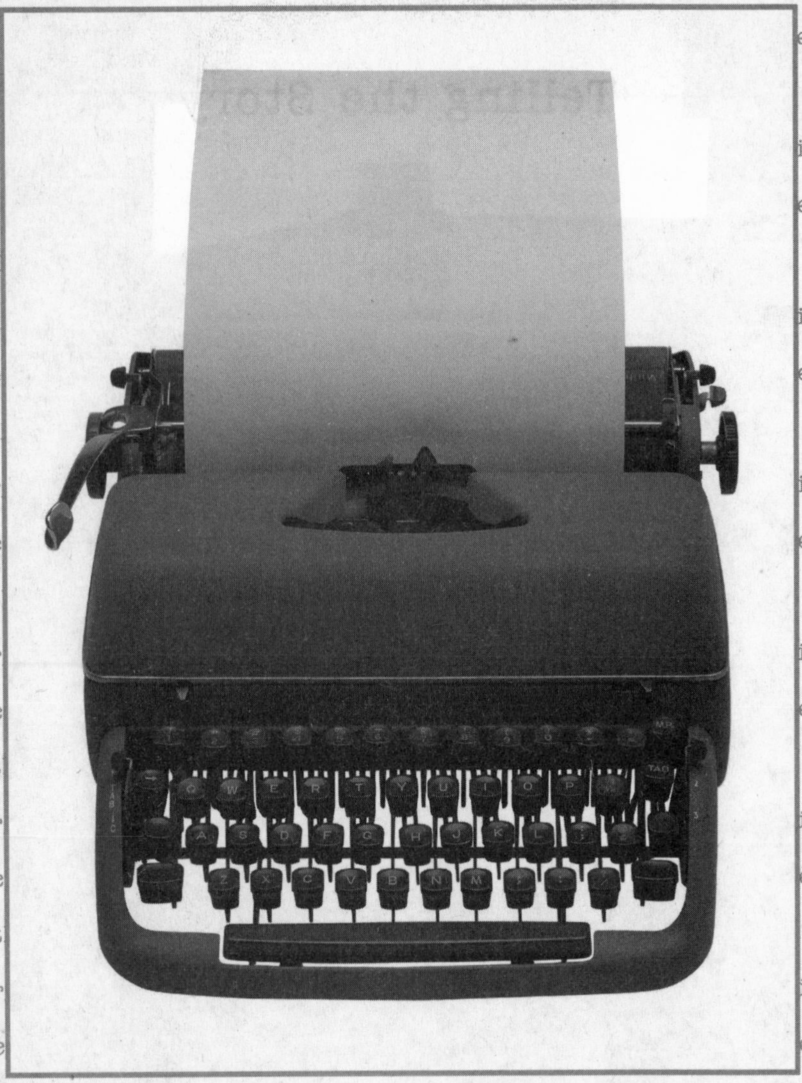

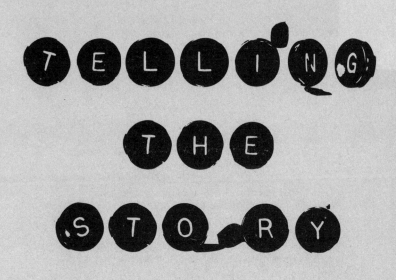

TELLING THE STORY

How to Write and Sell
Narrative Nonfiction

PETER RUBIE

Quill
A HarperResource Book
An Imprint of HarperCollinsPublishers

HarperCollins books may be purchased for educational, business, or sales
promotional use. For information, please write to: Special Markets Department,
HarperCollins Publishers Inc., 10 East 53rd Street, New York, New York 10022.

Designed by Jennifer Ann Daddio

Library of Congress Cataloging-in-Publication Data

Rubie, Peter.
    Telling the story : how to write and sell narrative nonfiction / Peter Rubie.
        p. cm.
    Includes bibliographical references and index.
    ISBN 0-06-053528-8
    1. Authorship. 2. Feature writing. I. Title.

PN145.R733 2003
808'.02—dc21   2003047865

03 04 05 06 07 WBC/RRD 10 9 8 7 6 5 4 3 2 1

ACKNOWLEDGMENTS AND THANKS

To my editor, Edwin Tan, for his encouragement and savvy guidance and care. To my agent, June Clark, for being there and making all the right moves at the right time. To B. Mark Smith, for his helpful advice. To Amy Yarsinske and Randall Silvis, for allowing me to use their proposals. And to my wife, Mel, for putting up with my grouchiness while wrestling with this particular bear.

The profession of book writing
makes horse racing seem like
a solid, stable business.

JOHN STEINBECK, ACCEPTING THE
NOBEL PRIZE FOR LITERATURE

CONTENTS

••••••••••••••••••••

Telling the Story

I N T R O D U C T I O N

....

It's all storytelling, you know.
That's what journalism is all about.

TOM BROKAW, NBC NEWS

 In Cold Blood. All the President's Men. Dispatches. The Perfect Storm. Name some books that have been huge best-sellers over the years and you'll find there's one thing they have in common: they read like a novel, but they are true stories. They all fall into a category now called "narrative nonfiction."

In recent times the success of books such as *Longitude* by Dava Sobel, the story of the invention of the seagoing chronometer; *The Perfect Storm* by Sebastian Junger, a modern-day twist on an old-fashioned, Jack London–esque adventure-cum-science story, relating the sea storm of the century; and Jon Krakauer's *Into Thin Air,* an account of climbing Mount Everest that ended in disaster, has given publishers pause when considering what sells best, and therefore interests the average American most. At one time it was bold, brassy fiction from writers like Harold Robbins, James Mitchener, James Clavell, and Danielle Steel. And certainly, brand-name authors of fiction are still selling well, as the John Grishams, Tom Clancys, and Stephen Kings of this world demonstrate.

But a casual list of other successful books includes narrative nonfiction titles such as Mark Bowden's electrifying reconstruction of the battle of Mogadishu, *Black Hawk Down,* as well as *A Bright and Shining Lie, Walking the Bible, The Soul of a New Machine, The Professor and the Madman, Greed and Glory on Wall Street, Indecent Exposure, Barbarians at the Gate, Den of Thieves,* and *A Civil Action,* to mention but a handful.

There are even substantial awards (ranging from $10,000 to $45,000) that are given out to deserving authors in the genre, two in memory of J. Anthony Lukas (the author of *Common Ground,* who died in 1997) and one in memory of Mark Lynton, a senior executive at Hunter Douglas in the Netherlands.

Writing narrative nonfiction—the novel of true events—is not nearly as simple as it seems. You have not only to construct a strong narrative with characters who readers care about emotionally, but also to pay attention to the veracity and integrity of your narrative. In a novel, on the other hand, what does it matter? It's all an invention based on real life, not an attempt to re-create it.

A Bottom-Line Business

The publishing industry has long bewailed the demise of the midlist novel, considered by many to be the nice, quiet novel of manners and observations of the human condition. Instead, major publishers, certainly, are more focused on blockbusters—those novels that can "break out" and sell in large quantities. Publishing always was, and continues to be even more these days, a bottom-line business. Numbers of books sold count, and the author who cannot move copies of his book will not last long in the major leagues of publishing. This reality may infuriate many, to be sure, and it's not one I defend in terms of encouraging and developing art, but it's nevertheless a fact that one must face. Raging about how things *should* be does nothing to change how they are.

The success and appeal of narrative nonfiction books has infused publishing with fresh blood. The books pounce on an untold or barely told incident and pry it apart, searching for a way to understand, in the microcosm of the story, more about the macrocosm of our world—who we are and why we do the things we do—while at the same time giving us a rattling good yarn.

Narrative nonfiction has also given readers and publishers a much needed blood transfusion, and respite from new regurgitations of the predictable "same-old same-old" that accountants demand in order to satisfy the insatiable appetite of the tyrannical bottom-line approach to big-time publishing. It allows experimental books of nonfiction to be marketed and sold in a predictable way, which keeps the bookstores happy, and yet allows some authors to indulge in experimental writing that would otherwise prove to be very hard to sell on a commercial scale.

Take, for example, one of the more celebrated nonfiction debuts of recent years: Dave Eggers's *A Heartbreaking Work of Staggering Genius.* Eggers's book (not unlike the man himself) is defiantly unconventional. It is an angry, witty coming-of-age memoir that is almost self-consciously inventive. Even as he describes the deaths of his parents and his attempts to care for his younger brother, he deliberately comments on his inability to do justice to the story he is telling, in a disarming (some would say disingenuous) attempt to outpace any conceivable criticism.

During a May 2000 Harvard panel discussion about narrative nonfiction, Walter Kirn, contributing writer to *Time* and literary editor of *GQ,* made some interesting points about narrative nonfiction writing and its appeal to the culture. "It's my contention," he said at the time,

> that we don't live in a very experimental time, literature-wise in fiction. . . . the [19]60's and 70's were times of invention of meta-narrative. We had Goddard films that took everything, cut it up into a million pieces, and threw it up in the air. [Now] we live in a very conventional time, aesthetically, when it comes to storytelling. I've noticed this in novels, and I think it's probably true in nonfiction. . . .
>
> I think we live in a fairly politically and culturally complacent and quiescent time. I don't think those edges or borders are being pushed yet. . . . A lot of this is a feature of not having great stories to tell. There

is not a Vietnam War going on. You have to seek far and wide to find some of these stories now.

The events of 9/11 have changed this, of course, creating a new and still unexplored cultural landscape that is forcing us to confront such issues as individual freedoms and rights to privacy versus the government's need to protect its citizens, and the free press's mandate to make those in power account for their actions.

Creative writing programs around the country have moved away from teaching the art of the short story, and instead focus on self-awareness (some critics might call it self-involvement). Memoir and the concept of the reporter as a participator in a story, not a removed objective observer, are becoming the norm. The courses try to teach the art of reconstructing pithy dialogue, writing in the first person, using the present tense, setting a scene, and so forth. It has become an academic institutionalization of what Gay Talese termed New Journalism, whose guiding principle is to "seek a larger truth than is possible through the mere compilation of the facts."

Some trace the beginnings of New Journalism to Norman Mailer's 1960 *Esquire* piece about Jack Kennedy's nomination, or to Murray Kempton's columns for the *New York Post* in the 1950s. Some argue it can be traced as far back as Nathaniel Hawthorne's 1862 dispatches for the *Atlantic Monthly* magazine from the front lines of the Civil War, making his work the progenitor of George Orwell, Ernie Pyle, John Steinbeck, and others. Contemporary book-length narrative nonfiction is usually considered to date from Truman Capote's *In Cold Blood* (1966), considered by many the grandfather of present-day narrative nonfiction, though oxymoronically described at the time of its publication as a "nonfiction novel." (A novel by definition is a fiction, that is, an invention, while nonfiction by definition is its opposite—*not* fiction but truth.) Capote's book became the inspiration for literary true crime as a successful subgenre of narrative nonfiction, but eventually led to the excesses of Joe McGinniss's *The Last Brother* (1993), a fictionalized biography of the still-living Ted Kennedy that invented his thoughts rather than report interviews with him, and Edmund Morris's *Dutch* (1999), the authorized biography of President Ronald Reagan, which bemused everyone with its fictional narrator and imaginary characters. Before that, Meyer Levin wrote *Compulsion* (1956), a novelistic account of the Leopold-Loeb murders; and before him, Theodore Dreiser based *Sister Carrie* on a real case that illustrated the difficulties of women struggling in newly industrialized America.

This book aims to give some thoughts on how best to meld careful journalistic research with fictional techniques. *Telling the Story* has grown out of my early experiences as a journalist and then publishing house editor, and my later experiences working with authors and editors as an agent who for over 10 years has specialized in representing journalists and books of narrative nonfiction.

A quick definition. You may hear or see the terms "creative nonfiction" and "narrative nonfiction" used interchangeably by teachers and some editors. Strictly speaking, "creative nonfiction" refers to short pieces for newspapers and magazines, while "narrative nonfiction" is used fairly exclusively in book publishing circles to refer to book-length projects. So, while all the information in this book can be applied comfortably to shorter works, it is primarily designed for the writer of long pieces, usually 60,000 words and over.

Something else to bear in mind: writing narrative nonfiction is not something that can be mastered overnight, and this book is designed merely as an introduction to the field. It puts some warning signs by pitfalls to be wary of, and hopefully opens a couple of doors through which you can pass in order to continue your studies in this field. The writer of narrative nonfiction has to be an investigative journalist, an adept researcher and interviewer, and a skilled novelist. That's a tall order for someone who has not done one or more of these things professionally before tackling a narrative nonfiction book.

Writing guides like this can be seen as opinionated and filled with rigid rules. I am not in favor of writing as a form of mass-produced, homogenized factory literature or formulaic successes. But in order to discuss issues of

. . . the . . .

technique and analysis it's important to have a structure and a language of technique to relate to, if only to reject it in favor of something that works better for you. Following the "rules" in this book won't help you write a best-seller or a brilliant piece of journalism. However, if you are an Infant Innocent, this is a good place to start. This book is intended as a tool kit, and a map and crude compass to help you find your way around a deceptively tricky world of writing, that is—as Paul Dickson, an award-winning journalist and author of *Sputnik: The Shock of the Century,* once described it— "possibly the most fun you can have with your clothes on."

Narrative Nonfiction:
The New Genre

. . . .

I got this idea of doing a really serious big work—it would be
precisely like a novel, with a single difference: Every word of it
would be true from beginning to end.

TRUMAN CAPOTE, ON *IN COLD BLOOD*

 While I was preparing to write this book I found myself traveling for a month, for various business and personal reasons. My
wife and I live in New York City, and we set off from there to
visit Seattle and British Columbia, in Canada, before returning to the East Coast to tour New England, eventually returning home via
New York State. We left a day later for England, the country of my childhood.

I hate to shop. My wife—a Southerner—loves the hunt of it. So, while
my wife went trolling for bargains, as usual when on my own in a strange
place I found myself haunting bookstores. Some were independents and
some were part of chain stores (and, by the way, great places to have a cup
of tea and rest up with a book while awaiting the return of the Southern
huntress triumphant with her spoils).

I decided on a whim to search for books by and about narrative nonfiction.
It was an instructive experience: as a genre, "narrative nonfiction" doesn't
exist in most bookstores in the United States, Canada, and England. Yet we all
know what we mean by it: factual writing that reads like a good novel.

A Gathering of Genres

"Narrative nonfiction"—what I would call "the novel of true events"—is really an umbrella term for a collection of genres that *are* found in the bookstore. It can be broadly divided into a number of subgenres—adventure, biography, history, military, memoir, travel, and true crime—though they shade into one another at times (travel *and* adventure, for example, or history, biography, *and* military). This list cannot be considered definitive, however, because narrative nonfiction is a *style* of writing, not limited to a given kind of subgenre. Richard Preston's best-selling *The Hot Zone*, for example, shades into adventure because of the dramatic, novelistic style that Preston uses to write the book, and it has a first-person slant on occasion that tilts it toward memoir. Yet it is neither of these things. *The Hot Zone* is clearly a popular science book. At its heart, it's an account of what happens when one of the world's most virulent viruses, the Ebola virus, breaks out in a laboratory near Washington, D.C., and how it is contained.

Regardless of genre definition, what all these books share is the commonality of being well-written, literate stories with characters, scenes, and a narrative arc, as well as being digests of connected facts.

In May 2000, Robert Vare, senior editor at the *Atlantic Monthly,* moderated a panel discussion at Harvard about narrative nonfiction. He said:

> I think [narrative nonfiction] . . . is essentially a hybrid form, a marriage of the art of storytelling and the art of journalism—an attempt to make drama out of the observable world of real people, real places, and real events. It's a sophisticated form of nonfiction writing, possibly the highest form, that harnesses the power of facts to the techniques of fiction constructing a central narrative, setting scenes, depicting multidimensional characters and, most important, telling the story in a compelling voice that the reader will want to hear.
>
> Nabokov . . . had the most illuminating remarks about narrative. He wrote, "The term 'narrative' is often confused with the term 'plot,' but

they're not the same thing. If I tell you that the king died, and then the queen died, that's not narrative; that's plot. But, if I tell you that the king died, and then the queen died of a broken heart, that's narrative."

. . . narrative nonfiction bridges those connections between events that have taken place, and imbues them with meaning and emotion.

In interviews in fall 2002, Random House executive editor Peter Gethers commented that for him, "narrative nonfiction is not a genre, it's a style. It simply means that nonfiction is told in a compelling way with an emphasis on story." Farrar, Straus and Giroux publisher and editor in chief Jonathan Galassi agreed: "Readers buy books for many reasons, but I don't think the author's approach to his or her material is primary among them, though it may have a powerful effect on a reader's enjoyment of the book."

Little did Walker publisher George Gibson know what he was starting one day in 1994 when he called up a magazine writer named Dava Sobel to talk about turning one of her magazine articles into a book. It was to be more than a history of the invention of the chronometer; it would also be the story of the man who did it. *Longitude*, published in 1995, slowly but steadily took off in the United States and spent 18 weeks on the *New York Times* best-seller list. But when Gibson tried selling the rights to the book in the U.K., it was turned down by publishers over a dozen times before Fourth Estate added it to their list. It went to the best-seller list in England as well. The success of *Longitude* was, in its own way, as important a milestone in the creation of narrative nonfiction as a hot genre as Capote's *In Cold Blood*.

The British edition of *Longitude: The True Story of a Lone Genius Who Solved the Greatest Scientific Problem of His Time* came out in August 1996. Since then, on both sides of the Atlantic, the book has started a gold rush for similar books among publishers. We have seen the rediscovery of books such as Ernest Shackleton's 1914 classic *South,* a tale of remarkable survival and endurance at the South Pole (which led to an IMAX documentary and a TNT television movie), and esoteric stories such as *Fermat's Last Theorem* by Amir D. Aczel and *Fermat's Enigma* by Simon Singh, both of which tell the story of the struggle to solve a seventeenth-century mathematical puzzle, and Janet Gleeson's *The Arcanum,* about the invention of porcelain.

Derek John, a director of AP Watt, the British literary agency, has been quoted as saying that he thinks the demand for such "compact, exquisitely written books is partly due to people having shorter attention spans in an overloaded culture." George Gibson concurs that "people like short books, given time pressures."

Peter Gethers has a slightly different take on things, however. He said,

I don't think writers like Junger and Krakauer have challenged conventional notions. They feed into a centuries-long tradition of nonfiction storytelling. I actually think a book like *The Perfect Storm*—which I loved—is quite an old-fashioned book, in the absolute best sense. For what it's worth, I was recently having a conversation with someone, bemoaning the state of the world. We tried to come up with things that are better now than they were 50 years ago. We came up with only three things: food, baseball stadiums, and nonfiction books. I think there's a thirst for books like Krakauer's and Junger's because there's a thirst for anything that's actually good these days. We thirst for good politicians, good movies, you name it. It's just that narrative nonfiction actually seems to deliver the goods lately.

Editors at publishing houses, however, were not about to use the oxymoronic term "nonfiction novel," which some marketing maven, clearly trying to finesse the unfinessable, invented for Truman Capote's 1966 true crime story, *In Cold Blood.* Instead, publishers coined the term "narrative nonfiction"—fact-based books that read like fiction. (As I mentioned earlier, "creative nonfiction," often taught in colleges, usually refers to magazine-length pieces. "Narrative nonfiction" commonly refers to book-length pieces.)

What most successful narrative nonfiction has in common is a narrative, characters, the promise of adventure and controversy, the revealing of secrets, peering backstage and behind the curtain, so to speak—for example, the ill-fated boat ride *(A Perfect Storm)*, the illicit taboo of an adult love affair with a missing father *(The Kiss),* going into battle in a modern war *(Black Hawk Down).* But there is a gray zone between fiction and nonfiction. Every time a journalist puts thoughts into the minds of his or her "characters," every time a reporter re-creates dialogue for scenes that weren't recorded and at which the writer was not present, no matter how scrupulously those thoughts and dialogue are based on extensive interviews with the principals about what they were thinking and saying at the time, the writer enters that gray zone of "faction," that is, fact and fancy.

Why Stories?

We use stories as a way of making sense of the world around us. We grow up on them, crave them like a fix. They are reassuring and comforting in some strange way, perhaps because of their structure and order, and predictability. As children we often want to be read the same story again and again, in an almost hypnotic fascination. But as we approach puberty it slowly dawns on us that like Santa Claus and the Easter Bunny, many stories are inventions. Yet despite this apparent betrayal, despite real life slowly impinging on our shrinking world of invention and fantastic possibilities, we still desperately want to believe in stories. That's why the con artist is so successful. He doesn't really sell us a bill of goods—he helps us sell ourselves by telling us a story we want to hear. We want to believe his story, and we help him shape it to our needs. The best litigators are not those who discover and assemble the truth for juries—they are those advocates who manage to spin the most convincing story from the same facts their opponents are using to tell a different story.

When the novel began, in the eighteenth century, the novelist often presented himself not as an author of untruth but as an editor of a true history—a scoundrel, in effect, passing himself off as something other than he was. *Robinson Crusoe* (1719) by Daniel Defoe, for example (considered by many to be the first novel), tries to present itself as nonfiction by being written in the form of a journal by a supposed real-life character. It was a game with its audience, who at the time trusted Defoe as a journalist but did not yet think of him as also a satirist. Because Defoe was a well-established journalist, his novel is remarkable for its journalistic attempt to present the story and its details as true. (The novel was partly based on the memoirs of Alexander Selkirk, who was cast away on Mas a Tierra in the Juan Fernandez Islands off the coast of Chile as a punishment for insubordination. Selkirk spent four years and four months on the island; Crusoe spends 28 years.)

Almost 300 years later, it could be argued that the novel has become a creature of artifice with fabulist qualities, for the most part locked into a genre mentality in order to be marketable to modern audiences. So-called non-genre fiction (and literary fiction is as much a genre as mystery or romance, it can be argued), such as Alice Sebold's rightfully acclaimed *The Lovely Bones,* has become the antithesis of *Crusoe.* It is written as magic realism, or allegory—forms that shout from the rooftops, "I am a lie!" A novelist is a prince of liars, but because he is forced to admit he lies, he somehow manages to reveal truths that realism (and journalism) cannot.

Jack Hart, managing editor of the *Oregonian* newspaper, in an interview in fall 2002 said: "I think literary fiction has fallen prey to campus navel gazing and has lost touch with ordinary humanity. And it has the audience to prove it."

Jonathan Galassi counts both Thomas Friedman *(The Lexus and the Olive Tree)* and Jonathan Franzen *(The Corrections)* among his authors. He said,

> I think a lot of fiction today tends toward autobiography—a very problematic development and in many ways a sign of weakness. Narrative nonfiction uses fictional strategies and tools to forward the development of an idea. I'd say the convergence between fiction and nonfiction is quite notable. . . . Recent successes in fiction, most notably Franzen's

The Corrections, indicate a swerve away from postmodernism . . . in
some ways a return to the heroics of nineteenth-century realist fiction,
particularly in the Russian vein, where the narrator's sensibility is not
the sieve through which reality is strained.

Narrative nonfiction books have themes that tend to the historical, but
certainly not completely. The reader learns something by tracing the story of
an arcane object or phenomenon, rather than just an historic figure or
important political development. In Hart's view, nonfiction has a ready
advantage over much introspective midlist fiction published today. "I like
Tom Wolfe's explanation," he said. "Narrative nonfiction 'enjoys an advantage so obvious, so built-in, one almost forgets what a power it has: the
simple fact that the reader knows all this actually happened.' "

Is Reality Really Real?

Once upon a time, in the mid-1960s, the art house movie documentary
Mundo Cane was shocking—a behind-the-scenes look at the real, brutal
face of the world that the networks considered unfit to broadcast. Turn on
the TV nowadays and *Mundo Cane* has been replaced by its grandchil-
dren—the antics of desperate human lab rats, their lives and failings will-
ingly dissected before millions by Dr. Phil on Oprah or the invasive camera
lenses of *The People's Court;* MTV's *The Real World; Big Brother; Survivor;*
and a myriad of other shows, each one progressively nastier than the last in
an attempt to be more real than its predecessor. How long before we reach
the world of Stephen King's novel *The Running Man?* And our reading tastes
are marching right along with our viewing tastes.

Instead of enjoying novels about the trials and tribulations of the rich
and powerful in the novels of Jackie Collins, Harold Robbins, and Sidney
Sheldon, the best-selling memoir of recent years for St. Martin's Press has
been *The Nanny Diaries,* which manages to combine memoir with a similar

salacious exposé of the weakness and foibles of the self-involved monied classes that the novelists used to revel in writing about. *The Nanny Diaries* is more effective and delicious for contemporary audiences because we know it is not just *based* on real life—it is a *depiction* of real life, and we can feel momentarily superior to those who usually act as though they are superior to us.

Craving Stories

But our thirst for reality may be creating a society that novelist Doris Lessing describes as having "a reluctance of imagination." If not reluctance, then it is at least a kind of cultural *fatigue* of imagination. We grow tired of the familiarity and predictability of the fiction we are offered. We crave new tastes, new experiences, new adventures, stories that touch our lives and involve us, not stimulate our imaginations. We want to know what is possible and what is extraordinary by examining true examples of those who have dared and overcome and pushed the envelope of human experience. In a sense, we're tired of the theory that fiction suggests and want to watch the reality of life in action.

Truth is, in today's marketplace it seems commercially more viable to write a memoir of growing up as the third generation of men in one family to be convicted of murder than a novel on the same subject. George Gibson is not convinced, however. "I disagree with Lessing," he said. "Short books can stimulate imagination just as much as long ones, maybe more, if they're well done. I also don't agree that a lurid memoir is more commercial than a novel." Jack Hart disagreed. "[Frankly] I'd rather read the true experiences of a third-generation criminal than a novel on the same subject."

For the moment, the memoir seems to be playing itself out as a hot subgenre within narrative nonfiction. How many more incidents of confessed, intimate faux pas lovingly crafted for public consumption can we stand? With a couple of notable exceptions, it is a literature of narcissistic self-involvement, revealing stories of more and more tasteless taboo breaking and exhibitionism as each new book tries to top the revelations of the one before. Blake Morrison, in his British collection of essays *Too True* (1998), said, "Confessionalism is masturbation [but] . . . with art . . . it become[s] empathy."

Where the novelist has to construct a fictional world and then make strenuous efforts in her writing not to jerk us out of what John Gardner calls "the fictive dream," the author of narrative nonfiction is given much more leeway by a reader "because it's true."

If a thing happens in a novel, and seems to be unbelievable or a fortuitous coincidence, the reader might well dash the book across the room in disgust at such clumsy writing, never to return to the story (or the author) that somehow betrayed him. However, in nonfiction the same clumsy writing and plotting may well be accepted by the same reader, who comforts herself with the thought that "after all, it's true." We read on, falsely secure in the arms of the narrator, trusting in his narrative re-creation, excusing poor craft when we shouldn't.

Making It Live

What's important in nonfiction is the content: the idea, the new paradigm, or the question and answer the work presents. Narrative nonfiction adds the dimension of story.

I gained a certain insight into writing narrative nonfiction while working as an editor for BBC Radio News. Radio is a wonderful medium for the writer because by and large everything spoken is scripted. When writing news for the "Beeb" it was important to state facts, but also, in a bold, colorful sentence or two, to create word pictures that would make the people and places come alive for the listener. These days, writers of narrative nonfiction are wise to do at least that, using some of the tools of fiction—narrative spines with beginnings, middles, and ends; characterizations; suspense; and even surprise. Truth becomes refracted, like light through a prism, and becomes something other, although still the truth.

Some of the most successful classical novelists, whether Defoe or Dickens, Tolstoy, Thackery, Austen, or Eliot, have relied on real events and real people to build their fiction around. Thackery and Tolstoy used the battle of Waterloo as a backdrop to their stories; but what really separates the nonfiction *Black Hawk Down* (about the battle of Mogadishu) from the fictionalized *The Killer Angels* by Michael Shaara (about the battle of Gettysburg)? Is it simply the ability to interview the participants? Surely not, as both books are keenly researched. I leave you to decide.

The novel's role is, in part, to answer the question *why* and give us the emotions of the people involved, putting us inside the minds of the key participants. However, Truman Capote's *In Cold Blood* daringly struck out in a new direction, establishing narrative nonfiction by usurping the presumed, re-created insights into people and events previously the domain of novelists, and claiming them for journalists who write novelized versions of true events. Along with *Longitude*, which reinvigorated this style of writing, *In Cold Blood* is the most influential of modern narrative nonfiction works.

The Saga of *The Lovely Bones*

So what of the modern novel, then? Some argue that in order to survive, it has been forced to become either more extreme and imaginatively surreal (like *The Lovely Bones*) or more overtly realistic (like Thomas Keneally's *Schindler's List*, and the potboiler *Exodus* by Leon Uris). Perhaps, as the mania for reality-based entertainment continues to ratchet up the stakes, the truth about the need for stories that are true but read like fiction is that fiction has been trivialized by the emphasis on genre expectations that dictate what should and should not be a part of the novel.

As a result, American novelists who wish to hit best-sellerdom (and that's practically everyone) hesitate to try and write stories that deal with the more profound philosophical questions of life, such as "Who are we?" and "Why are we here?" and "What is our purpose?" We shrug off fiction as superficial, an unchallenging, almost comforting invention. Art and commerce need to be in balance, yet commerce seems to be undermining art these days.

Alice Sebold's *The Lovely Bones*, for example, which might seem to contradict this idea, owes its outstanding success in part to an audience that suddenly recognizes it is starved of challenging and worthwhile fiction to read, the sheer accomplishment of its author, and a heartfelt but not preachy ability to tackle some profound issues. It was named a Book-of-the-Month Club main selection. Barnes & Noble included the book in its Discover program highlighting new writers, and Sessalee Hensley, the chain's fiction buyer, placed an initial order of more than 10,000 copies, instead of the 3,000 to 5,000 standard for that program.

Anna Quindlen, a Book-of-the-Month Club judge, told a TV audience on NBC's *Today* show, "If you only read one book this summer, read *The Lovely Bones*."

Added to that was an (unfortunately) serendipitous timing in its publishing: this outstanding novel about a murdered child who narrates her story from heaven appeared while several wrenching stories about murdered missing children were playing in the national media for weeks. The fiction, in a way, became an unconscious insight into the nature of truths we cannot fathom unless we have had the misfortune to experience them. Its burgeoning success, like a snowball headed downhill, gave it increasing sales and marketing momentum.

The Lovely Bones was also a case of bold publishing. The publisher (Little, Brown) originally anticipated a modest 10,000-copy print run, but had enough insight to print and ship many times that number after the book drew attention, so that when readers asked for the book in the store it was available.

It's worth remembering, however, that Sebold's first book was a nonfiction account of her rape in 1999, called *Lucky* and published by Scribner.

. . . the . . .

"Rape is one of the subjects people have a knee-jerk reaction to," Henry Dunow, Sebold's agent, is reported to have said. "A number of publishers expressed distinct misgivings." By late 2002, *The Lovely Bones* had been number one on the *New York Times* fiction list for several weeks, knocking Stephen King's *From a Buick 8* to number two, while *Lucky* was number two on the *Times* nonfiction paperback list.

What's the lure of the narrative nonfiction story? George Gibson thinks it's that "people love good stories, especially those that educate them at the same time or take them to places they'd never otherwise go, which is what great fiction does." Peter Gethers is more pragmatic: "There are still plenty of midlist novels being published. But I do think that one of the reasons for the rise of narrative nonfiction is that television seems to have taken the place of a lot of novels. People watch *The Sopranos* to get their fiction fix."

Despite all this, commercial sensitivity is vital in the final stages of polishing publishable material. One of the first questions an editor or agent asks of a manuscript is, "What genre is it?" Without knowing that, the editor or bookstore owner does not know where best to place the book in the bookstore, and the sad truth is, few bookstores place books in two different places at the same time (say, *The Physics of Star Trek* by Lawrence Krauss in both the science section and the science fiction section). In her book *Thinking Like Your Editor,* literary agent Susan Rabiner, the former editorial director of Basic Books, explains that in a meeting with book buyers for Barnes & Noble she discussed this very issue: "Over coffee I raised my complaint. Failure to stock *The Physics of Star Trek* in the *Star Trek* section as well as the science section would cost thousands of sales for both of us. Couldn't they at least shelve the book in both places? To my amazement, the answer was no, they couldn't."

The reason? Bookstores like B&N have buyers who buy books in certain fields. So the buyer for science titles might stock *The Physics of Star Trek*, but he or she has no involvement with the science fiction buyer, who stocks the shelf where *Star Trek* books belong. Depending on the store and the buyers, the same book could appear in either section of the store, but rarely both at once.

Categorizing Books—a Marketing Conceit

On average, some 50,000 trade books a year are published in the United States. Some are hardcover (sometimes called cloth); many more are paperback, either mass market (the small-sized books that fit in your pocket) or trade (the larger-sized ones that almost look like hardcovers). All of them can be categorized in some fashion.

The development of genres came about as a marketing necessity. "Category" and "genre" are marketing terms that mean more or less the same thing. Their purpose is basically to help you more easily find what it is you're looking for. They are also *guides* that let you know, generally, what you can expect to find in a certain type of book. The writer of narrative nonfiction, because it attempts to re-create a real set of circumstances, is allowed more experimental latitude in technique than the novelist these days; that appeals mightily to authors interested in writing popular experimental literature.

While genres are being constantly reinvented, it's important that an author become familiar with the classics of a genre as well as read the latest published books in the genre to get a sense of what readers expect. A genre can be hot, become overbought, and then be hard to sell into for a while. Memoir has become such a subgenre in recent times, while true crime, which was dormant for a number of years, is starting to attract interest from editors again.

When your book comes out you're not really competing with all the other books in the store. You're competing only with all the other books in your genre. So, without diverging too much from what's expected, you ought to be thinking about how you're going to make your book different from others like it. And that difference comes from knowing your genre well enough that you can spot a "hole," or good idea.

Know your audience. One of the biggest differences between books and other media forms is that, while movies and TV don't discriminate by age and gender, books, in general, are written with a specific audience in mind. Adventure and travel books, for example, which are often man-against-nature stories, are bought and read mainly by men. Only those books that become big sellers transcend those limitations.

Artistic Categories

All forms of art employ categories. In music, for example, you can write an opera, a tone poem, a symphony, a concerto, a folksong, a pop song, and so on. A composer is guided by the form of that genre, be it the sonata form, the fugue form, or the AABA melodic structure common in popular music.

You can mix genres, coming up with what is called a cross genre. Gershwin and Bartók, for example, borrowed heavily from other genres, such as folk music, spirituals, and gospel music, while jazz greats Duke Ellington and George Russell worked in the opposite direction, borrowing from classical forms. Each composer also influenced the work of others.

Because narrative nonfiction is character driven, it has a structure that echoes fiction and can be divided into a number of subgenres. Its narrative spine should either give us the *why* of a situation (such as *Into Thin Air* or *Black Hawk Down*) or track the story of an idea (such as *Longitude* or *The Professor and the Madman,* the story of the creation of the *Oxford English Dictionary*).

What follows are a series of thumbnail notes on the broad subgenres of narrative nonfiction. Many edge into one another, but it's important when you conceive, write, and eventually submit a book that you choose a particular subgenre and use only that to describe it. (Remember Susan Rabiner's story quoted earlier.)

Adventure

The true-adventure story is an amalgam of travelogue, memoir, and the old-fashioned man-against-nature or man-against-beast story popular in the late nineteenth and early twentieth century. As a growing part of the population is drawn to more and more extreme things to do for pleasure, so we are also drawn to read about more and more extreme and dramatic adventures with ordinary people in extraordinary places and circumstances, who often risk life and limb whether deliberately or not. *Into Thin Air* and *The Perfect Storm,* books that evoke the works of Jack London, Robert Louis Stevenson, and Joseph Conrad, are good examples of this, as well as the earlier *Kon-Tiki,* Thor Heyerdahl's story of trans-Pacific anthropology and seamanship on a balsa-wood raft.

Travel Books

These break down into narratives of adventures getting from point A to point B, travel guides, and destination guides. A travelogue will often have lyrical descriptions of faraway places and is aimed at an audience known as armchair travelers.

The books often lift the curtain and peer under rocks. Non-narrative books often provide mundane but important information on hotels, restaurants, places to go, interesting sights to see, and so forth. Travel guides are nondestination books that tell you how to travel in a particular way, such as by donkey across Tibet or by train across China (Paul Theroux's *Riding the Iron Rooster*), or by just staying put and experiencing something new and other (Peter Mayle's *A Year in Provence; Under the Tuscan Sun* by Frances Mayes; *The Flâneur* by Edmund White, about the joys of strolling aimlessly around Paris). Again, *Kon-Tiki* might fit here, or *Into Thin Air,* even though they are also considered adventures and might, at a pinch, also be considered memoirs, as they contain personal reflections and recollections.

Biography

Historian Doris Kearns Goodwin said, "The past is not simply the past, but a prism through which the subject [of a biography] filters his own changing self-image."

The subject's life should have had a profound effect on the people who came into contact with him or her, and some shadow of it should also touch the reader of the biography.

This is a popular category if you can find a suitable subject, but to carry it off the writer must be an expert on the subject. The same kind of investigative, analytical attention to detail used in true crime is foremost in biographies such as A. Scott Berg's *Max Perkins: Editor of Genius,* David Wise's *Spy: The Inside Story of How the FBI's Robert Hanssen Betrayed America,* and of course, in recent years, David McCullough's masterwork, *John Adams.*

Biographies take several forms. Some use the work and life of the biographical subject as an indicator of the subject's inner world. Others are more literary in nature, placing more emphasis on the narrative structure of the book in an effort to reflect its biographical subject.

The three types of biography all try to reveal the essence of the subject: *interpretive,* where the events of a subject's life lead us to a better understanding of the inner person and how that person fits in with his or her world; *objective,* which gathers facts and documents how the subject lived; and *dramatic,* which uses fictional techniques to re-create the subject and his or her times.

Dramatic biographies such as *Eleanor of Aquitaine: A Life* by Alison Weir or her earlier *Life of Elizabeth I* use known facts about the subject and her time that are interpreted by the biographer's imagination in an effort to reveal the intimate qualities of the subject.

The controversial Ronald Reagan biography *Dutch* broadly falls into this category. Edmund Morris's biography of former president Reagan involved the author creating himself as a fictional character in order to tell the president's story, and attracted a lot of criticism for its approach.

In general, a biography has to have a theme, and its subject has to fit into the context of the times the subject lived in. More than that, the subject of a biography should also be a symbol of some sort for the spirit of his or her age. The book should bring out some thematic element of that culture. Broadly, a good biography is one that illuminates and shows the times as much as the person.

The dangers of biography are inaccuracy and hero worship. The biographer needs to cultivate an objective eye that fits his subject into the world with compassion. Most biographies treat their subjects as one of three things: an example, a victim, or a source of wisdom.

Biography depends on two things: public and personal papers and sources, and living witnesses. Of course, in the case of the long-dead, you're stuck with only one of the two.

It's also a demanding form of writing, requiring that the author know the subject intimately, live with the subject for a long time, somehow make peace with his or her flaws, yet obtain necessary permissions from those relevant people who are living, and ensure that any quotes are accurately related and sourced.

The biographer must have the skills of a storyteller, to construct an insightful, compelling narrative; of a diplomat, to deal with the many witnesses who can shed light on the subject's life; and of a detective, in order to dig out facts and research on the subject, to be devoted to the subject and yet objective enough to explore the dark nooks and crannies of the life in question. The biographer also needs the literary and psychological brilliance to create a book that the subject could honestly admit was an accurate portrayal of who and what he or she is. Unless you are a skilled writer, and someone with a strong analytical background, biography is going to be a tough genre to use to break into publishing. It is also not without potential problems. For example, in 1958, Dore Shary's *Sunrise at Campobello,* despite being an award-winning biographical play about Franklin D. Roosevelt, was the subject of litigation. The playwright/producer was sued by the descendants of the former president, and Schary ended up having to pay close to $19,000 in compensation for "loss of privacy" brought about by the play.

History

Biography, history, and current affairs often edge into one another. To succeed in writing a credible work of history, both the narrative work and the more scholarly nonfiction have to be written by a recognized scholar or someone with credentials of some sort, as for example a Ph.D. You can have other credentials, though. A parish priest could write a major work on religion and get it published; a teacher could write a book about the history of education; a journalist could do a book about almost anything if he got his sources lined up; a parent of a sick child could research all there is to know about the child's disease and then write about it. You need to have some edge, however small, beyond your interest in the topic, though. In general, those who are passionate about something also tend to have studied it a lot and are often experts by default.

The appeal of the historical story for readers is the chance to meet real people as they really were. The historical writer also strives to portray the customs, culture, and knowledge of the period. In a time of political correctness it is sometimes difficult to maintain the integrity of portraying cruelty, ignorance, and hardship that clash heavily with contemporary values. Like the biography, the historical novel has relevance because of what the past has to tell us about the present. Arthur Miller's play *The Crucible,* about the Salem witch trials, was written in the early 1950s, but is also an allegory about the McCarthy House Un-American Activities Committee witch-hunt for communists. Most historical stories tell us something about who we are now, or cast light on events that we thought we knew, only to discover that we have been deceived in some way.

Military

This is really a subset of both history and biography. Perhaps two of the best examples of successful military books in recent years are *The Killer Angels* and, more recently, *Black Hawk Down.* Others include *Band of Brothers: E Company, 506th Regiment, 101st Airborne from Normandy to Hitler's Eagle's Nest* by Stephen E. Ambrose; *Reason Why: The Story of the Fatal Charge of the Light Brigade* by Cecil Woodham-Smith; and *Trafalgar: The Nelson Touch* by David Howarth.

These genres blur as history becomes more subjective and historians use the techniques of fiction to facilitate a deeper understanding of the past and its influence on the present.

How does one define or distinguish history from fiction, from historical fiction, from fictionalized history? How do the interpretations and biases (read: politically corrected attitudes) of the present infect our understanding of what was really going on in the past? These are all issues the historian and military historian must tackle.

Memoir

Memoir is a somewhat tainted genre these days, and has blossomed from the pure recounting of a specific life to incorporate a personal account of almost anything. For example, the excellent *Into Thin Air* by Jon Krakauer is considered an adventure book, but is described by the author as "a personal account of the Mount Everest disaster" of 1996. In other words, a memoir.

Discussing the phenomenal success of memoir as a subgenre during the 1990s, Robert Winder, deputy editor of the British literary magazine *Granta,* wrote, "Bookshops . . . groan with [the] confessions [of] criminals and addicts, abuse victims and sports fans, war heroes and domestic saints (or sinners) [who] queue up to get their lives off their chests."

It is a demanding genre to write well. A big fuss was made of Kathryn Harrison's book about incest, *The Kiss,* and also Frank McCourt's memoir of a childhood cursed with drink, violence, and poverty, *Angela's Ashes,* because they were so intimate and revealing of these terrible experiences. But they also upped the ante for the average writer of memoir because they were so well written; and *The Kiss* in particular (as well as, more recently, *Running with Scissors* by Augusten Burroughs) has a salacious quality that has set the bar higher for writers of commercial memoirs.

Nowadays, commercially successful memoirs are about traumatic events in a writer's life that a writer of exquisite skill can *transform into a universal experience we can all share.* It is the nearest thing to poetry a writer of prose can do. Read Isabelle Allende's moving book *Paula,* about the sickness and coma her daughter suffered.

Memoirs are about a child's sickness, a father's death, a loss of honor or career. We read of others' pain because the writers' sensibility allows them to extract from their dreadful experience powerful universal emotions that illuminate our lives. Editors who buy memoirs do so because the writers have successfully transferred the experience to the page in a strong emotional way, and in so doing, like the alchemists of old, have transmuted the experience from base lead into gold.

When a memoir such as *A Year in Provence* by Peter Mayle succeeds—it is not about personal pain but a growing and learning experience—it often edges into another genre. In this case, adventure and travel.

True Crime

The model for true crime books—and the book that still defines the genre—is *In Cold Blood* by Truman Capote, the original "nonfiction novel"—a term I must confess I despise. The book was the first one to use fictional techniques extensively to tell a true story. The experts who write true crime successfully are, or have been, lawyers, cops, investigators, journalists, forensic specialists, and so forth.

In *Editors on Editing*, St. Martin's Press senior editor Charles Spicer explains there are two basic types of true crime book: There is the *gut* story, that is, one that affects us on a primal level, such as Anne Rule's *Small Sacrifices*, about a mother murdering her children; or *Perfect Murder, Perfect Town* by Lawrence Schiller, about the JonBenet Ramsey child murder. And there is the *glamour* story, set in the world of the rich and famous, such as Allan Dershowitz's and William Wright's books about the trials of Claus Von Bulow—who was convicted, and then acquitted in a second trial, of trying to kill his socialite wife, Sunny—or the several books about Sante and Kenny Kimes, convicted of murdering the wealthy elderly Manhattan socialite Irene Silverman.

Beyond powerful and, of course, accurate characterization with identifiable villains, and if possible also heroes, the narrative nonfiction book should have some sort of unraveling investigation. It is the writer's job to learn the art of the newspaper reporter, not only capturing the spirit of what was said and done, but doing it accurately without boring readers with unnecessary detail or speech in the process. It is a fine tightrope to walk.

True crime books allow us to peer into the mind of the demented, though they are also very influenced by how much of a gripping story can be woven, who the characters are, where the story took place, and so on. They are usually psychosexual in nature. One of the elements of narrative nonfiction that many writers do not consider carefully enough is that it takes the techniques and skills of a journalist *and* a novelist to write a compelling story. *How* the story is told is as important as *what* happened.

T W O

Searching, Searching:
Discovering a Subject

• • • • • • • • • • • • • • • • • •

Nothing in the world can take the place of persistence. . . .
The slogan "press on" has solved and will always solve
the problems of the human race.

CALVIN COOLIDGE

If at first you don't succeed, try again,
and then try something else.

MASON COOLEY, U.S. APHORIST

 You would think, given the blizzard of information constantly swirling around us, that finding ideas for stories would be a pretty simple matter. Yet despite the assault of uncategorized, indistinguishable data that we are subjected to daily, much of it is of questionable accuracy and really not at all informative. In fact, very few pieces of information that cross our path are potent enough seeds to take root in the fertile earth of research and development. And of the ones that do take root and grow into newspaper or magazine articles, fewer still are likely to develop into successful books.

First of All—Check It Out

That doesn't mean we shouldn't pay attention to the constant barrage of information around us. Quite the reverse—it's just that we should employ a suitably skeptical and questioning attitude about an idea before committing too much time and too many resources to it. The first thing to do if a good idea strikes is to research whether or not it has been done before, and if so, to what extent and by whom. The simplest way to do this is to go to the Web. Try going to sites like Google.com, ixquick.com, amazon.com, barnesandnoble.com, or booksinprint.com, and running a search on the idea or topic, and see what turns up.

For example, entering the terms "narrative nonfiction" and "book" and "writing" and "how to" and their variations and combinations brought up over 1,000 hits on Google and some 80 or so hits on Amazon. Some of the Google sites were interesting leads to transcriptions of interviews or roundtable discussions with authors, editors, and agents on the subject. Yet there was not one mention of a book still in print and available that explicitly covered the topic. I actually knew of three books that might qualify, and two of those were old, as I mentioned in my initial book proposal: *The Art of Creative Nonfiction* by Lee Gutkind, published in 1997 (which I knew about because Wiley, his publisher, was also the publisher for my book *The Elements of Storytelling*); and *Writing for Story* by Jon Franklin, published in 1986. Both books focus on New Journalism and writing short creative nonfiction for magazines and newspapers rather than long pieces. I have been friends with agent and former editor Susan Rabiner for some years, and we share office space, so I knew about the third book, her own *Thinking Like Your Editor.* However, that book is about writing not narrative nonfiction, but serious nonfiction like *The Physics of Star Trek* or Stephen Hawking's *A Brief History of Time.*

In short, there were no books currently available on how to tackle writing a book like *Black Hawk Down* or *Longitude* or *The Right Stuff* by Tom Wolfe (described by the publisher as a novel, even though it is a dramatization of the true events of the space program of the sixties and seventies). This amazed me. I had decided not to write any more books about writing because I didn't feel I had much else to say other than what I had already written. Yet here was an idea that seemed to beg to be written, on a topic I specialize in as an agent and that no one had thought to deal with yet. My editor, Edwin Tan, and my publisher felt the same way. (It was only after I began writing this book that I stumbled across James B. Stewart's book *Follow the Story*, published in 1998, which is probably the only book that came close; and thankfully, his approach and mine are different enough that readers will learn from both books without much overlapping.)

The truth is, rather like looking for the mate of your dreams, most writers don't have a clue where good ideas come from; we just know them immediately when they cross our path. Recognizing and taking advantage of a potentially good, original idea (and I stress *original*) is as much a skill as coming up with the idea through voracious reading and discussion with others.

Looking for One Thing and Finding Something Better

Sometimes what you think you are going to write becomes something else. It is the smart writer who is flexible enough to adapt. For example, when Manuela Hoelterhoff, opera critic for the *Wall Street Journal* for 20 years or so, wrote *Cinderella & Company: Backstage at the Opera with Cecilia Bartoli*, Ms. Hoelterhoff intended to draw a portrait of an operatic mezzo-soprano who had achieved an unusually loyal and popular following in the opera world before reaching her thirtieth birthday.

For two years, the author immersed herself in Bartoli's world: from her 1995 appearance at the Houston Grand Opera in the title role of Rossini's *La Cenerentola (Cinderella)* to her Metropolitan Opera debut two years later in the modest role of the maid Despina in Mozart's *Così Fan Tutte*. Hoelterhoff had access to the singer, her mother (who doubled as Bartoli's vocal coach), Bartoli's Italian boyfriend, her manager, and a supporting cast of recording executives, agents, PR types, and orchestra conductors, all of whom seemed to be outlandish characters straight out of the commedia dell'arte.

The intended biography of the meteoric rise to fame of a young singer with a beautiful voice but a miniscule repertoire of roles became, instead, a much broader and more interesting portrait of the rarified world of professional opera at the turn of the twenty-first century. Even if opera does not particularly interest you, the book is so well written, witty, and fascinating it easily takes its place alongside anything Tracy Kidder or John McPhee has written. Ms. Hoelterhoff specializes in word pictures and a Dorothy Parker–like, incisive wit.

Two quick examples: On witnessing the large soprano Deborah Voigt (who can appear to be at least 300 pounds on occasion) singing next to the elfin-looking tenor Francisco Araiza in Verdi's *A Masked Ball,* she described Voigt as "looking as if she were ventriloquizing with a hand puppet." Kathleen Battle, who is commonly thought to be disliked in opera because of the apparently unpleasant way she treats people, is immortalized in a story about how she called her agent from the backseat of a limousine to have him tell the driver to turn down the air conditioner.

What Manuela Hoelterhoff did, of course, was recognize a good idea when it presented itself, and go with it despite what she had intended to write at the outset.

The Story-Sense Workout

More than anything, coming up with a subject that works both as a book and as an engaging and relevant story is a skill that must be developed. It is a "muscle" that must be paid attention to and nurtured, and like muscles hardened by working out in the gym, the story-sense muscle develops only from constant practice. It is not likely to be very useful the first few times you use it, but that should not discourage you from continuing to develop it. You are nurturing what journalists call "news sense" or "story sense," and that is an indefinable quality born of regular practice. As with good art, most journalists know a good story when they see it even though there is (happily) no formula that can be applied.

Journalists are intrigued, for example, by people saying no to them when there should be no reason to. Back in the 1960s, London's *Sunday Times Magazine* decided to run an A-to-Z series about remarkable people, events, and institutions of the twentieth century. One of those was a famous department store in London. When the store was asked to provide what was essentially a PR piece about its history, they point-blank refused to cooperate. This so intrigued the reporters of the *Times* that they checked into the store, and why it was being so evasive. The reporters uncovered the fact that the store, known only by its initials, took those initials from the owners, two Dutch brothers who had been major supporters of the German Nazi Party prior to and during World War II. The store was a favorite of British Jews and, undone by journalistic curiosity, lost a great deal of business when the truth about the store's past was reported.

In *Follow the Story*, Pulitzer Prize–winning journalist James B. Stewart says:

> Curiosity is the great quality that binds writers to readers. Curiosity sends writers on their quests, and curiosity is what makes readers read the stories that result. These days, when there is increasing competition for people's time, writers cannot count on anyone to read their work out of a sense of obligation, moral duty, or abstract dedication to "being informed." They will not read because someone else deems a subject important. They will read because they want to, and they want to because they are curious.

Curiosity is fueled by questions. Why wouldn't the London department store supply the *Times* reporters with a simple background piece as they were asked to do? When Amy Yarsinske wrote *No One Left Behind,* an account of the abandonment of U.S. pilot Michael Scott Speicher, the first casualty of the Gulf War still in Iraqi hands over a decade later, the question was, "Why is no one seriously trying to get him back?"

Curiosity, however, needs to go hand in hand with a passion for a subject. Jonathan Galassi, of Farrar, Straus and Giroux, summed it up: Authors of narrative nonfiction "should try to find topics that interest them deeply on a personal level, first of all, and work on ones that they see are related [to those passions] in some way—not always surface-obvious."

Writing about how *The Perfect Storm* came about, Sebastian Junger said: "My own experience of the storm [of the century] was limited to standing on Gloucester's Back Shore watching thirty-foot swells advance on Cape Ann, but that was all it took. The next day I read in the paper that a Gloucester boat was feared lost at sea, and I clipped the article and stuck it in a drawer. Without even knowing it, I had begun to write *The Perfect Storm.*"

For Jon Krakauer, *Into Thin Air* was even more personal. While on Mount Everest, writing an article for *Outside* magazine, he experienced a rogue storm that killed nine climbers from four expeditions. Three more would die on Everest before the month was ended. "The expedition left me badly shaken," Krakauer wrote. His article was published four months later in *Outside* magazine. "Upon [the article's] completion I attempted to put Everest out of my mind and get on with my life, but that turned out to be impossible. Through a fog of messy emotions, I continued trying to make sense of what had happened up there, and I obsessively mulled the circumstances of my companions' deaths." He went on: "Several authors and editors I respect counseled me not to write the book as quickly as I did. . . . Their advice was sound, but in the end I ignored it—mostly because what happened on the mountain was gnawing my guts out. I thought that writing the book might purge Everest from my life.

"It hasn't, of course."

If you're a professional writer who has been published in magazines and newspapers, you probably already have an idea of how to find stories.

Often, an editor at a magazine or a newspaper features editor will come up with an idea, and either commission it or ask a particular writer to write up a couple of pages "on spec"—that is, on speculation of an eventual purchase.

The book world does not tend to work quite that way. It's true that if you have an agent or if you're published, with a good relationship with an editor at a publishing house, it may be a little easier to run ideas past your agent or your editor and come up with something that is going to work for everyone. But the odds are you're not in that position. A client of mine, for example, had a major house publish her first book, which got an 80 percent sell-through. (That means over 80 percent of the books printed were sold to the general reading public through bookstores and the like, which is a success for a writer.) But total sales didn't reach 20,000 copies, so even though her editor loved the idea for her new narrative nonfiction, his new boss decided that he couldn't buy my client's new proposal. I gently pointed out to the editor that with an 80 percent sell-through rate, the only reason the book had not sold 20,000 copies was that the publishing company had not printed enough copies to allow her to sell that many. This made no difference to the corporate decision, however.

My job became finding another editor for the new book, which in this case was not very difficult. However, the point is made that publishing is an industry plagued with such situations, most of which are not within an author's control.

HarperCollins senior editor Dan Conaway feels that "the most important thing—virtually the only important thing, to me—is the quality of the writing, the depth and nuance and insight and drama that comes organically from great writing. I'm not called on to do 'ripped-from-the-headlines' books as my bread and butter, so I don't much care whether it's a fantastic story, unless it's fantastically well told. So-so writing always comes back to bite one on the ass, especially if one does as much editorial work as I do."

Peter Gethers of Random House feels similarly: "When looking at a submission, I basically look for the same things no matter what the category: a compelling story, characters I care about (or whom I find interesting), and if possible, some kind of emotional attachment rather than just purely an intellectual one. I suppose that's my definition of a good narrative nonfiction book—it establishes an emotional connection with the reader."

George Gibson, publisher of Walker & Company, says much the same thing. What he looks for in a book proposal, he says, is, "first, can the author write; second, is there a good story here; third, will it expand the reader's knowledge and understanding of the world?"

Deciding What's Worth Writing

So how do you find a good subject to write about? Mark Twain once said, "In the real world, the right thing never happens at the right place, at the right time—it is the task of journalists and historians to rectify this error."

If you are already selling consistently to magazines and so forth, on the surface it might not seem that difficult. But here's the problem: What may work well as a short piece may not work as a longer piece. So the problem falls into two parts: first of all, how to find a good subject to write about, and second, how to tell if that idea will work as a book.

Jack Hart of the *Oregonian* newspaper feels, "I'm not sure all narrative nonfiction needs to read like a good novel. It should be a pleasure to read, of course, but good narrative can do productive work even if it doesn't tap a good novel's great human truths and deep characterization. Explanatory narrative, like Rich Read's *The French Fry Connection,* is a case in point, as is almost anything by John McPhee."

In an interview in May 2001 in *Writer's Digest* magazine, author Colin Beavan described how he came up with the idea for his book *Fingerprints:*

> Basically, my agent and I were sitting around his office one rainy day,
> and I was having trouble coming up with some ideas. And he said, Well
> OK, I have this idea. So I left his office feeling obliged to do some

research because he was my agent, and he'd kindly offered me [the] idea, but I was like, "Oh God, the history of fingerprints?" I went to the library, and it was like synchronicity because one of the first books I came across talked about this kind of unsung hero of fingerprinting who had basically had his idea stolen from him. And then all of a sudden it wasn't this ungodly dry subject to me, but a real human story about justice and giving credit where credit is due.

. . . In narrative nonfiction the key is to find a story. If you want to write good narrative nonfiction, what you have to realize is that, just like fiction, it's about people—all stories are about people. And just like in fiction, in narrative nonfiction—although you're more constrained by the facts—what you're looking for are stories that intrigue people and characters that are interesting.

All knowledge involves change in the recipient. If it does not involve change, it is not knowledge, but information without meaning. If I say, "You are reading this book"—duh! that's not knowledge, it is self-evident. You have learned nothing. If I say, "If you continue to read this book you'll catch a nasty social disease," you have learned something that will effect a change, probably quite rapidly.

So too, topics for narrative nonfiction books should add to our understanding or reveal previously unknown things.

Peter Gethers commented, "I truly don't think there's much difference between good fiction and nonfiction storytelling. The best writers—ranging from Dostoyevsky to Stephen King to Truman Capote to Robert Caro—are also great storytellers." He went on, "The best narrative nonfiction involves human-interest stories about ordinary people who accomplish extraordinary things in extraordinary circumstances, even if it is about the story of an idea."

While *Longitude*, for example, is the story of the invention of the chronometer and the discovery of how to measure longitude, it is really focused on the trials and tribulations of John Harrison, the man who eventually solved the puzzle. Similarly, while Simon Winchester's *The Professor and the Madman* is about the creation of the *Oxford English Dictionary* and the codification of the English language, the story is humanized by focusing on two figures: James A. H. Murray, the editor of the dictionary, who faced the monumental task of compiling the initial version of the *Oxford English Dictionary,* and one of his most reliable and thorough volunteer contributors, Dr. William Chester Minor. Minor, however, had a secret: After serving as a physician in the Union Army during the Civil War, he fixed upon an obsession that Irishmen wanted to kill him. After the war he visited London, but his worsening psychosis led him to murder a complete stranger and he was tried, convicted, and institutionalized in an asylum for the criminally insane. Being well educated, and now with plenty of time on his hands, Minor was well suited to becoming a major contributor to Murray's enormous undertaking—creating the *OED.*

Three Basic Ways to Find a Story

There are basically three ways to find stories:

- First, you can either directly observe an event or be involved in one.
  This ranges from the experiences, say, described in fire battalion
  commander Richard Picciotto's first-person account of the World
  Trade Center catastrophe on 9/11, *Last Man Down,* to historian D.
  Graham Burnett's experience as the foreman of the jury in a murder
  trial in New York City, related in *A Trial by Jury.*
- Second, you can listen to the stories told by third-party observers who
  are witnesses or sources to something. Woodward and Bernstein's *All
  the President's Men* would fall into this category, or Robert Conot's
  1967 book *Rivers of Blood, Years of Darkness,* about the brutal 1965
  Los Angeles riot, an event considered by many to be a turning point
  in race relations in America.

- Third, you can consult written or published accounts. Almost any historical account, be it a biography or a re-creation of a historic event, would fall under this category. Books by A. Scott Berg, Alison Weir, and Simon Schama would fall into this category.

The truth is, outside of travel writing, it takes a sensational or bizarre personal experience to be worth considering as the basis for a book. If you have *really* been taken by aliens and experimented on, and you can convince me of the experience, it's clearly worth putting together a proposal on it. This worked for Whitley Strieber, for instance, when he wrote *Communion* and then the sequel *Confirmation*. (But because Strieber has already done this story, your story will need to be more than just a repetition of the experience. Compare these books with the more recently published *Captured by Aliens* by Joel Achenbach, for example. *Just* because it's true doesn't make something innately interesting to others.)

Such personal-experience writing is a form of memoir. Jon Krakauer's book *Into Thin Air* is really a memoir of a disaster he was involved with, as was Picciotto's. When thinking about writing a memoir, one of the major questions you should consider as objectively as possible is, why would someone else really be interested in my experience? One answer is overcoming adversity, such as in Frank McCourt's memoir *Angela's Ashes*. As moving and popular as that book was, it is interesting to note that many felt the sequel, *'Tis,* was disappointing. James B. Stewart makes an interesting point in *Follow the Story:* "What about my experience do I find puzzling, and what might I better understand given additional reflection and research?"

George Plimpton blazed the trail for a style of story that involves the reporter as observant participant. In the mid-1960s he wrote one of the seminal narrative nonfiction titles, *Paper Lion: Confessions of a Last-String Quarterback,* which details his adventures as a 36-year-old rookie quarterback wannabe with the Detroit Lions from their preseason training camp through to an intrasquad game a month later. It's a funny and perceptive book, and is still a model of what has been called "immersion reporting." The question that comes to mind with this kind of writing, of course, is why not just interview a professional and tell *his* story? In following the immersion path, there is a danger of the writer's ego getting in the way, and the writer bringing little perception or value to such a project. Some might argue that anything you, as a regular Joe or Jane, can actually talk your way into doing may not be that interesting to the rest of us. An exception might be an undercover or exposé sort of story.

For example, Barbara Ehrenreich went undercover to write *Nickel and Dimed: On (Not) Getting By in America,* a close-up look at the working poor that demonstrated that even at the height of the economic boom of the late 1990s, many unskilled workers couldn't earn enough to meet basic human needs. Ehrenreich decided that the best way to understand the plight of the working poor was to become one of them. She left her comfortable home and steady income as a writer, and tried to live on a series of jobs in restaurants, hotels, stores, and nursing homes, earning an average of $7 an hour. That was well above the minimum wage in 1998, the year of her experiment, yet even so she discovered that it was nearly impossible to live on such wages.

Narrative nonfiction is often the story *behind* a story. As in *The Wizard of Oz,* it is a drawing back of a veil from the appearance of a thing, to see the machinery beneath. What really happened, and why did it happen that way?

Mark Bowden worked as a reporter at the *Philadelphia Inquirer* for 20 years before writing his third published book, *Black Hawk Down.* "When I began working on [*Black Hawk Down*] in 1996," he wrote,

my goal was simply to write a dramatic account of the battle. I had been struck by the intensity of the fight, and by the notion of 99 American soldiers surrounded and trapped in an ancient African city fighting for their lives. My contribution would be to capture in words the experience of combat through the eyes and emotions of the soldiers involved, blending their urgent, human perspective with a military and political overview of their predicament. . . . I wanted to combine the authority of a historical narrative with the emotion of the memoir, and write a story that read like fiction but was true.

Why They Did What They Did

All successful stories involve some sort of relationship between people, what they do, and why they do it. If you can't satisfy and develop those elements, your book will fall flat. It may take a while, but once you develop what journalists call "news sense," you'll start to see potential book ideas everywhere.

There is a danger in searching for a narrative, however, when we have only the part of the picture that has grabbed our interest. Narrative is seductive, and the temptation is to use it for its own sake. The danger is that we will distort reality by forcing it into a narrative template. We may find a protagonist where none really exists. We may create a climax to a story that has never been resolved. When looking for a narrative nonfiction book that appeals to him, Jonathan Galassi explained, Farrar, Straus and Giroux is "interested in the significance of the subject and its relation to the approach of the author—style, research, point of view, attitude."

The larger questions to consider are: Who is the audience for this book? What other books in this field can be used as models for your proposed book? Were they successful? Is the audience (that is, the market) easily definable, reachable, and large enough?

It should go without saying—and yet here I am, saying it—that it is a seriously bad idea to try and second-guess the commercial viability of an idea. Trying to write something because you are sure it is going to be a bestseller, while the topic is one you do not particularly care for, is a bad idea for many reasons. Not the least of them is that you will have a miserable time writing a book you'll have to live with for perhaps a year or more. You are not likely to inject much passion into it, and passion is the one thing editors and agents, and readers, look for in successful books.

At a panel discussion at the Washington Press Club in 2002, award-winning journalist Paul Dickson (author of 40-plus books, including *Sputnik: The Shock of the Century*) commented that "every day when you wake up, you've got to think of the reader." To make his point, he told the story of writing what he now calls a "snakebite book":

> One time—I had [already] won three awards [for investigative journalism]—I wrote a book that was tough, it was investigative, [it] used every tool I had as a journalist, but no commercial publisher was interested, so I did it with a university press. And I remember going to the zoo, and there was a sign in the zoo over a poisonous snake that said that "every year in America, 1,906 people are bitten by poisonous snakes," and I realized that fewer people had bought my book [that year than had been bitten by a poisonous snake]. . . . You've got to think of the reader.

Sources

Anything that someone else witnesses or knows about and tells you falls under the rubric of "source" material. The person telling you is your source. Be warned that while you should cultivate conversation with everyone you meet (in a work sense), and listen nonjudgmentally to them, most people have stories they are busting a gut to tell you and most of these stories are hopelessly useless in book-publishing terms. The most useful sources are usually people you have to cultivate: a cop, or firefighter, or emergency worker, or doctor, or scientist, or nurse, or secretary, or . . . almost anyone *except* someone who does public relations for a living. These PR types desperately want to give you stories that are stripped of any real interest except what works for them and their clients, and they also want to control you and the way the story is presented. Taking someone out for a drink, schmoozing on the phone, or just listening to something someone wants to tell is a perfectly acceptable and time-honored way of getting an idea for a story from a source.

Sources can be named or unnamed, but we'll talk more about that in the research chapter.

Networking and Using Local Resources

Become familiar with your local colleges and universities. Know who teaches there and what they teach. Read the campus newsletter, and start trying to find out what seem to be the hot topics of the day in a particular discipline, whether it's animal husbandry (remember Dolly, the cloned sheep?) or architecture and engineering (do we need to rethink how we build tall buildings now that terrorists crash airplanes into them?). Who had a spectacular failure? Do you recall the stories about physicists who claimed to have produced cold nuclear fusion a few years ago? What happened there? Colleges are filled with athletes, scientists, artists, and others who all have stories about themselves, or know stories about others, and have thoughts and opinions on a wide variety of subjects.

Put the word out—mention to friends and colleagues that you're look-ing for a new idea for a book. They'll probably inundate you with stuff you can't use, but there's always that one intriguing tidbit . . . !

Make sure that you read not just newspapers and national magazines like *Scientific American, People,* and the *National Inquirer,* but strong regional magazines or magazines that cover specific areas of interest, like *Outside, Pacific Golf,* and *Texas Highways.* Not only that, these days there are magazines that cover almost any topic you can think of, and if there isn't a magazine for it, you've got to wonder whether that's because there might not be a large enough audience for your subject. Bear in mind, though, that if a magazine article catches your eye, you should wonder whether the author of that piece is working on his own book, from which the piece is either an excerpt or a teaser. Look also to the Web, for Web zines such as *Salon* and the like.

Tabloid TV like Oprah and Ricki Lake can be a place to start. Features on the History Channel, the Discovery Channel, *Dateline, 60 Minutes,* PBS's *Nova,* or *Frontline* can all start the old gray matter ticking with short intriguing pieces. It's also worth talking with scientists, doctors, police officers, firefighters, and lawyers, all of whom often have stories and ideas that could form the basis of at least an article, and might also be expanded later into a book.

The truth is that we rarely see a story as a whole, at least at the outset. Something about a story will speak to us, will catch our eye in the same way that a potential girlfriend or boyfriend might. Often we don't know exactly what it is that caught our attention, but somehow it is something that we can make our own. Sometimes it is the situation that speaks to us. How did he get into that situation? we think. And how on Earth did he get himself out of it?

Browsing Sources Old and New

Try to avoid old stories, unless there is something new to tell us. My client Judy Pearson, for example, discovered that despite the many books on spying during World War II, no one had ever told the remarkable story of Virginia Hall, an attractive Baltimore socialite with a wooden leg who was first a British undercover operative and eventually an OSS operative in France during the Nazi occupation. The sudden availability of never-before-published source material made all the difference in deciding whether or not this was a viable project.

James Srodes is a Washington, D.C., journalist who also writes biographies. He is the author of a number of books, including *Allen Dulles: Master of Spies* and *Franklin: The Essential Founding Father.* He commented that he reads endlessly, often going over ground that others have covered, looking for things that they may have overlooked. "I love to prove other people wrong," he said.

> I'm a journalist, so I guess I'm something of a professional smart-ass. I look for overlooked stories, to see where someone else has screwed up, to find a new angle on something that could be otherwise considered familiar. I read all the time looking for the "aha" factor. . . . When I was researching my biography of Benjamin Franklin, for example, I noticed that many previous biographers . . . came away unsatisfied as to who Franklin was. Aha, I thought, I can do this [write a biography of Franklin], and my interest quickly turned into a passion.

One of the simplest things to do is keep abreast of current events. When you pore over magazines and newspapers, consider whether there is an interesting story that has a human-interest angle. In the true crime category, for example, a brutal murder in a nearby neighborhood might really catch the local headlines. But what is there about the crime that would interest someone in a state several thousand miles away? If you live in Phoenix, Arizona, for example, and something happens there, why would a book about that subject sell in Alaska or Vermont?

Looking for stories in magazines and newspapers is not about trying to steal someone else's efforts—or at least it shouldn't be. Newspapers and magazines, by their very nature, only introduce you to a topic and maybe raise some questions about the why and wherefore in telling a news story. What makes a potential book is the answers (or search for answers) to unanswered questions the story has raised. A good example of a book that came from the seed of a small newspaper article was John Berendt's *Midnight in the Garden of Good and Evil.*

Look around you. What are the trends and social forces that you see at work? In early 2002, for example, everyone was chasing Enron stories—the biggest financial story of the decade, it was claimed. The books centered around tales told by some of the people involved in the financial scandal. But what about the larger ramifications of the story? What did the story tell us about who we are and why we do the things we do? What could a book tell us that a magazine article could not? If you can find answers to those questions, then maybe you have a potential book on your hands.

Truth is, though, that such a story is so big, and would attract such immediate national attention, that unless you have some personal experience you want to confess or reveal, other, more experienced writers will undoubtedly beat you to the punch on such a story and it's probably not worth your time pursuing it.

A Topic Is Not a Subject

A client of mine is a leading immigration lawyer. He writes a column for the *New York Daily News* as well as the Spanish-language *El Diario.* Yet a policy book about immigration needs to overcome the obstacles of audience indifference—not to say hostility following 9/11. The average American citizen doesn't care about immigration, except in terms of how it is impacting his or her immediate environment. It may make a good basis for an article in a magazine, but not for a book.

During a conversation we had, the author and I decided that one of the key aspects of immigration these days is civil rights. In effect, as part of the fallout of 9/11 there is a continuing assault on civil liberties, particularly of non–U.S. citizens.

If the government can take someone away and put them in jail indefinitely without trial, without access to a lawyer, and without an explicit charge, all in the name of homeland security, most Americans would say it is a necessary price to be paid for safety—until the day the government does it to them, someone they love, or a respected and beloved neighbor. The INS is able to not only imprison noncitizens on a whim and a suspicion, it can deny asylum to those who face certain disaster in their homeland if they are returned. But still there is nothing we could turn into a book here, only a topic. And topics do not make great book subjects.

A book would use fictional techniques to introduce us to, say, a family of three from Iraq who sought asylum because they had fallen victim to death threats from Saddam Hussein's secret police. After many dangerous adventures they arrive on American shores, pleading for their lives, only to be rebuffed. They are sent back to Iraq, where the father of the family is summarily executed. Not knowing where else to go, the mother and son return to the United States and once again plead for asylum—this time successful in their attempt. A dry, intellectual idea that might work for an academic press has been clothed in passion and human interest, and is therefore far more likely to successfully catch our attention and make its point far more vividly: that what happens to others, if we let it, will happen to us eventually as well if we are not careful. The book proposal now strives for universal appeal, even though it tells a specific and localized story.

This touches on a major obstacle writers don't grasp enough: Passion may be a prerequisite to writing, but a topic, however passionate one feels about it (you know them—health care, gun control, abortion, immigration, welfare cheats, and so on), makes a lousy book until it is humanized.

The way America treats its working poor is a national shame, Barbara Ehrenreich felt, and she found a powerful and emotionally grabbing way of taking a topic and making it relevant. "When someone works for less pay than she can live on—when, for example, she goes hungry so that you can eat more cheaply and conveniently—then she has made a great sacrifice for you, she has made you a gift of some part of her abilities, her health, and her life," Ehrenreich said.

The trick is to write a book that is compelling enough that people will read it. In an interview she gave to *Publishers Weekly*, Ehrenreich said,

> You don't start out thinking about who the audience is—or at least I don't. It's too constraining. I've written about economic issues a lot since the '80s, trying to show through statistics that people couldn't live on the mini-

mum wage. I wrote expository books, interviewed women, approached it from an economic point of view. But nothing I did seemed to make much difference. I mean, abolishing welfare was not what I had in mind. . . . I realized the next step was to get out there and try to draw some attention to these issues by personalizing them. . . . [Writing the book] really changed the way I saw the world. I began to see all the invisible people—I know this sounds like [the movie] *The Sixth Sense*—but I became aware of a world of discomfort and pain all around me: in the grocery store, at restaurants. I also found that writing in the very immediate first-person was a lot of fun.

Good Idea—Great Article, Weak Book?

Another difficult truth is that a good idea might make an excellent article but a weak book. You need to be able to look for and find the universal in the details of the specific in order to transmute an article into a book. Will anyone want to read the book? Will it even be relevant to readers three years after you sell the idea to a publisher?

So how do you know whether your idea is a magazine idea or a book idea? It's true that many nonfiction books start out life as articles. *Longitude, Into Thin Air, Black Hawk Down, The Hot Zone,* and *No One Left Behind* all began life as articles or a series of articles. However, in general, if a story is particularly timely, it will probably work better as a magazine or newspaper piece than as a book. If a story can have relevance two years from the time you start working on it, and hopefully a continued relevance beyond that (to create backlist life), then maybe it's a book. The magazine article may tell us what happened superficially, or portray a character, for example. But what is the deeper story? What will cause us to look back on an event or issue and see our current world afresh?

It took years, for example, for the British government to admit the truth about the sinking of the Argentinian cruiser *Belgrano* during the Falklands War.

In early 1982, the Royal Navy nuclear submarine HMS *Conqueror* torpedoed and sank the Argentinian cruiser *General Belgrano*. The ship sank within an hour, leaving approximately 290 crew members dead and a further 30 dying of burns and exposure in the icy waters of the south Atlantic.

After a great deal of stonewalling and blatant misinformation on behalf of the British government, the full story came out: The *Belgrano* was sunk when it was outside the 200-mile total-exclusion zone that Britain had declared around the Falkland Islands after an Argentine force seized the colony, and despite then–prime minister Margaret Thatcher's claim that the ship was inside the exclusion zone and steaming to engage British ships, the *Belgrano* was in fact heading for home and *away* from the exclusion zone. It was sunk to make a political point, by all accounts. The best way to tell that story in book form would be to zero in on several characters, some from each ship and some who were privy to the decision-making processes in London and Caracas, showing what happened and how decisions they made affected the lives of others, both known and unknown to them.

The 12-Point Book-Idea Checklist

Here are 12 points to consider when taking into account whether or not a story is worth pursuing as a book.

1. Play to your strengths. Write something you can be considered an expert about, and if that's not possible, make sure you have experts intimately involved in the telling of your story.

2. Play to your passions. Look for ideas and stories that genuinely interest and move you. If you're really a good writer—and as Peter Gethers comments, "Part of being a good writer is to have good instincts about things that are interesting and moving"—then readers will be attracted to your idea because of that passion.

3. Who is the audience for this book? What other books in this field can be used as models for your proposed book? Were they successful? Is the audience (that is, the market) easily definable, reachable, and large enough?

4. Will the book be relevant, say, three years after you manage to sell it to a publisher? Does it have backlist life, as well as front-list appeal?

5. Is the protagonist an interesting person? There is nothing more boring for an audience, or more challenging for a writer to capture on paper, than a character whose one claim to fame is a fleeting, dubious moment of glory in an otherwise humdrum, very ordinary existence. The central characters of *The Professor and the Madman*, for example, made the book stand out because author Simon Winchester was able to take a man without formal education, the editor Murray, and contrast him with a psychotic but highly intelligent murderer, Minor.

6. Is the antagonist interesting? If the story is true crime, for example, is the victim interesting? Those who are picked at random by killers are of less interest than those who were chosen by the killers for a specific reason.

7. Find an interesting setting, in terms of geography. Jon Krakauer's *Into Thin Air*, for example, takes us to the summit of Everest. Flying in a Thai Air jetliner, he stared out the window at the peak of Everest, 29,028 feet above sea level and level with the window. "It occurred to me that the top of Everest was precisely the same height as the pressurized jet bearing me through the heavens. That I proposed to climb to the cruising altitude of an Airbus 300 jetliner struck me, at that moment, as preposterous, or worse. My palms felt clammy."

8. Find an interesting, different world. For example, in the late 1980s, Ebola fever, an African virus with a 90 percent kill rate, broke out in

a research facility in the suburbs of Washington, D.C. A biohazard SWAT team from the U.S. Army was called in to work with scientists from the Centers for Disease Control to secretly contain and decontaminate the place. In Richard Preston's *The Hot Zone,* we are introduced to the fascinating, frightening world of lethal viruses and the secret world of the men and women who try to defeat them and make them harmless.

9. Find a story that has complications, or at least twists and turns. John Harrison, for example, the protagonist of *Longitude,* had no formal education or apprenticeship to a watchmaker. Yet he managed to solve the foremost puzzle of his time, how to accurately and effectively determine longitude at sea. It should have been a simple matter for him to claim the prize set out by the British Parliament for the first person to achieve this goal. However, for many years Harrison's every success was deflected by members of the scientific community of the time, who deeply distrusted the simple answer of two clocks set to differing times. The commissioners responsible for awarding the prize changed the rules several times in order to favor scientists who they felt were more deserving of the award, despite the fact they had not solved the problem. It took the intervention of King George III, when Harrison was an old man, 40 years after he initially solved the problem, to settle the matter in Harrison's favor. The complication, needless to say, must be a basic one: an injustice (as in Harrison's case), a theft, a setback, something that relates to the human condition involving jealousy, hate, love, pain, or the like.

10. If possible, find a story that has a resolution. Stories that are still hanging may make good magazine articles. (Although this is the most flexible of all the points, for someone just starting out it is one that is worth paying attention to if you hope for success.)

11. Find a story that ideally has a local, or regional, focus but will at the same time appeal to a national or global audience.

The Professor and the Madman, for example, is essentially centered around the Oxford region of England, which is where Murray lived, with occasional forays to London, and is some 30 miles or so from Broadmoor, where Minor was imprisoned. Yet the story clearly had global relevance.

12. Is it a major national story, like the Enron or WorldCom story? If so, almost certainly many major writers will be already working on it, and unless you have an inside track or something unique to bring to the table, it probably won't be worth your while pursuing it. Publishers hate to "crash" books—that is, bring them out quickly. It usually takes nine months from delivery and acceptance of the manuscript to its landing on the shelves. Shorter time frames make everyone's life miserable, and so only experienced professional writers are usually contracted to write books that have a particularly timely aspect to them.

THREE

Researching Your Subject: Poking and Prying with a Purpose

• • • • • • • • • • • • • • • • • •

Research is formalized curiosity. It is poking and prying with a purpose. It is a seeking that he who wishes may know the cosmic secrets of the world and that they dwell therein.

ZORA NEALE HURSTON, AFRICAN-AMERICAN WRITER

 I learned several valuable lessons about researching and reporting stories during my early years as a journalist in England in the 1970s: Don't believe anything you read or are told until it is confirmed from at least one other objective source. ACYA—always cover your ass. Get time, date, place; confirm correct spellings; get contact telephone numbers, cites, and so forth, in case you have to revisit a document or a person you interviewed. Keep careful notes and hang on to them for at least five years.

My first job as a journalist was on a weekly newspaper—the *Slough Observer*—in England. It was the nearest thing to perpetual studentship I could find at the time, and besides, I loved the idea of writing for a living. It had taken a few months to decide what I wanted to do (not economics, that was for sure, which is what I had been studying at university), and when I finally got a job as an apprentice reporter, it was late in the year. A typical British winter, cold and damp, was starting to settle in.

My second day on the job, I was bawled out for bad spelling in front of the assembled newsroom staff by the editor in chief. The news editor, Bob, took me aside and told me about my predecessor, as inexperienced as I, who had been asked by the editor in chief to confirm the spelling of someone's name in a story the reporter had written. The reporter was not sure, and did not have a contact telephone number. So the editor had ordered the reporter to get on his bicycle and cycle five miles in cold rain—on deadline, of course, so he had to cycle the five miles right back, not stopping off in the pub for a quick one—to confirm the spelling with the man in question in order for the newspaper to go to press that week with accurate information. It was a lesson I took to heart that has never failed me: ACYA—always cover your ass.

First Stop: The Library

Like a treasure hunt, research starts with small steps in the library and on the Internet. However, online research can be a quagmire. I'm lucky enough, because of a connection to New York University, to have access to the NYU library facilities. I can search for published articles on LexisNexis, ProQuest, and other databases, which has proved extremely useful.

Go to your local library and avail yourself of their Internet services if you can; it's a great first step. Many have access to these databases. (A little trick here: If you print the articles you may pay 25 cents or more for each page. Instead, if you e-mail the article to yourself you can print it out at home for free.)

There are many sources and places to find various indexes of information, and most of these are on the Web now. One of the best places is the Library of Congress, which is a huge resource and probably one of the first places to visit for leads in researching just about anything.

Once I've discovered some source material, I start reading and making notes of questions that occur to me, thoughts that flitter across my consciousness, and so forth. To write effective narrative nonfiction, you are looking to immerse yourself in the world of your subject, and then place their story within that world. In that sense, like all good fiction, narrative nonfiction takes us to strange new worlds and introduces us to people we haven't met before. Consider, for example, John Berendt's *Midnight in the Garden of Good and Evil,* set in steamy Savannah and filled with a fascinating assortment of colorful eccentrics that the city seems to nurture; or Richard Preston's *The Hot Zone,* a chilling story of an Ebola virus outbreak in a suburban Washington, D.C., laboratory.

How to Research: Reading and Talking

Research takes two forms: sifting through documents and talking to people. These are not easy things to learn to do well. They take practice and diligence, a great deal of thought, and frankly, a certain ethical mind-set. Don't just trust the Internet, which is famous for having a great deal of poor source material plastered all over it. Don't accept one version of something as gospel just because it appeals to you. Confirm it with several independent sources if you can.

Commenting on the research he did on his book *Into Thin Air,* for example, Jon Krakauer wrote: "At one point during my research I asked three other people to recount an incident all four of us had witnessed high on the mountain, and none of us could agree on such crucial facts as the time, what had been said, or even who had been present."

Journalist Iris Chang, who wrote the best-selling *The Rape of Nanking,* about Japanese atrocities in the Chinese city of Nanking in the 1930s, grew up in the academic community of Champaign-Urbana, Illinois. She explained that she had first heard the story of these atrocities from her parents. "Neither of my parents witnessed it," she said,

> but as young children they had heard the stories, and these were passed
> down to me. . . . Throughout my childhood *Nanjing Datusha* remained

buried in the back of my mind as a metaphor of unspeakable evil. But the event lacked human detail and human dimensions. It was also difficult to find the line between myth and history. While still in grade school I searched the local public libraries to see what I could learn about the massacre, but nothing turned up. That struck me as odd. . . . It did not occur to me, as a child, to pursue my research using the mammoth University of Illinois library system, and my curiosity about the matter soon slipped away.

It took another 20 years before Chang became again caught up in the story, realizing from her research that the story was not just myth, but documented, accurate oral history—despite Japanese insistence that the holocaust in Nanking never happened. She became determined to bring the truth of the incident to light, and her research was remarkable, involving both thousands of pages of documents and many interviews.

Random House executive editor Peter Gethers (who is also a published writer) had an interesting point to make about research. "The key to research," he commented, "ultimately, is not what you use but what you don't use." He added that even though "one has to be thorough and accurate . . . it's necessary to walk the fine line between accuracy and overdetailing."

In *How to Write,* the Pulitzer Prize–winning writer Richard Rhodes makes an interesting point about researching facts:

On the first day of my college course in . . . the methodology of writing history . . . Louis P. Curtis, the historian who taught the course, proposed that we prove what every English schoolchild knows, that Charles I, king of England from 1625–1649, was beheaded. . . .

The class reconvened. Everyone had discovered a fact that proved that the English people had beheaded their Scottish king. Mr. Curtis listened patiently to our reports. Then he summarily demolished them. An order for paint doesn't prove a beheading. A conviction of treason and a death sentence doesn't prove a beheading. Not even an eyewitness account proves a beheading. All might be misinformed or mistaken or fraudulent. History, Mr. Curtis shocked us by saying, is past, gone, unrecoverable in its authentic facticity [sic], and the writing of history is necessarily provisional, a matter of sifting the limited evidence and deducing what is probable and plausible and what is not. No accumulation of documents proves anything in and of itself.

Standards of Evidence Versus Proof

In other words, there are standards of evidence that responsible people may agree to, but there can be no final proof. As a trained and experienced journalist, my first reaction on reading this was to dismiss it out of hand. Some things are self-evident, after all, and pretty much scientifically proven, right? The world is round, the Earth travels around the sun, the Holocaust happened, and so forth. And yet even now, I reminded myself, in the early twenty-first century, there are people busy trying to prove the reverse of all these things. Caution is particularly necessary when we shift from day-to-day congress to the realm of creating, or more accurately, re-creating on the page events that by their nature are interesting (and commercially viable) because as readers we don't know much about them or the characters involved in them. The truth is, however, that whatever the facts do—or do not—prove, one can't write a piece of narrative nonfiction without thoroughly collecting and assembling them. Even in writing convincing historical fiction, for example, it is the veracity of a key fact or two in the narrative, an observation that really nails the scene into its time and place, that leads us to believe in the authenticity of the story, and thus its credibility.

In his essay "Rewriting the Rules of Nonfiction," *New York Times* award-winning reporter and book author Kurt Eichenwald talked about researching his book *The Informant: A True Story:*

When writing such books, every fact—from the weather conditions, to the color of the wallpaper, to the types of meals eaten by the characters—has to come from somewhere. Oftentimes, it requires the reporter to be as dogged in pursuing minutiae as in trying to crack the big secrets of a criminal investigation. In many ways, the reporting of such books is like working on the world's largest jigsaw puzzle. Everything provides a piece—an interview here, a receipt there, a document, a video—and all of these pieces must be brought together into a cohesive narrative, one that doesn't show any of the seams. What that means, of course, is an enormous amount of rewriting. Each new discovery of information must be run through the narrative and accounted for.

Connections?

Scientist Stephen Jay Gould once commented that his chief talent was the ability to see connections between things that to most people seem unrelated. Along the same lines, the British science reporter and writer James Burke always looks for the story in his material, and focuses not just on one aspect, but on the thread of events and their potential meaning. Using a kind of six-degrees-of-separation game with science and history, he tells a story that is not so much cause and effect as change and serendipity, which leads to inventions and discoveries. Burke attempts to demonstrate three phenomena: seemingly inconsequential events can lead to major innovations; inventions lead to new discoveries; and the technological advancements resulting from these discoveries can have profound effects throughout history on people and society. He created stories, in other words, like Stephen Jay Gould, from materials that at first blush do not seem to go together; but his stories are based on his expert knowledge and his ability to research strange and unusual things and connect them.

Here's a thumbnail example. In 1707, off the southern coast of England, a British admiral, Sir Cloudisley Shovell, decided to turn right when he should have turned left (the ability to accurately determine longitude not yet a part of the sailor's tool kit). As a result, his fleet foundered on the rocks and 2,000 men were lost at sea, including the unfortunate admiral.

The British government decided this longitude thing needed to be taken in hand, and it offered a prize (in today's money, worth several million dollars) for the person who solved the problem. The competition inspired a clock maker called Huntsman to find a better kind of steel for a spring to make watches keep better time.

The steel Huntsman discovered was great at cutting other steel, and was used by an Englishman called Wilkinson to bore out very thin cannon barrels. Napoleon used these cannons so effectively that his armies were able to conquer a large part of Europe. They needed to be provisioned, however.

In 1810, a French wine maker called Nicolas Appert solved that problem. He discovered that you can pack and preserve food by boiling it and putting it in a corked champagne bottle. This discovery allowed the emperor's well-fed army to travel longer and farther afield.

Several years later, following Napoleon's defeat in 1815, a British company was preserving food in cans because they had bought Appert's patent. They obtained it serendipitously, because they had actually gone to France to buy the patent to the first continuous-paper-making process, which in turn brought about the invention of the first-ever toilet roll.

So, one could say that the invention of the toilet roll was the direct result of having to solve a terrifying (and bowel-loosening) navigation problem at sea.

Who Knew? Who Cares?

A good researcher combines the skills of a reference librarian and a police detective. The first step in conducting any kind of research is to think through the project and plan some general lines of research. In researching history or biography or a current event, for example, it's a good idea to ask two questions:

Who would know about this?
Who would care enough about this to help put it in print?

When Judy Pearson started research on a biography of Virginia Hall, America's most famous female undercover agent of World War II in France, she was amazed to discover no one had ever written a book about Hall. Judy uncovered a fascinating story that, in brief, took a Baltimore socialite with a wooden leg, who worked in Europe for the U.S. State Department during the 1930s, to London. She was recruited as an operative of the SOE (the British equivalent of the OSS) and then smuggled into France. She became the number-one target of the Nazi Gestapo, which had orders to kill her on sight, and had to escape by walking into Spain before going on to London. Back in London, she was recruited as an undercover operative for the OSS (later to become the CIA) and smuggled back into France to help prepare for the D-Day landings by operating behind the lines.

Judy first got in touch with Hall's niece, who was prepared to help with the book and had previously unpublished material she gave Judy. The author also got an unprecedented commitment from the head librarian of the CIA Museum allowing her to become the first civilian given access to recently declassified wartime OSS papers. She also planned to go to London, France, and Germany in order to find documentation about Hall from the SOE, the French Resistance (which Hall helped set up), and Gestapo files. With this kind of travel involved in researching the book, it was imperative to think through where she was going, why, and what she hoped to look for when she got there.

The Five Basic Resources for Research

There are five basic resources for research:

- Published books
- Unpublished manuscripts, letters, and the like
- Limited-edition documents, such as reports by organizations, newsletters, restricted memos, and court documents
- Magazines, newspapers, and other periodicals
- Interviews

The Four Basic Ways to Carry Out Research

There are four basic ways to conduct research:

- Reading and viewing source material (books, papers, films, pictures, and so forth). Biographers, historians, and investigative journalists do it all the time.
- Interviewing people face-to-face, or by letter or e-mail. I did it for this book; Richard Preston did it for his book *The Hot Zone;* so did Mark Bowden *(Black Hawk Down)* and Sebastian Junger *(The Perfect Storm),* to mention but a handful.
- Firsthand observation. A great example of this is D. Graham Burnett's memoir of jury duty on a murder trial in Manhattan, *A Trial by Jury.*
- Deductive reasoning, which connects the dots drawn by the other three methods. This last is the most fraught and dangerous because it does not involve something empirically tangible but involves supposition, which can land an unsuspecting writer into a lot of trouble if he or she isn't careful.

One of the most interesting examples of this last kind of research informing a book is Sebastian Junger's *The Perfect Storm.* This is how he describes tackling the problem:

> Recreating the last days of six men who disappeared at sea presented some obvious problems for me. On the one hand, I wanted to write a completely factual book that would stand on its own as a piece of journalism. On the other hand, I didn't want the narrative to asphyxiate under a mass of technical detail and conjecture. . . .
>
> In the end I wound up sticking strictly to the facts, but in as wide-ranging a way as possible. If I didn't know exactly what happened aboard the doomed boat, for example, I would interview people who had been through similar situations, and survived. Their experiences, I felt, would provide a fairly good description of what the six men in the *Andrea Gail* had gone through, and said, and perhaps even felt.

A classic example of this technique is a chapter toward the end of the book titled "The Zero-Moment Point." It is the point where the boat sinks and the crew drown. The whole chapter is based on the experiences of people who almost drowned, and the science of what happens to a boat when it sinks and to a human being's body when it drowns. For all that it is pure conjecture, it is conjecture rooted in hard fact, and does not pretend to be anything other than a way of trying to understand what happened to the crew of the *Andrea Gail* at the moment of its demise. I'm a little uncomfortable holding up this kind of substitute research and writing style as a paragon of how to deal with such narrative problems, but there is no doubt that Junger's experience and integrity as a reporter make all the difference in carrying off this kind of storytelling in the book.

Journalist and author James Srodes, at a panel discussion on writing nonfiction at the National Press Club in Washington in May 2002, talked about writing and researching biographies:

My message is context, context, context. You have to build a timeline, and you have to be able to . . . say with some authority who these people are, and what they knew, and more importantly what they didn't know. What other people knew and what they didn't know, and what was going on [at the time]. . . .

You [also] have to discipline yourself to grab context where you can and make it work for you while you're following the timeline of your subject's life.

As an example, he mentioned writing the biography of Allen Dulles, one of the founders of the CIA. "Writing [the biography] was largely the story of how we came to get the intelligence services we have today, against the life of this rather extraordinary man."

It's important to watch out for those blind alleys of information that beckon seductively off the main trail of the story you are trying to tell. If you're not careful, before you know it you have stopped writing about the life of, say, Thomas Jefferson and instead you are writing about the War of Jenkins's Ear.

How to Take Notes

A skill worth developing when plumbing the depths of material is good note taking. Most reporters are never taught this; they just learn by trial and error and the fear of screwing up on deadline. When I worked on an evening newspaper with a midday deadline for stories for the first edition, I often had to jot down an opening paragraph in my notebook, then phone in the story and dictate it to a typist by reading the written lead paragraph from my notebook and then creating the rest of the story extemporaneously from my notes. You shouldn't have to write a book that way, but writing newspaper articles on the fly certainly taught me the value of keeping good notes.

Here are some tips on note taking:

- When you tape-record an interview, always first ask permission of the person you're interviewing. Some people don't mind, others can be intimidated by the idea. In some states it's actually illegal to tape someone, even over the phone, without their express permission. ("Do you mind if I record this so I get what you say accurately?" is always a good point.) Always carry a fresh supply of batteries with you, and from time to time actually check to see if the machine is recording. If you're using a tape recorder, for example, look carefully to see if the tape wheels are turning.

- Think about converting your interviews from tape (or mini disc) into wave files on your computer. Then, using a wave editing program, you can cut and splice the interview, and bookmark and otherwise move along to any point you want in the recording pretty rapidly. It may take a couple of days to get comfortable with the program, but it's worth it if you have extensive recorded interviews. And they can't deteriorate with time and are easily stored by burning them onto CDs.

- If at all possible, get photocopies of original material you may use to refer to when writing your story. If not, then at least be thorough and record enough information so that you can make sense of what you wrote when you return to your notes in a few months' time. Don't make your notes so cryptic you have no clue what the notes are exactly about, or where they came from.

- If possible, take notes in spiral-bound notepads no larger than the size and thickness of the average mass-market paperback (approximately five by seven inches). Spiral-bound pads are easily found in stationery stores, and the top-spiral-bound notepads in particular make it much easier to turn the page as you're taking notes. According to journalist and author Richard Rhodes, this is what Tracy Kidder told him was his preferred method. "Don't try to tape-record," Kidder said. "People freeze up, and besides it'd take years to transcribe all that tape. I just buy a stack of pocket-size spiral notebooks and make notes whenever I can."

- If you do use paper, make sure you use only one side. There's nothing worse than forgetting to turn over the page (we've all done it, trust me) and inadvertently throwing away something you need because it's on the back of something you don't need.
- Write down full notes on the sources of your information, partly so you can find it again and check its accuracy if you need to, and partly so that you can establish its veracity if challenged.
- Type wherever possible. For example, if you're doing library research, use a laptop computer if you can so that you don't have to worry about not being able to read your handwriting later.
- Work to a system. I recommend one that relates to the project you're researching rather than, say, the sources of the information you've found. (Don't categorize all information from the Baltimore Public Library as "Baltimore," and all information from the CIA Museum as "Museum," but instead use "Hall's life prior to 1939" and "Hall's work for the OSS.")
- Truman Capote claimed that he had trained himself to remember as much as a four-hour interview verbatim. Personally, without aids I can't remember 10 minutes these days, and I suspect most people are nearer to my side of the spectrum than Capote's. However, the acclaimed journalist David Halberstam *(The Best and the Brightest)* was reported to have said that when interviewing people who don't want to be recorded in any way, he often used his memory, and then transcribed notes soon after.

Interviewing

As a young reporter, I used to hate to interview, immediately after the event, the relatives of people who had died traumatic deaths. It made me feel like a vulture. The kid was hit by a truck; she drowned while swimming in the local swimming pool; his airplane crashed; her car was smashed in a 10-

car pileup on a highway in the fog; he was mugged and killed for $5 in the mean streets of Bedford-Stuyvesant in New York City . . . What could the survivors, in their grief and mourning, add to the facts of the story? Why would they even want to talk with me in the first place?

Funny thing is, nearly all the relatives of these people wanted to talk to me, and the stories and details they gave me always enriched and humanized the story. What's more, it showed me that my initial fear that sources would not talk to me was wrong. In fact, people *want* to talk about themselves and their experiences, for the most part. It's a natural human instinct, and when people believe that what they have to say is not being judged or treated with scorn or contempt, it's sometimes hard to shut them up. What turns out to be much harder than getting them to start talking is keeping them focused on topic.

The fear that people don't want to be interviewed by a reporter and will spurn them is an understandable qualm on the reporter's behalf, but it's an indulgence that most professional journalists can't afford, because they have to answer to editors who need the story. If someone says, "Go away," so what? If they hang up on you, call again, persist in getting the information some other way.

My first news editor, Bob, told me a story about his experience of what used to be called in England "foot-in-the-door" journalism that helped keep much of my later career as a writer in perspective. Bob was a short, thin man in his forties at the time I knew him, who sometimes liked to smoke a pipe while he edited. He had an easy laugh and a great sense of humor and was one of the most mild-mannered people I ever worked for. He was a terrific journalist who could smell a good story the moment he saw it, and also knew when he was being bullshitted. He went out of his way to make life comfortable for those who worked for him, while not compromising standards in any way.

Early in Bob's career, working for a British Sunday tabloid newspaper not unlike the *National Inquirer*, he was given the job of interviewing a woman who was one of the wives of a convicted bigamist awaiting court sentencing. He spent all day camped out a few doors away from the woman's house, in his cramped Volkswagen Beetle, parked in a suburban street of semidetached houses and small, postage-stamp gardens guarded in a number of instances by plastic garden gnomes. Many of the people in the street regularly read Bob's newspaper on Sundays.

Bob saw her arrive home late in the morning carrying shopping bags, and immediately went to her front door and rang the bell. When she answered the door, he said, "Hi, I'm Bob from so-and-so newspaper and I'd like to interview you about—" This was as far as he got. She said, "I don't want to talk to you, and my old man works nights and is upstairs trying to sleep. If you wake him up he'll come down here and beat the shit out of you. You've been warned." With that she slammed the door closed—almost.

Taking the concept of foot-in-the-door journalism a little too literally, Bob put his foot between the door and the doorjamb, thinking that when the door bounced off his foot he would get a few more precious moments to press his case as to why she should talk to him. Unfortunately, the door latched shut with his foot still caught in it. Now he was stuck, and his foot was starting to hurt.

He rang the bell. She ignored him. He rang the bell again, and again and again. Eventually a large and very unhappy truckdriver jerked open the door and said, "Oi! She told you to piss off." As Bob limped quickly away, he was chased by the truckdriver. In fact, Bob did not have time to get out his car keys and had to run—or rather quickly hobble—down the street for some way before he was able to hide behind a bush for what seemed like ages while the truckdriver stood in the doorway of his house, hands on hips, glowering and surveying the street, keeping an eye out for Bob's return. Eventually he went inside and Bob was able to sneak over to his car and make his getaway.

What happens to you if you're turned down by a potential interviewee is not likely to be worse than what happened to Bob, and he survived to have a good career as a journalist after that incident.

Don't assume that people won't talk to you or don't want to. A musician acquaintance of mine named Gordon regularly toured with Miles Davis many years ago when Miles worked a lot in Europe. One night he sat in with me and some friends as we played a jazz gig and we all had a ball, of course. Afterward, Gordon explained that he played very little in England because everyone assumed he worked all the time as a result of his connection to Miles, and no one bothered to call him and ask him to do gigs, which he would have been perfectly happy to do if he was available.

One of the remarkable things about *Cinderella & Company* is that all the people interviewed for the book already knew Hoelterhoff's reputation for being an acerbic writer, but they were nevertheless happy to talk freely with her. Of course, she was well aware of the plethora of arrogance that is rampant in opera and used it to her advantage. Truth is, her subjects didn't care what she thought or said about them as long as they were portrayed as major players in the book. This is particularly true of the powerful agent Herbert Breslin, whom Hoelterhoff admits she so hated that she used to go through the *New York Times* obituary pages looking for his, "a little squib tucked under the fold, somewhere beneath retired postmasters and minor-league ballplayers from the 1950s." She describes Breslin as a "motor-mouthed, bullet-headed, forever tan egomaniac," and his monologue on how he got his main client, Luciano Pavarotti, to show everyone how real money could be made in opera is breathtaking in its overt shamelessness.

Two things are important when interviewing someone: Be as prepared as you can before you start the interview, even to the extent of writing down some questions if you need to; and try to be a sort of fly on the wall while you're conducting the interview. The notion of going into an interview to get someone to confess, or otherwise spill the beans, is frankly foolish for the most part. People are far more likely to confess in an attempt to explain themselves. Truth is, most people want others to like them and will provide all sorts of information to someone they don't find threatening or judgmental. But you have to be willing to listen without comment or contradiction or argument, at least at first. Let people hang themselves with their own words. Encourage them to speak; don't insert yourself into the interview if you can help it; just prod it along. Toward the end of the interview you can always say something like, "I'm a bit confused." Then, referring to your notes (I recommend that you take notes even if you are recording your interview with a tape recorder or MiniDisc Walkman for the sake of accuracy), ask: "I thought you said earlier blah-blah. That seems to contradict yada-yada. Help me out here." Then sit back and record the response.

Robert Conot, the author of *Rivers of Blood, Years of Darkness*, about the 1965 Los Angeles riot, decided he was going to compile "a complete historical account" of the event. To that end he spent from August 1965 to May 1966 gathering material that filled "an entire filing cabinet."

This represented, in addition to information culled from documents compiled by various agencies, interviews and discussions of varying length with nearly 1,000 persons, and the written accounts of occurrences, as well as personal opinions, of some 500 more.

[I] became familiar with the south-central area a considerable period of time before the riot, and, by exercising prudence, was able to move about the area even while the riot was still in progress, thus observing some of the happenings firsthand.

His sources included the Los Angeles County district attorney's office, the California National Guard, the California attorney general's office, the Los Angeles Fire Department, the L.A. Police Department, the L.A. County Probation Department, the Bureau of Public Assistance, the California Fair Employment Practices Commission, the complete transcript of the McCone Commission hearings on the riot, the records of some 200 felony trials, the L.A. County Human Relations Commission, the Bureau of Public Assistance, plus hundreds of interviews.

How Accurate Is the Recollection?

The passage of time is an important element of storytelling, although the story needs to be true to its period. When interviewed, people tend to edit themselves, aligning their memories more with the tenor of the time they are being interviewed, rather than trying to re-create exactly what they thought at the time they are now recollecting. This can lead to anachronistic story-telling that seems to read well now but is untrue for the period actually being reconstructed. We are more enlightened now, it can be argued; but that is no reason that good guys of yesteryear can't be portrayed as display-ing opinions and traits we would find objectionable now. At its extreme, biographers of historical figures such as Jefferson and Lincoln struggle with this issue a lot.

One of the most potent tools at your disposal as an interviewer is silence. Don't rush to fill in a silence in the interview (unless it's a radio or TV interview you're conducting, of course). Just wait without talking. The strain of the silence almost always prompts the interview subject to fill it in some way.

For some people, the aggressive approach works, but it has a limited success in my experience, and most of the journalists who use it regularly are, frankly, assholes. In an exposé there may be room for such an interview technique, but not in many other places. Still, if that is your style, I guess you must go with it if it gets results. I would also avoid overt flattery unless you really mean it. Most people can smell insincerity a mile off and that's likely to shut down any meaningful interview early on because your subject will feel contempt for you.

I've found that if you treat people with respect they will respond much better to you and give you what you want or help you get it, most of the time. Most interviews are done *on the record,* that is, the source is willing to be identified and quoted directly.

When dealing with institutions, you sometimes have to resort to *attribu-*

tion—that is, "A White House spokeswoman said," "An executive from Enron, who refused to be named, explained," and so forth.

Lastly, there is *off the record,* which means essentially that someone will give you leads and background information but cannot be quoted or used directly in constructing your story. That doesn't mean you can't use that nameless person's information to pry a response or confirmation out of someone else, who will be on the record, however.

What do you do when someone refuses to talk? Here's an interesting phenomenon: When telemarketers call on the phone or knock on the door, even when we don't want to do business with them, most of us take time to explain we are not interested. The telemarketer argues back, "But just give me a minute," and before we know it, because we have maintained the relationship in some manner, we have provided the opportunity to the salesperson to hook us. The only way to avoid the situation is to politely but firmly say, "No thank you, I'm not interested," and then close the door or hang up the phone, severing any further connection.

If your interviewee is still with you, even if he or she has so far refused to answer a question or cooperate, then the door is still open. Threats rarely work and are unnecessarily antagonistic, as I've discussed. Outright lying is not something worth attempting because you usually get caught, and that will make interviewing others harder as your reputation for dishonesty precedes you. Shading the truth is acceptable, however. Woody Allen once gave a wonderful description of how he won a fight by using his chin to smash his opponent's fist, quickly following that with a crushing blow from his groin to his opponent's knee . . . It's all in the perspective.

What Bob taught me to say was something like this: "Look, we're going to write this story about you whether or not you give me an interview. I've already got two people [or however many there are] who claim such-and-such, but frankly that doesn't quite make sense to me. It's really in your interest to talk with me because we really want to do a fair and accurate piece, and we need to hear your side of what happened."

Listen Quietly, Be Tenacious

In writing *Black Hawk Down,* Mark Bowden explained, he had been fascinated by the battle in Mogadishu, but as he had "no military background or sources, [I] assumed that someone with both would tell the story far better than I could."

Sometime later Bowden read that at a Medal of Honor ceremony for two of the Delta Force soldiers killed at Mogadishu, the father of one of the men had insulted President Clinton, telling him he was not fit to be commander in chief. After a meeting with the father of another dead soldier who knew little of what had happened, Bowden made up his mind to learn more.

Some three years after the event he made requests to the Pentagon media office, which were ignored. He then filed a Freedom of Information request for documents, which still hadn't arrived two years after that. "I was told that the men I wanted to interview were in units off-limits to the press. My only hope of finding the foot soldiers I wanted [to interview] was to ask for them by name, and I knew only a handful of names. I combed through what little had been written about the battle and submitted the names I found there, but I did not receive a response."

At such a dead end, what was a good reporter to do? As in all good stories about reporters, persistence paid off in an unexpected way. He was sent an invitation by the father of one of the dead soldiers to the dedication of a building at the Picatinny Arsenal in memory of his son. It would take Bowden a day of traveling, and with his lack of success up to that point, the story had become less important. "Still," he said,

> I had been moved by my conversation with Jim. I have sons just a few
> years younger than his Jamie. I couldn't imagine losing one of them,
> much less in a gunfight someplace like Mogadishu. I made the drive.
>
> And there, at this dedication ceremony, were about a dozen Rangers
> who had fought with Jamie in Mogadishu. Jim's introduction helped
> break down the normal suspicion soldiers have for reporters. The men

. . . the . . .

gave me their names and told me how to arrange interviews with them. Over three days at Fort Benning that fall I conducted my first twelve interviews. Each of the men I talked to had names and phone numbers for others who had fought there that day, many of them no longer in the army. My network grew from there.

He visited Somalia and got the Somali side of the battle. He discovered the battle had been videotaped and he was able to listen to radio traffic, from which he transcribed actual dialogue. Eventually he watched the 15 hours of army video of the battle. Along with documentary material he recovered, the material "gave me, I believe, the best chance any writer has ever had to tell the story of a battle completely, accurately, and well."

John McPhee is possibly the most successful and most respected writer of narrative nonfiction around today. He has been doing it since 1964 and has garnered a multitude of awards and nominations, including two National Book Award nominations. In *The John McPhee Reader,* the editor, William Howarth, describes why McPhee is so successful at his job. McPhee, he explains, is a person who "inspires confidence, since people rarely find someone who listens that carefully to them. . . . He cultivates a certain transparency in social relations, a habit derived from practicing his craft. To see and hear clearly, he keeps his eyes open and mouth shut."

One of the best descriptions of a self-effacing interview technique can be found in *The John McPhee Reader.* William Howarth wrote:

When McPhee conducts an interview, he tries to be as blank as his note-book pages, totally devoid of preconceptions, equipped with only the most elementary knowledge. He has found that imagining he knows a subject is a disadvantage, for that prejudice will limit his freedom to ask, to learn, to be surprised by unfolding evidence. Since most stories are full of unsuspected complexity, an interviewer hardly needs to feign ignorance; the stronger temptation is to bluff with a show of knowledge or to trick the informant into providing simple, easily digestible answers. . . . [McPhee] would rather risk seeming ignorant to get a solid, knotty answer.

As a result, some of his interviewees have mistakenly believed he is thick-witted. At times his speech slows, his brow knits, he asks the same question over and over. When repeating answers, he so garbles them that a new answer must be provided. Some informants find his manner relaxing, others are exasperated; in either case, they talk more freely and fully to him than they normally would to a reporter. While McPhee insists that his air of density is not a deliberate ruse, he does not deny its useful results. Informants may be timid or hostile, unless they feel superior or equal to their interviewer. By repeating and even fumbling their answers, McPhee encourages people to embroider a topic until he has it entire. In an ideal interview he listens without interrupting, at liberty to take notes without framing repartee or otherwise entering the conversation.

What better example of the art of research than that?

Order Out of Chaos: Building the Skeleton of the Book

••••••••••••••••••

Obviously, where art has it over life is in the matter of editing. Life can be seen to suffer from a drastic lack of editing. It stops too quick, or else it goes on too long. Worse, its pacing is erratic. Some chapters are little more than a few sentences in length, while others stretch into volumes. Life, for all its raw talent, has little sense of structure. It creates amazing textures, but it can't be counted on for snappy beginnings or good endings either. Indeed, in many cases no ending is provided at all. . . . Even in a literary age like the nineteenth century it never occurred to anyone to posit God as Editor, useful as the metaphor might have been.

LARRY MCMURTRY, *FILM FLAM: ESSAYS ON HOLLYWOOD*

 Originally, this chapter was going to be about writing a book proposal, so it may seem a little out of sequence, if not premature, to start discussing the structure of your narrative nonfiction book before covering how to create a proposal for it. After all, nearly all nonfiction is sold in proposal form first and then written from the outline included with the book proposal—except, of course, that as more research is done, and the writer gains more knowledge of his subject, the book begins to deviate from the proposal in detail, if not in broad outline.

And that's the point here: A proposal is a separate entity from the finished manuscript, and how to create one doesn't really fit into a sequence of chapters concerned with the techniques of writing a book. Placing a chapter on proposal writing here could be seen as interrupting a logical structural flow.

Aha! A comment about the structure of this book, as an example of structuring books in general. How cunning. The chapter on writing a proposal could fit anywhere, theoretically, but my editor and I agreed that actually it should be at the end of the book so as not to interrupt the flow of chapters dealing with how to *write* a book of narrative nonfiction, rather than *sell and market* one.

Art Must Have Its Own Logic

"Let's get the rules straight first," Butch Cassidy says to the gang member who challenges him to a knife fight, in William Goldman's movie *Butch Cassidy and the Sundance Kid.*

"Huh?" says the gang member. "There are no rules to a knife fight."

"OK," says Butch, and delivers what Goldman describes in his screenplay as "the biggest kick in the balls ever seen in the history of motion pictures."

Similarly, there are no rules in writing. Do what works for you—and your readers. Here's a clue to whether or not you're right: Are you getting published? If you're not getting published in some form, then you're not the best judge of your own material. I'd go further, and venture to say that if you're reading this, clearly you lack at least the confidence, if not the expertise, to carry off extravagant storytelling and are looking for some guidance about this book-writing business. Don't confuse the ideas that follow with rules— they're not. They're analytical tools to help shape and tame your creative endeavors if you're having trouble getting them down on the page.

It's a universal law, like gravity, that all art must abide by its own internal logic—a natural structure inherent to the piece of art you're creating, be it overtly pastoral or avant-garde in the extreme. Without a coherent internal structure that creates and follows its own rules—which may not be at all obvious sometimes—there is no creativity, only random chaos.

Second Thoughts?

So, having come up with a book idea, and some initial research around it, you should pause for a moment and consider if you want to live with your subject for a year or more. If you have the right book idea for you, that won't really be an issue, because you'll be excited by each revelation you uncover. However, it's worth remembering that the historian David McCullough (author of the best-selling biography *John Adams*) once contracted with Simon & Schuster to write a biography of the artist Pablo Picasso. The more he researched Picasso, however, the more McCullough decided he didn't want to spend time with the artist. Luckily, he had a better idea—a biography of Harry S. Truman—and managed to convince his publisher to let him write that book instead. (Thus are the origins of some great books.)

Another bad reason to write a narrative book is for its timely news value. With a potential eighteen-month lag from signing up a book with an editor to seeing it arrive on a bookstore's shelves, the breaking-news value of any book is going to be dubious at best. Of course, tell us the story, but don't leave it there. What does this story mean to the rest of us? How does the story somehow become *more,* take on a symbolic or universal quality, despite the specifics of its details?

For all that *Into Thin Air* is about the disaster on Mount Everest, it is also about the challenges of mountaineering and why people are attracted to the sport. In 1953, Sir Edmund Hillary became the first man to reach the summit of Mount Everest after nearly 100 years of people dying in the attempt. By 1996, there were traffic jams of people paying upward of $70,000 each to be tour-guided to the top. Jon Krakauer set out to explore why. "The notion that climbers are mere adrenalin junkies chasing a righteous fix is a fallacy, at least in the case of Everest," he wrote. "What I was doing up there had almost nothing in common with bungee jumping or skydiving or riding a motorcycle at 120 miles per hour. . . . I quickly came to understand that climbing Everest was primarily about enduring pain. And in subjecting ourselves to week after week of toil, tedium, and suffering, it struck me that most of us were probably seeking, above all else, something like a state of grace."

The best reason to write about something that happened in a story form is that the telling of the story will afford us the ability to reflect on the true meaning of the event, and how it was perceived at the time.

The Man in the Bar . . .

One of the best ways to start ordering your thoughts and material is to practice what can be called the "man in the bar" technique. In other words, tell the story as if you were telling it to an interested listener over a drink. I find this an interesting experience at dinner parties with friends who make the foolish mistake of asking me what I'm writing at the moment. To my way of thinking (and many writers would disagree with this), if I can't hold their interest when retelling in miniature what has fascinated me so much about a subject I am devoting time to write about, that's a clue there's something adrift somewhere.

Many writers don't like to talk about works in progress, and the reasons are myriad. I'm always terrified I'm going to bore people to death with the crude fumblings of my effort of the moment, and manage to convince myself at the same time I must be mad continuing to work on something no one is interested in hearing about.

But telling the heart of the story becomes an interesting task when someone genuinely wants to know what I'm working on. Obviously from memory, and with a determination to make the story as "sexy" as possible, I

. . . the . . .

start to tell the bare outlines of the story and why it fascinates me. If I can't do that, if I don't have a grasp on the elemental story I'm trying to tell, I'm going to have real problems writing it. As I tell the story I find a natural structure starts to emerge. This is an extension of the first piece of advice I was ever given on how to write a news story (by Bob, my wonderful news-editor mentor on the *Slough Observer*): Write the piece as if you were writing a letter home to your mother. Start with the most interesting thing first. "Dear Mum, Guess what happened to me today? I met a man who blah blah blah."

Find Your Audience

A writer is no less a performer than a singer or actor, and like them, a writer should try to take into consideration how his audience is going to react to his work. This is not pandering or compromising your art but honing your material so it appeals to a group of harried but interested recipients. As you assemble your material and start to construct the book, you should ask yourself: Who's going to read this book? Why? How can I make the book compelling to this audience?

Narrative nonfiction should do more than just tell a story that perhaps has been recounted already in a newspaper or magazine. It needs to peel the onion, get under the skin in some way.

People are much more likely to read short pieces in magazines about things that they might not want to buy books about. Why pay $25 for a book that says you're screwed, basically, unless it also suggests ways you can get unscrewed? You can frighten people (think of *Silent Spring,* Rachel Carson's classic, or Richard Preston's *The Hot Zone*), but it's hard to write a book that leaves the reader no hope or optimism or something profound to think about. Regardless of what publicity you get for yourself, the content of your book is a factor in its commercial viability.

Take the case of *Creating a Life: Professional Women and the Quest for*

Children by Sylvia Ann Hewlett. The book discussed the growing fear among middle class and professional women (and provided statistics to prove its point) that women who sacrifice families for careers may well wake up childless at 45. Great things were expected of the book and its author. The publisher, Miramax Books, paid the author a six-figure advance and printed 30,000 hardcover copies. In its first two months the book generated the kind of publicity authors dream about. It was featured on the TV show *60 Minutes* and the covers of *Time* and *New York* magazines. It was promoted on *Oprah*, *Today*, *Good Morning America,* and *NBC Nightly News*. It was debated on the editorial and op-ed pages of the *Los Angeles Times,* the *San Francisco Chronicle,* and the *New York Times*. But after two months, the most talked-about book in America in the spring of 2002 had sold somewhere in the region of 8,000 copies—a poor performance under the circumstances. Why did things go so wrong?

The explanation seems simple: Women were just not interested in shelling out $22 for a book that front-loaded depressing news about their biological clocks and had a couple of cursory final chapters (which they probably never got to) on what they could do about the situation.

Jonathan Burnham, the editor in chief of Miramax Books, was quoted in the *New York Times* as saying: "What people [came] away with [was] the frightening data. They [were] taking in the bad news and not paying attention to the prescriptive elements."

Ironically, many experts also felt the tsunami of media coverage actually dampened readers' interest. "The woman who feels devastated that her life didn't work out doesn't want to read about it," Roxanne Coady, the owner of R. J. Julia Booksellers in Madison, Connecticut, was quoted as saying in the *Times*. "The woman who gets it as a cautionary tale gets what they need from the press." And there's the rub. Who needed to read a book that made you feel bad when, instead, you could get what you needed to know from the press coverage?

A Good Title

A title and subtitle are important elements of a book. Originally I had decided to call this book *The Elements of Narrative Nonfiction: Writing the Novel of True Events*. As I began working on the book it struck me as a clumsy title. And so, after some discussion, we decided upon the current title. The original title was good enough, though, that I could use it as an axis around which I could start to gather focused information and conduct interviews. A good title and subtitle will help focus your book, and without such a lens attached to your creativity you will struggle to decide what should be in the book and what ultimately does not fit. Each time you're unsure of how to apply information or interpret it, it's useful to think to yourself: What's the title of what I'm writing, again?

Your Spine—the Table of Contents

A couple of tricks that may help involve using colored three-by-five or five-by-seven index cards. Each group of colored cards represents a chapter (pink for chapter 1, blue for chapter 2, green for chapter 3). You can reuse colors after a while. Once you've done this you can shuffle the chapters around and find the best structure for the material.

Gather your index cards and notes, and lay them out on the floor before you. Start moving them into some sort of order, both chronological and in terms of sequences of action. Have you conducted all the research you need to do? Are there holes in the timeline, or parts of the action you can't re-create or track? Can you show the events of your story in enough detail? What have you uncovered that no longer seems to be relevant to the story you're telling? Can it be discarded?

Assemble the information into a rough table of contents (TOC). This is essentially your spine, and it should comprise chapter headings, and per-

haps a line or two about what will be in the chapter in question. Allow yourself the luxury of writing pretty freely, jotting down anecdotes, stories, facts,
and so forth that you can gather under these chapter headings. If you can't
fit new material into the existing TOC, either create a new heading or put it
under a miscellaneous heading, to be inserted later (maybe). Start accepting that some of the information, even the more interesting or entertaining
aspects of what you've found, may have to be left out of the book because it
simply doesn't fit.

Structure Is Organic—Trust Your Instincts

Do you remember that scene in the first *Star Wars* movie when Luke has to
make a near impossible shot as he battles the death star? He hears Obi-
Wan's voice tell him, "Use the force," and he calms himself down and listens to his instincts, which guide him in delivering the coup de grâce to the
death star. The point? Sometimes it's best to just relax, like Luke. Gather
your material around you, reorder and reshuffle it as you would a bunch of
Scrabble tiles, and let the natural structure of a story emerge organically
from the way the material all fits together naturally. This leads to that, that
leads to the other.

How will you know? The right structure is the one that comfortably lets
most of the facts and information you've gathered all neatly slot into place.
This may sound simple, but it shouldn't automatically be assumed that it's
easy. If the structure of the narrative (that is, the story) isn't right, then people won't understand the importance of what you're writing and make sense
of the facts you've assembled.

The structure of the narrative is what's going to get people to the facts,
and a reader isn't going to get to the facts without the story. For many writers the story seems to come naturally as they gather their material and try to

mentally synthesize it for themselves. It all depends on what you're writing about, who the characters are, and what they've done.

At a roundtable discussion on narrative nonfiction sponsored by the English Department of the University of Pittsburgh in 2001, Brendan Cahill, then a senior editor at Grove/Atlantic, commented that "there's definitely a concern that the story and the truth is what's being served. . . . I think what creative [that is, narrative] nonfiction allows you to do is to create an arc of storytelling to allow the facts and people's thoughts and emotions to all have a coherence to the interpretive framework that the writer uses to recap and then tell or relate it to the reader."

Structure is a reassuring thing. It's what helps the reader trust the narrative voice; but most of the time readers are not and probably should not be, aware of the artifice of a structured story. Books that obviously play with this convention are Dave Eggers's *A Heartbreaking Work of Staggering Genius* and some of the books of Tom Wolfe and Hunter Thompson. In such cases, style is as important as content, but the writer has to establish somehow (through published articles mainly) that he or she is a recognized stylist. This kind of writing became known as gonzo reporting (that is, idiosyncratically subjective) and it slowly morphed into memoir. It's a tough choice to emulate as a role model. These authors write the only way they know how to, because it's an extension of who they are, not just to produce a book of self-conscious artifice.

The Two Kinds of Structure in a Narrative

A narrative has two distinct kinds of structure: *what* it is and *how* it's put together. *What* your narrative is begins with your outline. It includes what sets your story in motion, that is, the instigating event; the goal your protagonist is ultimately striving for; the conflict he or she faces and the opposition the protagonist must overcome to achieve that goal; how they over-come this obstacle to achieve their goal; and what it costs the protagonist to succeed—the stakes, in other words.

How a narrative is put together is concerned with the kinds of drama you create for your scenes, the action that you put in them, the kind of lan-guage you choose to use, the tone of the piece, and so on. Without these ele-ments working together in deliberate harmony, your narrative will not have an enabling structure.

You need to figure out the "bookends" of your story—when it starts and ends—so that you get a sense of the time frame you're writing about: a week, 24 hours, two years . . . *The Perfect Storm,* for example, is ostensibly about three days or so in late October 1991, yet it ranges far and wide from those days, going back as far as 1850 at one point. The passage of time is hazy in the book. *Black Hawk Down,* on the other hand, tracks from midday, October 3, 1993, to 5:45 A.M., October 4, although it follows on with epi-logues about people in the States and the release of the captured pilot Durant, which took a few days longer. The passage of time is generally very explicit and helps the storytelling immensely.

Robert Conot described organizing *Rivers of Blood, Years of Darkness,* his book on the 1965 L.A. riots:

> In order to coordinate and cross-reference material from the many diverse sources with the actions that occurred during the riot—in some cases [I] discovered that . . . files contained a half dozen or more descriptions of what proved to be a single incident—[I] began an hour-by-hour plotting of the riot. This graph, two feet wide, ultimately grew to 25 feet in length. Among other things, it enabled [me] to discover an apparent witness to one of the riot deaths recorded by the district attor-ney's office as a homicide by person or persons unknown. . . .
>
> With one or two exceptions, all of the agencies who had personnel involved in the riot displayed a commendable frankness and honesty. As

Deputy Chief Richard Simon of the LAPD told the McCone Commission: "We feel it's better to tell the truth. Even if the truth is not good, it's better than rumors, which are generally horrible."

Having worked out a strict chronology for your own edification, you will undoubtedly also find there are more questions that need to be asked in order to verify what happened when. You may well find, though, that the story is not just *what* happened, but *who* it happened to. And it is in the ordering of the best way to tell the stories of the characters who animate your narrative that the best structure will likely emerge.

In his essay "Rewriting the Rules of Nonfiction," Kurt Eichenwald talked about how he structured his book *The Informant*:

[The Informant] was a story about a criminal investigation that was replete with lies. In this case, the FBI secured the assistance of the highest-ranking corporate executive ever to serve as a cooperating witness. For more than two years, that man, Mark Whitacre, provided the government with an unprecedented array of evidence about corruption at the nation's most politically powerful corporation, the Archer Daniels Midland Company.

But, unknown to the FBI and ADM, the entire time that Whitacre was working for the two organizations, he was simultaneously losing his mind. Eventually, the case spun out of control, as Whitacre became trapped by his own lies, and the government struggled to find out where the truth began.

Wrapping lies within truth was complex for narrative nonfiction, but, fortunately, many others had shown the way to soar while using this narrative technique. Indeed, in attempting this project, I was standing on the shoulders of giants—great authors who had blazed the trail for writing powerful narrative nonfiction.

For me, one of the most influential was undoubtedly Ken Auletta's 1986 masterpiece, *Greed and Glory on Wall Street*.

Eichenwald added that he made a decision to educate himself by reading as many narrative nonfiction books as he could. He began with Truman Capote's *In Cold Blood,* and went on to *The Final Days* by Bob Woodward and Carl Bernstein; *Indecent Exposure* by David McClintick; J. Anthony Lukas's *Common Ground; Barbarians at the Gate* by Bryan Burrough and John Helyar; *Den of Thieves* by James B. Stewart; and Jonathan Harr's *A Civil Action.* Eichenwald continued:

> With *The Informant,* I wanted the format to reflect the substance: What better way to tell a story where truth and lies meld together than by using a narrative technique that closely followed those used by novelists? And so, after my review of nonfiction works, I pored through dozens of novels. . . .
>
> As I began writing my book, the most complex choice involved the decision of where to begin the story. Using the dictates of most nonfiction, the answer would have been easy: I start where the action begins. Instead, I drew charts of the storyline, attempting to find the starting point that would allow me to hide the truth for as long as possible. Once I started down this path, the setup became easy. The story evolved into five plots, with each new one redefining the facts of the last. In essence, I was putting the readers in the position of the characters in the book who were deceived. With that plan in mind, I set off on my reporting extravaganza, seeking out the details that would allow me to write what is essentially a nonfiction novel.

The Architecture of a Narrative . . .

Before he died, my friend Gary Provost, a terrific writing teacher and author, used to talk with his students about structure in very simple terms. Think about the house or apartment you're living in, he would say. It will almost certainly still be standing after you're gone, despite sometimes punishing weather. It's made up of bricks and concrete, and steel truss rods and wooden framing, all dependent on one another. The difference between the building you live in and a chaotic pile of wood, brick, and concrete that make it up is forethought and organization—a coherent sense of orderliness.

What's more, that orderliness is not only functional; it can be molded into a shape that is pleasing, graceful, perhaps even beautiful, to boot. Someone thought ahead of time about how to put together your building: where to put a foundation, the best place to put beams so that they take the right amount of weight and stress, the best way to construct a frame that would hold everything together, where to cut holes for windows and doors, and so on.

Every part of the building supports every other part, and your building was carefully put together to achieve that effect. That's structure, and it applies to your book just as much as it applies to the building you live in.

The building blocks of writing narrative—the beams, bricks and mortar, and walls of your book—are scenes, exposition, half scenes, bridging passages, sequences, chapters, sections, actions, and so forth.

Something that may have occurred to you about structures, if I may prolong the architecture analogy a bit longer, is that they are made up of small things (for example, scenes) that make up larger structures (such as sequences), which in turn make up even larger structures (chapters and book sections), so that by cementing one brick on top of another in a certain way we can amazingly create self-supporting arches and hollow buildings as well as just walls.

The Four Basic Elements of Organization

There are broadly four basic elements of organization when telling a story:

- The first, obviously, is the recognition that you are taking the reader on a journey, using storytelling (or fiction) techniques.

- The second is a good eye for visual detail. The telling detail or two or three will give us just the right sense of place, of time, of character (if possible) to set the scene and give it meaning. Don't just dump a bucketload of researched details over the reader as if drowning them in facts and hope that will suffice.

- The third is a good ear for aural detail. Obtain and accurately use quotes and dialogue that convey to us the characters you're portraying in your narrative. Don't make up these quotes, or use stiff, generic, or artificial dialogue just because it's true. The spirit of how something is said is as important as what was said. (There's an old Yiddish joke about a Russian immigrant in a citizenship class at Ellis Island in the 1950s. When asked to write a sentence in English, from Trotsky to Stalin, he writes: "You're right, I was wrong, I should apologize." When the teacher reads it out in class the old man says, "No, no, you got it wrong," then puts the following inflection on the sentence: "*You're* right? *I* was wrong? *I* should apologize?")

- Lastly, use your heart to help your intellect. Have some compassion for your subjects and their situation and you will ultimately get much closer to the truth of the story you are writing, and certainly make it a lot more emotionally involving to a reader.

Organizing Principles

It's not necessarily the best idea to tell the story chronologically, or in the same sequence you discovered the information when you began your research. As I mentioned earlier, you need to decide for yourself first what the story is, and then how best to tell it.

One of the ways to make that decision is to consider why you're telling the story in the first place. What is the story's significance? And thereby hangs an organizing principle that may guide you as to how to tell the story.

In *The Perfect Storm,* for example, Junger starts by introducing us to the poor, blue-collar fishing town of Gloucester, Massachusetts, and through that the crew of the *Andrea Gail*. Gloucester becomes the point of a triangle, in a sense, where the human elements of the story—the crew of the lost ship—personify the town; the town in turn becomes the personification of the East Coast fishing industry; and the dangerous and difficult conditions set the scene for the story, in this case experiencing a terrifying storm of the century. As the book progresses in chapters, we switch from the worsening deterioration of the weather to a history of how tough it is to earn a living as a fisherman because of the arduous and dangerous conditions of the job, to the specific though intuited story of the doomed crew, who sail, quite literally, into the heart of the storm.

In a similar vein, though less obviously, *Into Thin Air* is a memoir principally structured around Krakauer's decision to write about climbing Mount Everest as a reporter for a magazine. It is infused with glimpses of mountaineering, particularly man's attempt to defeat Everest, and becomes in some ways an involuntary meditation on why people climb not only mountains in general but this one in particular.

Richard Preston's *The Hot Zone* covers the period from 1967 to 1993, though not chronologically. He outlines the presumed origins and history of the Ebola virus in Africa, and its effects, almost as a living predator, much like the shark in *Jaws*. But he intersperses that chronology with more contemporary events involving Lieutenant Colonel Nancy Jaax, a U.S. Army biohazard specialist who works alongside her husband, Colonel Jerry Jaax, the SWAT mission team leader, during a near catastrophe involving the virus at a lab just outside Washington, D.C.

We move further along the scale to *Black Hawk Down*, which is structurally something of a model of complex but linear chronological narrative. Here the author's task was to re-create the battle of Mogadishu, and he humanizes the story by focusing on various individuals who were at various places during the battle, piecing the narrative together in a mosaiclike fashion. This is not a million miles away from the structure of the 1993 movie *Short Cuts,* inspired by characters in the short stories of Raymond

Carver. It may seem strange mentioning movies, but if there is one unarguable point it is that films are all structure, and a study of them can really inform the structural possibilities open to a narrative writer, be she journalist or novelist. Robert Altman's movie crosscuts between two dozen or so principal characters, most of whom cross one another's paths. Quentin Tarantino used a similar structure in *Pulp Fiction*, as did John Herzfeld in *2 Days in the Valley* and P. T. Anderson in *Magnolia*. Each movie followed an assortment of characters, in some cases manipulating time sequences by going back and forth in story chronology as the characters' paths crossed, in others just having their lives intersect when we changed viewpoint and essentially entered familiar scenes through new doorways.

The most obvious structure is a chronological structure: start at the beginning, progress to the middle, detail the denouement. However, sometimes the story's chronology works most effectively when told backward, as in Martin Amis's novel *Time's Arrow* and Harold Pinter's play (and then film) *Betrayal*, or more recently Christopher Nolan's *Memento*.

There is also what could be called the circular structure. *Sunset Boulevard* follows this shape. We begin with a body facedown in a swimming pool, and a voice-over of the drowned man announcing that this movie is essentially going to tell us the story of how he came to die. It goes back in time, and gradually progresses to the point where we rejoin the scene that began it all, but able to see it in a completely different light with the hindsight of what has gone before.

Forrest Gump does something a little similar, starting with the title character sitting as an adult on a bus stop bench and then telling his story.

In *The Rape of Nanking,* Iris Chang wrote that

> the book describes two related but discreet atrocities. One is the Rape of Nanking itself, the story of how the Japanese wiped out hundreds of thousands of innocent civilians in its enemy's capital.
>
> Another is the cover-up, the story of how the Japanese, emboldened by the silence of the Chinese and the Americans, tried to erase the entire

. . . the . . .

massacre from public consciousness, thereby depriving its victims of their proper place in history.

The structure of the first part of my book—the history of the massacre—is largely influenced by *Rashomon* [a famous movie by Akira Kurosawa].

In that movie, a rape and murder are recounted from the perspectives of the various people who were involved in the crime. Each tells the story slightly differently.

Susan Rabiner, Chang's editor at Basic Books, recalls (in *Thinking Like Your Editor*) that

[Iris's] main problem lay in how to present Part One, the events of the rape itself. Would dividing the categories of violence by time . . . prove to be a viable organizing principle? This plan made for effective story-telling. But it didn't sit well with Chang. . . . Should she choose a fixed number of representative moments of inhumane treatment? . . . That was a possibility. The rape occurred over a period of six weeks. Could she tell the story chronologically? . . . Again, not a bad plan, but one that screened her from getting at what she really wanted to say. . . .

The book's structure emerged when she re-examined the material she had. The Nanking massacre survived as an historical military event because it was witnessed by so many neutral noncombatants—Americans and Europeans living in the city who refused to leave despite the invasion by the Japanese. Further, while conversing with a relative of a high-ranking German diplomat in Nanking at the time, she discovered he kept a diary, kept through the early stages of the atrocity. This diary later became front page news, and it seemed appropriate that she choose an organizational plan that made full use of her own contributions. . . .

In essence she told the story of what occurred three times, from three different perspectives, in what she referred to as the Rashomon style. . . . Why did this organizational style work so well for Chang? Because it got to the core of the problem as she saw it—that even today reactions to the atrocity vary, depending on the perspective and politics of the commentator.

In a somewhat similar fashion, D. Graham Burnett, in *A Trial by Jury*, explains that his book was really two stories interwoven: "that of the case— a trial story, a courtroom story, a drama focused around a violent death; and that of the deliberations—the story of what happened behind the closed door of the jury room. Each of these stories [was] complex, and they [were] of course entangled. I set out to write this book in order to tell the latter, but to do so I [had to] rehearse elements of the former."

The Basic Unit of a Book's Structure

I used earlier the analogy of book structure as architecture. If words are bricks, while they may seem to be the basic units of a structure, in truth, a basic unit takes shape only once you combine various bricks together. In literary terms, it's a matter of how words are utilized: the *thought* they combine to express and capture on paper is really the basic building block of a literary structure.

There's a tendency for some writers of nonfiction to write in what can best be described as an ever-present tense. This is used mostly for analytical writing, but it deliberately ignores the passage of time and makes any kind of narrative turgid reading because it seems to lack movement. A sense of time adds pace to the story. And how chapters break is important in pacing a story. James Clavell's novel *Shogun* is a wonderful example of cliffhanging writing—he heightens the suspense at the end of the chapter, and you finish it wanting to plunge ahead to the next so that you find out what happens next.

Ideas and Images

A narrative is really a combination of two things: ideas and images. A documentary filmmaker uses something similar. When learning to write fiction, you'll often hear the adage "Show, don't tell." In other words, if you're writing a narrative, find ways to show in verbal pictures rather than by didactic explanation what it is you want to convey. Of course, when writing nonfiction it's not always possible to write this way, but the instinct to try to use an image to humanize your fact or piece of information is laudable.

For example, in 1971, in an article in the *New Republic,* Senator Walter Mondale wanted to convey the fact that the United States had 6 percent of the world's population and about half the world's resources, but an income distribution that awarded 77 percent of total income to the top half of the population and only 23 percent to the lower half.

This is how he set up those facts:

I went to a small elementary area school in our small ghetto in St Paul. They had a splendid cafeteria and a very balanced meal, a warm meal, salad, and about every fifth child could not afford it. One child, whom I will never forget as long as I live, was about six or seven years old. She had a filthy dress on, and she sat at this table amidst the other children eating their good meal, eating a chocolate cookie. She had a little dirty bag that she had brought, that her mother had sent, and two other chocolate cookies. And I asked the principal, how can this happen? And he said, "We still don't have the money to pay for lunches when the families can't afford it." I assume there are millions like her in the country, that sit amidst their friends at lunch who have a decent meal, and they don't. It's a disgrace.

Whether or not you agree with his politics, there can be no denying that the imagery greatly enhanced the emotional power of the factual argument Mondale was making.

In *Thinking in Pictures: The Making of the Movie* Matewan, screenwriter and film director John Sayles said:

> When thinking in pictures it's important to consider whether a certain image will have the same meaning to someone else as it does to you. No matter what your experience of the Vietnam War, *Platoon* [by Oliver Stone] is a rugged movie to enter into, a meaningful assault on the senses. But the images in it are bound to have a different resonance for people who have been in combat than for people who haven't. The trick is not to ignore one group and concentrate on the other, to become either a caterer to the elite or a panderer to the masses, but to pick and build your images so that *anybody* can get into the story on some level, so that maybe people are drawn in deeper than they thought they could or would want to go. And you have to do all this without lying to them.

A narrative has this crude structure: Start with the problem to be overcome; in the course of developing a solution to this problem, show how the situation becomes more complicated; end by showing how ultimately the solution (or *a* solution) is applied and the problem resolved. When outlining your story you are searching for a protagonist and antagonist, who have conflicting goals and problems and whose stories will humanize the narrative, provide emotional nourishment for the reader, and broadly follow the structure of narrative as I've outlined it above.

Ideas and Images, Scenes and Chapters

Ideas and images, then, are the rhetoric of narrative storytelling, its meaning and emotion. The choice of image is very important because image is often used as a metaphor for a psychological state—in other words the emotion of the moment. So a boring, static image will produce—yes, you guessed correctly—a bored, disinterested reader. Any old image obviously won't do, then. What you need is not adjectives and adverbs (I recommend hunting them down mercilessly in your prose and killing them seriously dead!) but action words, or verbs. Instead of saying, "The thug *was kicking* the dog," for example, it's more powerful to say, "The thug *kicked* the dog."

By interweaving image and idea, we create a scene, which has a natural beginning and end. A series of related scenes is called a sequence. Very often, two or three sequences make up a chapter.

All writing, of course, is what you want it to be, but some things just seem to work on the page while others don't. That's because the things that work conform to internal rules of logic, such as that good drama is rooted in conflict. Things that don't work ignore these rules—no conflict, little drama.

At the Washington National Press Club in 2002, talking about writing *Sputnik: The Shock of the Century*, author Paul Dickson said, "When I started working on the book, the conflict was [obviously the Cold War enmity] between the United States and the Soviet Union. But the further I got into [the book], I realized that the conflict was [really] between [President] Eisenhower and the people who wanted Space for peace . . . and Wernher Von Braun and the Army. The conflict was really in America. There was this huge invisible tug-of-war that was going on in the country . . . which in many ways was our destiny."

Chapters—the Rogue Element of Structure

Chapters, however, don't use the same kind of internal-logic rules about what is dramatically successful as do scenes of action, exposition, and so forth. Chapters can be just about anything. A writer friend once submitted a proposal for a book and the interested editor asked him for not one but the first two chapters as a sample of the book. My friend had already written a thirty-page chapter and didn't want to do any more work, so he somewhat cynically broke the chapter into two 15-page sections. This actually worked much better for the reader, and while prompted by a feeling of sloth on my friend's part, it all worked out for him, because in our fast-moving, 30-second-sound-bite-influenced world, readers like to know there are places to take a breather before plunging back into the book, even if they don't use them all. The 15-to-20-page chapter length is the equivalent of potential rest stops along a parkway.

A chapter consists of a series of interlinking scenes or sequences, each following on as a direct result of what happened previously. In brief, a scene moves the story forward while at the same time giving the reader information about the characters. If it doesn't do either of these things, and hopefully both at the same time, it shouldn't be there and is ill chosen.

In its simplest form, the best way to tackle writing scenes is to start the scene when the action starts, and end it when the action ends. Don't lead up, explain, or editorialize if you can avoid it.

In *A Trial by Jury*, for example, we are taken fairly chronologically through the story, though with the first-person narrator's explanations for what is happening. In a sense, the book is a memoir of an event. Chapter 2, "How It Began," comprises a series of interconnected sequences.

First we have the sequence that depicts the author arriving first thing in the morning at the jury selection room in the Centre Street court building. The second sequence involves seeing the defendant for the first time as Burnett is called in to be considered a potential juror in the trial, being part of the voir dire process. The third sequence is being chosen as a juror on the case.

As you build your narrative it's useful to ask yourself, Do the scenes in my story relate to one another, or does this particular scene actually relate to a sequence I've put earlier or later in the book?

You'll discover that you may well have written some scenes that either are out of place and should be moved around, or can be discarded.

. . . the . . .

Half Scenes

As you might expect, a half scene is something that's midway between a scene and exposition, that is, authorial editorializing of some form or another. The half scene is exposition that is flavored with description. It's commonly used when you have something that's important for the reader to know but not important enough to devote a whole scene to. Here's a fictional example, but the technique is the same for narrative nonfiction:

> *That evening, Rachel remembered, she met with the police officer who was investigating the accident. The Starbucks was thinning out by then, and they found a small table in a corner where they sat huddled together with their backs to the rest of the customers. The cop was a dour old-timer who looked close to retirement and had the jowls of a bloodhound; his face was shot through with thready veins, and he had the red nose of a habitual heavy drinker. He sighed as he told Rachel what she had already guessed—the skid marks of the car showed that the "accident" looked like a deliberate hit-and-run.*
>
> *"We just don't have a lot of manpower to spend on these kinds of cases. But I want to assure you I am going to track down every lead I get. It's going to take time, though. We think she could have been mistaken for someone else."*
>
> *And there it was, the fact that would haunt Rachel for years to come. Someone in suburban New Jersey had deliberately tried to kill her sister, an ordinary housewife, because she looked like a stranger she didn't know and had never met. But who? And why?*

We could just have said, *That evening Rachel discovered that someone had tried to kill her sister, mistaking her for someone else.* But by giving us a brief picture of the cop and the setting, and letting the reader hear him tell Rachel the information as dialogue rather than as exposition, we created a half scene, which was made to come alive through a brief taste of dramatization.

Action in Structure

Action is simply what movement occurs in a sentence. *She opened the front door* is an action. *She bought a cup of coffee at Starbucks* is an action. *She adjusted the seat and turned on the ignition* is an action. *"Screw you Freddy," she whispered* is an action. In a strong narrative we look for a new action in every sentence. This is what defines pacing. Lots of actions, fast pace; fewer actions, slower pace. If you write a sentence such as *She started up her car; it was silver with a dent in the trunk, and had red upholstery,* then unless those details are going to have meaning in the narrative later on, you've belabored the point. All anyone needs to know at this point in the narrative is that she started up her car.

The antithesis of this is pushing the pace too fast, and leaving out something. For example: *She started up her car. The sandwich left a bitter taste in her mouth.* Excuse me? Hello? Where did that come from? The writer forgot to have her go into a store and buy a sandwich.

While she waited for her coffee, Ginny bought a sandwich. I'll eat that on the way home, she thought. Here we have one action after another, baby steps leading us logically forward.

Another thing you want to think about in terms of pace and sentence actions is the order in which you place the sentences. Focus on cause and effect. Every sentence should be a stimulus for another action. So make sure you write sentences and actions in their logical order. *She ducked. Rafe threw the plate at her.* This has her reacting to something that hasn't happened yet. The sentences should be reversed.

Building Conflict

Drama is made up of conflict—no conflict, no drama, boring narrative. It's important to think about the way conflict drives a narrative. How you create conflict and where you place it in your narrative is important to a narrative's structural success. Stories are about characters trying to go in a direction, while some force, some opposition, is saying, "No, you can't do that."

Here are a couple of tips about creating conflict:

- Conflict will occur naturally when two people (particularly with clashing goals) are forced together into a small space. For example, astronauts face certain disaster because their orbiting space station has a fire and loses precious oxygen among other potentially life-threatening events (*The Unmaking of Mir* by Thomas Mallon).
- Put pressure on the narrative by imposing a time limit, like a ticking clock on a bomb. You have only so much time before disaster strikes. Force the protagonists to act in a way that could get them into trouble, make them make mistakes because of haste and worry, increase the inherent drama and conflict of their situation. *Black Hawk Down* has a ticking clock. First one bird goes down, then a second, then the rescuers need to be rescued; meanwhile men are dying and taking horrendous wounds in a bitter firefight that seems endless.

A book that managed to combine both was *Our Story: 77 Hours That Tested Our Friendship and Our Faith* by Jeff Goodell (editor) and the Quecreek Miners. This is the book that told the story of nine Pennsylvania coal miners who were trapped underground for more than three days. Told using the miners' own words, it is an unsentimental and accurate account of a horrifying situation and a triumphant escape.

Equal but Opposite

Conflict is best conceived as two equal forces in opposition. In fact, a protagonist is pretty much defined by the strength of the opposition (or antagonist) he or she faces. The greater the conflict, the higher the stakes for all involved and the more potent the emotional content of the narrative. Ideally, whatever is trying to stop your protagonist from reaching her goal is so formidable that all the way through the book we worry who's going to win the battle. *Take It from Me: Life's a Struggle but You Can Win* by Erin Brockovich and Marc Eliot is an interesting example of a narrative nonfiction self-help book that is also part memoir in the *Angela's Ashes* vein.

Three Basic Types of Conflict

From a structural perspective we can divide up conflict into three basic types:

- *Human Versus Human.* This is the most common conflict. Two people in a scene may not be fighting, but they have conflicting goals and mounting pressures to attain those goals. Any true crime, such as *Small Sacrifices* or the military adventure *Black Hawk Down*, would qualify.
- *Human Versus Nature.* Guys trying to conquer Mount Everest, or beat a storm at sea, or survive a devastating flood would qualify here. The obvious examples are *Into Thin Air* and *The Perfect Storm.*
- *Human Against Himself or Herself.* These stories are principally about internal conflict, and are very hard to write well. The danger is that the writer's fascination with the character won't translate onto the page and the story will become wordy, self-involved, and boring. The trick here, so to speak, is to find ways of dramatizing in an external fashion what is going on in the internal story. Such narratives are

about regret and guilt; about people who don't have the strength to
do what they have to do, such as quit drinking or stop taking drugs.
Internal stories, and internal monologues in particular, are minefields
and can undermine a reporter's validity if he or she isn't careful. It's
a good idea to somehow telegraph to the reader that the internal
monologue is the result of careful research: *As she later recalled,
Debbie was thinking that . . .* In general, this type of story often
works better as an article than as a book, but there are powerful
exceptions. Some biographies and memoirs, particularly of
experiencing personal suffering, would fit neatly into this category.
The Diving Bell and the Butterfly: A Memoir of Life in Death by Jean-
Dominique Bauby and even *Angela's Ashes* by Frank McCourt might
be good examples.

Writing the Book: Flesh and Blood on the Bones

● ● ● ● ● ● ● ● ● ● ● ● ● ● ● ● ● ●

But suppose, asks the student of the professor, we follow all your structural rules for writing, what about that "something else" that brings the book alive? What is the formula for that? The formula for that is not included in the curriculum.

FANNIE HURST, *ANATOMY OF ME*

 Creativity is best defined as bringing order out of chaos, whether it's personified in the anarchic work of a Jackson Pollock or a Damien Hirst or in the bucolic nineteenth-century landscapes of Constable and Turner. Regardless of art's effect on the viewer/reader, for art to have any worth the artist had to have a purpose when creating the work, even if that purpose was banal. For example, Damien Hirst shocked and polarized the London and New York art worlds in the late 1990s by presenting exhibits of a sectioned cow and a shark in formaldehyde. In creating such art, he said, his aim was to "make art that everybody could believe in."

We read and hear about the rules of writing all the time. Someone says, "You've got to do it this way"; someone else says, "Oh, ignore all those guys and do it any way you like." You're faced with a choice between creative tyranny and artistic anarchy. Rarely do teachers mention fitting the techniques of how you tell your story to the *purpose* of the narrative you're writ-

. . . the . . .

ing. It's too hard and too sophisticated a concept for most students to grasp or employ. It requires intuitively understanding how something should be presented in order to show up its inner life, rather like a photographer finding just the right lighting conditions and expression on a subject's face.

In recent years I've become more and more conscious of a single governing principle on how to choose the best narrative technique from the many options available—it is simply this: What best engages the imagination while at the same time increases the emotional intensity of the narrative?

If you're reading this book you've already figured out there has to be some logic and structure to writing and that you shouldn't have to reinvent the wheel in order to write your book. It's a sure bet that other people have already discovered that some things work better on the page than others, and for good reasons. Does that mean you should create a narrative in a particular way every time? Of course not. But writing is a little like cooking; for example, there is a right way and a wrong way to cook with wine and cream in the same dish. One way, the food is tasty—the other way the cream curdles and it all looks and tastes like crap.

The so-called rules of writing are concerned with being able to analyze and discuss what makes a successful piece of creative writing and, more important, why something that should be working isn't. What's more, these rules need to be adapted and modified for every piece of creative writing you do. Writing is not (and should never be) one-size-fits-all, nor would I ever make that claim. What I'm trying to do in this book is present some windows into philosophical principles of drama that hopefully will help you write a stronger narrative and give you, at the least, some things to reject in favor of other solutions that occur to you. This is nowhere truer than when discussing the tricks of narrative writing.

The Organic Book

When a newspaper reporter writes a story, he doesn't usually have a lot of time to spend on crafting the piece. He must write his article quickly, accurately, and with a minimum of description and detail. Writing a book-length piece of narrative nonfiction is a different kettle of fish. The reader often knows ahead of time the broad outlines of the story you're telling, and so you are writing not just to convey *what happened* but, more, to take the reader to new worlds to meet interesting people—the *who, why,* and *how* of things. The reader wants color and emotion and characterizations, and the techniques of a novelist help in that regard. Complete books have been written on each of the various techniques I outline below, so regard them only as essential introductions or reminders.

A book is really an organic thing; piece by piece, scene by scene it grows, sometimes in surprising ways, much as we try to plan it out ahead of time. As we've discussed earlier, while the outline is the structural skeleton of the narrative, the flesh and blood that turns that skeleton into a living thing are not chapters, as you might assume, but scenes. The dramatized scene is the basic unit of creativity you need to focus on once you've got a structure for your book. You know what is going to happen; now you need to focus on how best to present that information, in cinematic terms.

Writing in scenes is the antithesis of academic, analytical narrative. Analytical writing uses an authorial voice to *tell* us a fact or piece of information. Dramatic writing, on the other hand, uses emotionally powerful language and images to animate a *distillation* of real life (as if we were watching a movie) that *shows* us that information. A recent movie, *Adaptation,* with Nicholas Cage, very much played with this idea philosophically and is worth a peek.

In the book *A Murder*, to give another example, Greg Fallis, a mystery writer and former cop, sets out to take the reader through a routine murder investigation. He alternates between, first, an authorial voice that describes in almost textbook style the various aspects of a police murder investigation and, second, scenes that bring to life through dramatization certain aspects of the story he is telling, from crime to investigation, to trial and punishment, to aftermath.

Unlike with fiction, there are occasions when an authorial narrative voice can be interspersed between scenes, dispensing journalistically the information we need to follow the story. Too many beginning writers, however, resort to the journalistic voice entirely, rather than creating scenes of emotional impact and dynamism, and the result is a rather flat narrative that *tells* almost everything and *shows* little.

Basic Needs of a Scene

In general, a scene should revolve around a primary character in the story, providing a sense of what she needs—both in the scene and in the larger terms of where she is headed at story's end—and of what's trying to stop her achieving that goal. If nothing gets in her way, the scene falls flat because she won't have "earned" her information.

> *"Where's Bob?" Suzie demanded.*
> *"Oh, he's over there," Jim said.*

Not much of a scene, and no dramatic tension. We quickly cease to care.

> *"Where's Bob?" Suzie demanded.*
> *"Get lost," Jim said.*
> *"But he's going to die if I don't give him his medicine."*
> *"Look at me? Do I look like I care? Leave me alone."*

A clichéd scene, it's true, but at least one showing some signs of drama, emotional involvement, and a momentum that will urge us to read on to see how Suzie deals with this setback. Why? Because she has to earn her information and Jim is saying no to her.

If your main character doesn't have a goal or doesn't want something badly enough, the scene won't work because there will be no point to it. If the characters don't care, where's the emotional engine? A reader's emotional involvement in your story parallels that of your protagonist to some degree. If the character isn't emotionally involved in the scene, the reader will likely feel the same way.

So how do you decide when to create a scene? *If there is no conflict and little emotion, don't bother with a scene.* Sum up your information in a sentence or two if you can. Create a scene when there has to be conflict and emotion.

- *Major events are about to take place.* In a memoir, for example, don't just write, *On Tuesday, I decided it was time I ended my marriage of 23 years, so I packed my bags, got in the car, and drove away.* Instead, re-create the scene. Or in a true crime narrative set the scene the moment the body is about to be discovered.
- *Characters are in conflict with one another.* Writers sometimes shy away from showing an argument or fight scene. They'll lead us up to it, and lead us away from it, but avoid the fight scene itself. Trouble is, the fight is what we really want to read about, not the other stuff.
- *There is great emotion being evoked.* Don't just write, *Billy woke up finally from the coma, and the next week left the hospital for home.* Let's see Billy wake up finally.

Small Sacrifices

The opening chapter of Anne Rule's *Small Sacrifices* has the following short scene, which I've condensed further for the sake of brevity. It could have been summed up this way: *At about 11 P.M. on May 19, 1983, a distraught*

blonde woman brought her three children to the McKenzie-Willamette ER
suffering from severe gunshot wounds. By the time the trauma staff were
through, one child was dead and two others lay near death.

This is how Anne Rule wrote it:

The bad call came into the Springfield Police Department at 10:40 P.M.:
"Employee of McKenzie-Willamette Hospital advises of gunshot victim at
that location. Officers dispatched. Arrived 10:48 P.M."

Rosie Martin, RN; Shelby Day, LPN; Judy Patterson, the night recep-
tionist; and Dr. John Mackey, physician in charge, comprised the evening
shift in the emergency room at the McKenzie-Willamette ER in Springfield.

McKenzie-Willamette as it existed in the late spring of 1983 was a
little cramped, a little out of date. Paint on walls and baseboards had
been scrubbed dull and drab; and the waiting room furniture was
chrome and peeling vinyl.

Facing the two sets of doors that led to the circular driveway off
Mohawk Boulevard, the three treatment rooms were to the right: Day
Surgery nearest the street, Minor Treatment in the middle, and the Trauma
Room at the back. On the left, Judy Patterson's desk was just behind a
small waiting area near the street doors. Five feet or so behind her desk
there was a small bathroom and beyond that a larger waiting room. . . .

That velvet black spring night Dr. Mackey and his staff, working in an
almost obsolete ER, would be the first to encounter what was unthinkable
for Springfield, what would be unthinkable for even a big city. None of
them would have much time to think during the hours they fought to save
the injured, their white shoes sliding on floors slick with fresh blood. Only
later would terrible musings rush in to destroy all hope of sleep.

Shelby Day is a slender, soft-spoken woman near forty, with six
years' experience in the McKenzie-Willamette ER. She wears white slacks
and pastel, patterned smocks. When she remembers the night of May 19,
1983, tears well unbidden in her eyes.

A car arrived at the ambulance emergency entrance, honking its horn. When Shelby and Rosie Martin, another nurse, ran out to see what the commotion was about, they were confronted with a "slender blonde woman in jeans and a plaid shirt" beside her car.

> She was pale but she was in control.
> "What's going on here?" Rosie Martin asked.
> "Somebody just shot my kids!"
> . . . The two nurses and the young woman gazed at each other for a fraction of a second, and then the emergency personnel went into action.

The Power of the Scene

A scene can be one page or 20 pages long. There is no definitive length. As a general rule of thumb, the scene should start when the action in the scene starts, and end when that action ends. Add as little setup, explanation, or editorializing as possible. In the above example, it starts, "The bad call came in . . ." We don't get a set of cops whiling away the time waiting for the call and eating doughnuts or chatting to their buddies. Straight in.

When you think your story through in scenes rather than explanation (that is, exposition), you are beginning to focus on creating the emotional bricks of your drama, which are cemented one to another. Through the depiction of conflict (people saying no to each other, in effect) and character development, you are infusing your story with emotional power. A scene, which can be considered a brick in the construction of the building you are creating, translates the emotional life of your characters into visually powerful, engaging, and dramatic material. In other words, scenes work the same way in your book as they would in a film.

Before starting to write your scene, ask yourself four questions:

. . . the . . .

- Whose viewpoint is this scene going to use?
- How does this scene advance the story?
- What problem does the main character have to overcome?
- What is this scene about? (What is its purpose?)

Your choice of what to dramatize should be guided by the answers to these questions, which in turn should almost always take into account how your protagonist, antagonist, or both advance the story. Does the scene move us closer to learning something important about these characters? Does the scene move one or the other toward their long-term goal?

Try to dramatize facts and events that make your characters confront opposition and obstacles that create moral or ethical dilemmas. In other words, questions of right and wrong.

Basic Elements of a Scene

A key aspect of a scene is that it takes place at a set time in a set place. If events don't happen at a specific time and in a definite place, you're not writing a scene, you're writing an abstract narrative.

Here are some examples of scenes:

- Last month in the desert near Las Vegas
- May 19, 1983, in the hospital emergency room
- Saturday afternoon backstage at the Majestic Theatre in Manhattan

Each example contains a distinct time and a recognizable geographic setting. If you change either of these characteristics, you create another scene. For example, if you go from May 19, 1983, in the ER to May 21 in the ER, even though the geography is the same, the changed time sets up another scene. Going from 11 P.M. on May 19 in the ER to 11 P.M. in the station wagon outside, we have again changed scene.

Everyone and everything is in the scene for a reason, and everyone in the scene has their own agenda. For example, in the scene above from *Small Sacrifices*, nurse Shelby Day is our eyes and ears—and feelings—as the scene in the hospital emergency room develops. We're in the hands of a professional doing her job, but her job involves critical emergency care of small children bleeding to death from gunshot wounds. Seeing the scene through the eyes of the nurse is a clever choice, and is important, because she can not only show us calmly what is going on, but also assess the mother and question her behavior. (The mother will eventually end up on trial for the murder and attempted murder of her children.)

Three Aspects of Scene Writing

There are three things about scene writing that you should focus on:

- *What has caused the event in the scene?* If the incident that provokes your scene has no real connection to something that happened in a previous scene, or if the scenes could be extracted from the narrative and not affect what happens next, then the narrative is going to be episodic. The scenes may share some thematic consistency, but that's not enough for a flowing narrative. Cause-and-effect is the key here.
- *Your character should be in that place at that time because of something that happened in a previous scene.* It can be one scene ago, or several scenes ago, but the action in that earlier scene should act as a spur to future action in the story, even if readers don't know it at the time they first read it. (The technical term for this is "foreshadowing.")
- *Does the reason (or impetus) for the scene happen within the scene (rather than before it)?* If so, the scene is likely not really linked in any emotional way to any other scene in the narrative and will result in an episodic narrative.

. . . Telling . . .

On the other hand, a strong scene in a narrative will broadly have these elements in common:

- It will cause a subsequent scene to occur, creating cause and effect.
- It will be driven by the main character's needs and wants. There's a reason he's at that place on that particular day. What is it?
- It will explore various ploys by the character to get his own way. We'll understand these ploys, not by having the author tell us what the ploy is but by seeing and hearing the character, in terms of movie imagery, and judging for ourselves. The character may try a few strategies to get what he wants before succeeding—or failing.
- The character must have changed his position, relative to the end of the story, for the scene to be worthwhile writing. By the end of the scene we must be moved forward in some way.

Even though a scene is a self-contained unit, it's important to remember that each scene links to the next. Scenes don't just dramatize specific events in a story, they show us what happens next. If the scene doesn't, in some way, have an element of "... and then" in it as a response to what happened in the previous scene, you should wonder whether one or other of those scenes ought to be in the narrative, despite the brilliance of the writing.

Goals—the Meat of Drama

When there's no conflict on the page, there's no reader interest in what happens. The reader also has no emotional involvement in the story. In other words, they don't much care what your characters do, why they're doing it, or what happens to them. Nothing compels the reader to stay with that story. Conversely, the more extreme the conflict, the more emotionally involved in your narrative your reader becomes. One way to do this is to make sure your characters have individual goals that will clash and conflict. The playwright Harold Pinter once described a theatrical drama as the fight for dominance among a group of characters. With some modification it works admirably for narrative nonfiction as well.

It's important that your characters have goals that clash. The conflict is the best part of your book. That's what people read it for. It's the emotional payoff, and to shortchange the reader is to leave him frustrated and annoyed. In narrative storytelling you can't be afraid of conflict. It's the meat of drama.

A narrative can be thought of as a series of connected conflicts (with bridging passages in between) that are eventually resolved by one final, cathartic conflict. As you move through your narrative you are constantly figuring out the details of what you should write next, and how best to write it. Character goals are the guiding principle here. In a true crime book, for example, the cop's *overarching* goal is to catch the crook. The crook's is to get away with his or her crime. They may have *intermediate* goals, such as planning the crime and then executing it, or making sure all the forensic evidence has been gathered, all the witnesses interviewed and accounted for. And they will have *minor* goals, such as the cop's need to appear as a witness in another case so that he can wrap up that case and get on with investigating this one, or the crook's need to steal a car so that he can get to where he is going to commit his crime.

The *depth,* or severity, of the conflict a character has to cope with will provide a parallel emotional depth for your reader.

In general, consider three questions:

- *Is there opposition* in the scene, and in your narrative in general? Forward momentum is the overcoming of opposition. Consider the Indiana Jones movies; solving one problem moves the story forward, only to land us immediately with a worse problem to solve. Out of the frying pan into the fire.
- *Is what you're writing interesting?* As you research your book you'll come across interesting material all the time. Sometimes there is no

conflict in the material. If such material seduces you, be sure that even though it's interesting to you, it enhances what you're writing in some way and has earned a right to be included.

- *Is the information essential to understand the scene or the narrative at that point?* If you can leave it out and understand what's going on, perhaps you should reconsider including the material. Should it be a dramatized scene? Perhaps it's worth only a sentence or two.

Exposition

As a rule of thumb, it's a good idea to try to limit exposition in your narrative. However, unlike fiction, in narrative nonfiction you need to put things in a context because you are re-creating real life; and real life is often complex, so scenes that approximate it sometimes need a context.

Because it explains or editorializes, exposition works in the narrative the same way that adjectives and adverbs do in sentences: It enhances and clarifies. The right piece of exposition, like the correctly chosen adjective, can be powerful and effective. Used poorly, it becomes a crutch to the writer, preventing him from developing an otherwise imaginative way of delivering this information—if it's needed at all—or an anchor retarding the forward momentum of the narrative, and something that dilutes the emotional power of his story.

Here are some things to consider about exposition:

- Don't introduce expository material unless the reader needs it to understand what's about to happen in the narrative.
- If possible, figure out a way of dramatizing the information the reader needs, using a scene or half scene.
- Try to begin the scene before giving the exposition. Put your character in a time and place, and frame the setting before introducing what amounts to a cinematic voice-over.

Viewpoint

Your narrative also needs a viewpoint—what is called, in fiction, a point of view. This does not mean an attitude or opinion, but a camera-lens position, for want of a better explanation, through which we watch the story unfold. Point of view (POV) can make a great deal of difference on how a story is told. It can impact profoundly on a story's emotional power, so choose wisely.

Imagine, for example, if reporters Bob Woodward and Carl Bernstein had not told *All the President's Men,* their account of the Watergate break-in and its aftermath, through their eyes but had chosen, instead, the viewpoint of their famous, still unidentified White House source, Deep Throat—or had used President Nixon's POV instead.

By and large narrative nonfiction uses three broad POVs:

- *The memoir voice, or first person:*

   Let me tell you about an experience I had the other day . . .

- *The subjective third person*, a kind of over-the-shoulder camera-lens position that also allows limited access to a character's thoughts and feelings:

   John moved carefully toward the door. His growing feelings of apprehension, as he explained later, came from a dread of discovering the gore that he was pretty certain was going to lie just beyond it.

- *The omniscient third person:*

   While George was out doing the family shopping, across town, Ricky and Billy were getting ready to rob the convenience store that George was heading to. Little did any of these people know

*how abruptly their lives would change when their paths crossed
less than an hour later.*

The subjective third-person approach is much harder to do convincingly than a first-person voice. Why? Because in first person you can tell a reader what *you* think and feel, but you can't convincingly tell a reader what *someone else* is thinking or feeling, unless that reader has some way of knowing how the narrator ("I") could accurately know this information. The question "How does she know that?" will distract a reader from enjoying the narrative and destroy the "narrative dream" you have been trying so hard to create in your reader's mind.

"I" in the Narrative

Inserting the author directly into the narrative is a challenging thing to do, and is best avoided unless what you are writing directly involves you in some way.

You can use "as told to the author" or "as reported to the author" or even a more generic tone, but it's best to try and leave the narrative voice in an objective third person. In *In Cold Blood,* for example, Capote never once inserts himself, and takes very much the journalistic novelist's approach.

During the auction of the murdered Clutter family's belongings, for example, he writes this:

The last thing to go was the contents of the livestock corral, mostly horses, including Nancy's horse big, fat Babe, who was much beyond her prime. [Nancy was the sole surviving member of the family, who was on a sleepover the night of the murder.] It was late afternoon, school was out, and several schoolmates of Nancy's were among the spectators when bidding on the horse began; Susan Kidwell was there. Sue, who had adopted another of Nancy's orphaned pets, a cat, wished she could give Babe a home, for she loved the old horse and knew how much Nancy loved her. The two girls had often gone riding together aboard Babe's wide back, jogged through the wheat fields on hot summer evenings down to the river and into the water, the mare wading against the current until, as Sue once described it, "the three of us were cool as fish." But Sue had no place to keep a horse.

"I hear fifty . . . sixty-five . . . seventy . . .": the bidding was laggardly, nobody seemed really to want Babe, and the man who got her, a Mennonite farmer who said he might use her for plowing, paid seventy-five dollars. As he led her out of the corral, Sue Kidwell ran forward; she raised her hand as though to wave goodbye, but instead clasped it over her mouth.

Editors usually try and curb a tendency for the author to personalize a narrative, because it usurps the story, distracts the reader, and takes away from your story. Most narrative nonfiction is about something you're researching, not about you. To treat the material otherwise is often to impugn the integrity of what you're trying to report. It's best to leave the voice in the third person, and then reveal any part the author played in the narrative in publicity interviews when you publicize the book later.

Paul Dickson commented:

In the first chapter of *Sputnik: The Shock of the Century* I'm a character. I [wrote myself as] a kid seeing Sputnik overhead. [Instead of being a nameless observer] I'm talking to people, and that's one way of getting your reader into the book. Once you're out of that moment, then [the author becomes an] observer but you've given the reader a sense of belonging to the story. I've always done discursive footnotes—for example, this interview was done on an October night, etc.—and you can use that discursive footnote in the back to insert yourself and give the reader the sense of validation that you really did talk to the person.

Jim Srodes added: "When you use 'I' you're creating a new character, and I don't know that 'I' is enough of a character to be in the book. You have to ask yourself, is 'I' that important? You certainly have the opportunity to give your views and your impressions, but *(a)* 'I' gets in the way, and *(b)* it's a tough character to create. It's easy to create a small boy looking at Sputnik [but] it would be almost impossible to carry him off [over the course of a book]."

This is clearly not the case with Krakauer's book *Into Thin Air,* however. His story and the narrative in general are intimately intertwined. Indeed, Krakauer described *Into Thin Air* as a "personal account." The opening sentence sets the narrative tone:

> Straddling the top of the world, one foot in China and the other in Nepal, I cleared the ice from my oxygen mask, hunched a shoulder against the wind, and stared absently down at the vastness of Tibet. I understood on some dim, detached level that the sweep of earth beneath my feet was a spectacular sight. I'd been fantasizing about this moment, and the release of emotion that would accompany it, for many months. But now that I was finally here, actually standing on the summit of Mount Everest, I just couldn't summon the energy to care.

At the end of *Longitude,* Dava Sobel does the reverse of what Dickson did in *Sputnik.* Having spent the whole book telling a historical story of the life of John Harrison and the struggle to vindicate his discovery of how to measure longitude, she begins the final chapter this way:

> I am standing on the prime meridian of the world, zero degrees longitude, the center of time and space, literally the place where East meets West. It's paved right into the courtyard of the Old Royal Observatory at Greenwich [in London]. At night, buried lights shine through the glass-covered meridian line, so it glows like a man-made midocean rift, splitting the globe in two equal halves with all the authority of the Equator.

For a little added fanfare after dark, a green laser projects the meridian's visibility ten miles across the valley to Essex.

The purpose of inserting "I" here is to show that this historical story has ramifications far into the future and is, in some ways, a continuing story that still touches our lives.

Richard Preston's *The Hot Zone* is a little more complex with its use of "I." Because he is a science reporter, Preston is used to being the narrative voice that explains complex scientific issues to a reading public who looks to him for engaging information. *The Hot Zone* is an extended piece of detective work, with Preston the detective. He has to explain what it is we are looking for, why it is so dangerous, and the clues that lead to its discovery.

In many ways, it is not dissimilar in approach to Frederick Forsythe's seminal thriller, *The Day of the Jackal.* In Preston's book, the Jackal—the freelance assassin the good guys must hunt down and stop before it's too late—is a prehistoric virus named Ebola. We need Preston's authorial voice to fully follow and appreciate the power and horror of the story he is telling. So he occasionally inserts himself in the narrative, but not obtrusively so. For example, Colonel Nancy Jaax is one of the army specialists we follow throughout the narrative as they track down the virus. Toward the end of the book Preston writes:

One day in spring, I went to visit Col. Nancy Jaax, to interview her about her work during the Reston event. We talked in her office. She wore a black military sweater with silver eagles on the shoulder boards—she had recently made full colonel. A baby parrot slept in a box in a corner. The parrot woke up and squawked. . . . .

She waved her hand at some filing cabinets. "You want to look at some Ebola? Take your pick."

"You show me," I said.

She searched through a cabinet and removed a handful of glass slides, and carried them into another room, where a microscope sat on a table. It had two sets of eyepieces so that two people could look into it at the same time.

I sat down and stared in the microscope, into white nothingness.

"Okay, here's a good one," she said, and placed a slide under the lens.

I saw a field of cells. Here and there, pockets of cells had burst and liquefied.

"That's male reproductive tissue," she said. "It's heavily infected. This is Ebola Zaire in a monkey that was exposed through the lungs in 1986, in the study that Gene Johnson and I did."

Looking at the slice of monkey testicle, I got an unpleasant sensation. "You mean, it got into the monkey's lungs and then moved to its testicles?"

"Yeah, it's pretty yucky," she said. "Now I'm going to make you dizzy. I'm going to show you the lung."

The scene shifted, and we were looking at rotted pink Belgian lace.

Not much denying that's a powerful way to learn information. Preston may be "I" in the narrative, but in many ways he has also put himself there as Everyman. We are seeing the world through Preston's eyes—and very powerfully.

Description

One way of increasing the intensity of the narrative is to think about how closely you focus the camera on the characters and details of the scene. As with moviemaking, you can have the equivalent of long shots, middle-distance shots, and close-ups, depending on how much detail you choose to reveal about the subject, and the place and setting.

The relationship between the pacing of a story and narrative intensity is quite complex, and includes such things as kind and amount of description, exposition, and awareness of the passage of time. Description, in particular, done poorly can sink a narrative quicker than heavy shoes on a drowning man; how much you use, and what you are using it for, are key.

By way of example: My wife is a professional actress, and she has been in a Broadway play at the Majestic Theatre on West 44th Street in Manhattan for several years now. The Majestic is an imposing building, dating from the nineteenth century, with a confined narrow backstage area and a large proscenium stage painted black, with a dizzying array of holes and trapdoors outlined all over it. From the stage you look out into the audience and see theater seats that sweep up three tiers high to the roof.

The cast rehearses regularly to keep their performances sharp and to bring in new cast members. I've seen a couple of rehearsals, which are not usually open to the public, but I'm known enough now by cast and crew that I've become a kind of fly on the wall.

I was watching a rehearsal one afternoon when I had a sudden insight about descriptive writing. I was sitting quietly in the empty theater, staring at the bare stage. After a moment a couple of actors came out and began to rehearse their lines. As ever, it was witty and fun and I quickly got caught up in the story.

Once the scene was finished, stagehands slipped onstage and positioned tables and chairs. A backdrop fell into place, wing flats moved into view, and suddenly we were in a room in an opera house in late-nineteenth-century Paris. This time, the actors who came onstage wore partial costumes and carried hand props, the guys on the floods painted the stage with various spotlights, and the sound guy cued prerecorded sounds. As much as I had enjoyed the scene before, this time the scene was that much more compelling because the lights, costumes, props, and so forth all heightened the theatrical experience.

While the scene played out I suddenly recalled hanging out at a party with my wife and some of the actors now onstage. Over drinks, the actors had begun swapping anecdotes about times the show had not gone as planned. There was the time, for example, when nearly all the electricity failed, except for one follow spotlight: no scenery rose from predetermined holes in the floor, no ankle-deep artificial fog flooded the stage, no boat came out from the wings—the actors were forced to re-create the climax of the play, in what was essentially a black box without props or equipment, to create a dungeon setting. But they carried it off.

And it occurred to me that, despite all the "gubbins" I was watching the actors wear and hold, and that set the scene onstage, an audience would stare at actors out of costume enacting a scene on a bare stage much longer than they would stare at a fully dressed stage devoid of actors.

The point of this story? Description in a narrative is no substitute for characters in a story. In fact, to be effective, description needs to be subject to the viewpoint of a particular character. It's a function of who is doing the seeing and how they are feeling, enhancing a narrative but not there for its own sake, just as a decorated stage is boring without actors performing their parts.

The most important thing to remember about description is to keep it short and pithy. Beginning writers seem to fall in love with description in their early drafts and forget that description, like adjectives, should be sprinkled on like salt, not smeared on like butter.

Dialogue

If description helps to paint the picture and create the image, dialogue helps to create the audio track. It's another form of "show" rather than "tell" and helps to dramatize a scene and heighten the reader's emotional response to the story. Re-creating dialogue, however, can be a minefield of ethical issues for the conscientious writer. We've already seen several examples in this chapter of how dialogue is handled. Go back and look at Capote's *In Cold Blood* sequence and Preston's *The Hot Zone*. Here are a couple more to consider.

Sebastian Junger's approach to dialogue when writing *The Perfect Storm* is fairly typical of writers of nonfiction. He wrote:

There are varying kinds of information in [this] book. Anything in direct quotes was recorded by me in a formal interview, either in person or on the telephone, and was altered as little as possible for grammar and clarity. All dialogue is based on the recollection of people who are still alive, and appears in dialogue form without quotation marks. No dialogue was made up. Radio conversations are also based on people's recollections, and appear in italics in the text. Quotes from published material are in italics, and have occasionally been condensed to better fit the text.

Reconstructing dialogue from scenes the reporter didn't witness can be tricky. Journalist Chris Harvey interviewed several writers about writing dialogue and wrote about it in a 1994 essay, "Tom Wolfe's Revenge." One of them, Jon Franklin, commented, "If you've got several people from the scene who are willing to talk and a working knowledge of psychology, it's possible. . . . People can remember surprising amounts of detail from traumatic or emotional occasions. . . . A person can often remember quite a lot of detail about a wedding day or a day he buried a parent. If you were in a serious accident, you can remember the bug smears on a truck."

To gauge the accuracy of their memories, Franklin told Harvey, he asks the sources details he can check. "If it's a funeral, ask about the day and the weather, and go back and check. If they're accurate in those kinds of details, it certainly makes me feel better, and suspicious if they're not."

In *The Hot Zone*, Richard Preston said the dialogue in his book came from "the recollections of the participants." It was extensively cross-checked, he added.

At certain points in the story, I describe the stream of a person's thoughts. In such instances, I am basing any narrative on interviews with the subjects in which they have recalled their thoughts often repeatedly, followed by fact-checking sessions in which the subjects confirmed their recollections. If you ask a person, "What were you thinking?" you may get an answer that is richer and more revealing of the human condition than any stream of thoughts a novelist could invent.

If a reporter is re-creating a private scene—such as a conversation between two people in their bedroom—it's a good idea to speak to both people. The reporter must also make it clear in the story who the sources are and that this is their recollection of the conversation.

It's important to distinguish for the reader things said at the time and things later remembered as said, perhaps provided in an interview. In an afterword to *Black Hawk Down,* for example, Mark Bowden explained that all dialogue in the book was either

> from radio tapes or from one or more of the men actually speaking. My goal throughout [was] to recreate the experience of combat through the eyes of those involved; to attempt that without reporting dialogue would be impossible. Of course, no one's recollection of what they said is ever perfect. My standard is the best memory of those involved. Where there were discrepancies in dialogue they were usually minor, and I was able to work out the differences by going back and forth between the men involved. In several cases I . . . reported dialogue or statements heard by others present, even though I was unable to locate actual speakers. In these cases the words spoken were heard by more than one witness, or recorded in written accounts within days after the battle.

The following excerpt from *Black Hawk Down* uses both narrative quotes that were recollected and radio tapes that are contemporaneous to the moment. The Rangers are already in a firefight in the backstreets of Mogadishu, in hostile territory. The first Black Hawk helicopter has just been shot down.

Nelson watched dumbstruck as the chopper fell.

"Oh, my God, you guys, look at this," he shouted. "Look at this!"

Waddell gasped, "Oh, Jesus," and fought the urge to just stand and watch the bird go down. He turned away to keep his eyes on his corner.

Nelson shouted, "It just went down! It just crashed!"

"What happened?" called Lt. DiTomasso, who came running.

"A bird just went down!" Nelson said. "We've gotta go. We've gotta go right now!"

Word spread wildly over the radio, voices overlapping with the bad news. There was no pretense now of the deadpan military cool, that mandatory monotone that conveys *everything under control.* Voices rose with surprise and fear:

—*We got a Black Hawk going down! We got a Black Hawk going down!*

—*We got a Black Hawk crashed in the city! Six One!*

—*He took an RPG!*

—*Six One down!*

—*We got a bird down, northeast of the target. I need you to move on out and secure that location!*

—*Roger, bird down!*

It was more than a helicopter crash. It cracked the task force's sense of righteous invulnerability.

More About Conflict in the Narrative

A definition of drama is that it is a process whereby we watch a character resolve his or her problems and dilemmas. As I mentioned earlier, problems and dilemmas arise when someone or something says, "No, you can't do that."

It might not be a person. It might be a mountain personified, such as Mount Everest in *Into Thin Air,* saying, "You can't climb me because I'm going to put sudden storms and arctic weather in your way and try to stop you." It could be a prehistoric virus saying, "Mess with me, and I'll kill you quickly and painfully and you won't be able to do anything about it."

Throughout a book, something or someone should be saying no to your characters. If you don't have a series of scenes with some sort of conflict in them, you don't have a narrative. Each time someone says no to your protagonist it increases the narrative's emotional potency.

However, while a scene is made up of characters dealing with rejection and obstacles, at some point you have to have something happen within that scene that resolves that conflict, that has those oppositions to your protagonists' ideals and ambitions turn around and say yes. The mountain's weather system calms and the climbers can make it to the summit; the police officer finally manages to convince the reluctant witness to come forward and tell everyone what she saw.

The Writer as Amateur Psychologist

Sigmund Freud defined the psyche as that part of ourselves which is responsible for our individual thoughts and feelings. For the writer of narratives, who is innately an amateur psychologist studying people and trying to figure them out enough to capture their individuality on paper, a point worth remembering is that despite outward appearances and our wishes to the contrary on occasion, we are not unified beings. We revel in our individuality. We say and do things that are constantly contradictory and paradoxical, and it is the writer's job to capture that but still make sense of the complexity of the human condition. Political correctness, while at its best an attempt to instill sensitivity into the thick-skinned, at its worst imposes a tyranny of bland homogeneity that attacks the roots of individuality, because individuality is anarchic, messy, and sometimes nasty. If political correctness infects writing, it becomes a form of literary cowardice if you're not careful, leading to no controversy, no conflict, and anachronisms in your narrative.

According to Freud, character *is* conflict. When we dream, we discover another self, far less shackled by convention and civilized behavior than when we are awake. Murder, cruelty, and sexual urges of all sorts arise directly or in distorted forms within the dreaming theater of our minds. And they arise, Freud says, because they are reflections of our desires. From this yarn comes the warp and weft of the whole cloth that will eventually comprise narratives about ourselves and our world as we seek to understand and portray the actions and thoughts of characters which may seem contradictory.

Transitions

I've mentioned scenes, sequences, and exposition. It's important to think about the way we connect them, which is called transitioning. The purpose of a transition is to keep the reader happily entangled in the narrative dream you are weaving. What I mean is that you need to write an engrossing narrative that does not, by clumsy writing, awkwardly jerk the reader from the world you have painstakingly created on the page.

A transition can be as simple as *Meanwhile, back at the laboratory* or *Ten years earlier, on a rainy Wednesday morning*. Another way you can transition from sequence to sequence, or scene to scene, is to use a half scene. Don't waste a lot of time getting us from one place to another if the point is to go from one scene to the next with little or nothing of importance happening in between. If it's not important, don't bother to write it down. One of the simplest ways to transition is to simply leave a white space between one section and the next, or a space with asterisks of some sort, like this:

* * *

Such a break in the text denotes a passage of time, a change of scene, and so forth, and a word or phrase is all that is needed in order to orientate the reader to the time and place of the scene that is about to unfold.

Pacing

Pacing describes the speed at which you tell your story.

A narrative has a current, just like a river, and you can adjust the speed of that current depending on how you write your narrative. There are several techniques you can use to achieve this end, including exposition, half scenes, flashbacks, flash-forwards, transitions, and editing out the unnecessary stuff of your narrative. As Elmore Leonard defines it, the unnecessary part of your narrative is the stuff that everyone skips in order to get to the good stuff—what happens next, though not at the expense of character development.

Each scene will have a climax, and one definition of pace is how rapidly a narrative moves from climactic point to climactic point. The overall pace of the narrative is also defined by how each scene builds toward a dramatic narrative resolution.

One of the things to ask yourself if you have some doubts about what you're writing is, will anyone care? Does what you're writing have some humanity to it?

Foreshadowing

Foreshadowing is something that comes through planning your story's twists and turns, and in the rewriting process. At its simplest, foreshadowing ties one seemingly unrelated incident to another, which occurs later on, making us see that second event in a whole new light. The playwright and author Anton Chekov nailed the essence of foreshadowing: If you pull a gun out in Act I, you need to fire it in Act II (or III). If a character in a domestic drama suddenly pulls out a gun in Act II and shoots her husband, the reader is entitled to say, "Where did that come from?" When considering plot twists and surprises in your narrative, it's important to foreshadow what is to come. Readers should always think to themselves after the enjoyment of the surprise, That's clever, why didn't I think of that? Their response should not be, Where did *that* come from?—because there was no hint of the surprise ahead of time.

Flashbacks and Flash-Forwards

These can be considered a kind of transition between sections of your narrative, although I prefer to think of them as structural tools. Flashbacks and flash-forwards change the time frame of the story and can cause a lot of trouble for writers. The central question is, how do I get my reader from the present into the new time frame, then back again? The first rule should be: If you can avoid using one of these, don't.

A flashback is often clumsy and annoying to readers and plays havoc with viewpoint. Despite all this, there are times when you have no choice. It's not necessary, for example, to always tell your story in a chronological fashion; sometimes an event in the past becomes relevant only part of the way into the storytelling process. You may need to structure your story synopsis chronologically, but you don't have to tell it that way.

> *As Jimmy limped down the street, a squeal of car tires behind him made him instinctively cringe, and he was instantly thrown back to that time, a year ago, when he was trapped in the cabin of his Ford Escort watching the terrifying weight of a 30-ton Mack truck, its tires locked and shrieking, slide inexorably toward him.*
>
> *It had been a fine spring morning, and . . .*

The key to writing a good flashback is to lead the reader gracefully through the transition into the past and bring him back through the same door that you used to get into the past. In this case it was a sound that did the trick. Anything like that would do the job as effectively.

One of the great strengths of using flashback in particular is the ability to hone in on just the meat of the event. You take us back to the precise moment something happened; the moment the event ends, we return to present time. That can help pick up the pacing of the book and allow you to omit extraneous material in the narrative.

The danger with flash-forward is that it has a tendency to be portentous without being helpful. It may seem to enhance narrative suspense, but nine times out of ten it doesn't really. *Little did Jimmy know that in less than an hour he would see a 30-ton Mack truck bearing down on him like an express train while he sat helplessly in the crushed cabin of his Ford Escort . . .*

The problem with flash-forwards is that they don't often make a lot of sense. The best advice is, use them like seasoning in cooking. A little goes a very long way.

Beginnings and Endings

Writers are often told to start a story "with a bang," and some authors think that instruction should be obeyed literally. However, the purpose of beginning a story with a dramatic moment is to engage the reader's emotions from the opening paragraph, and then hold their interest by posing a problem or a dilemma of an extreme moral or ethical nature. How did this character reach this traumatic point in her life? And how will she solve this problem? It is the reader's emotional commitment to what the main character is going through, and his intellectual fascination with how that character will solve her problems, that will compel the reader to keep turning the page.

Consider this:

Shortly after six o'clock on a rainy March evening in 1946, a slender, gray-haired man sat in his favorite bar, the Ritz, finishing the last of several martinis. Finding himself adequately fortified for the ordeal ahead, he paid the check, got up, and pulled on his coat and hat. A well-stuffed briefcase in one hand and an umbrella in the other, he left the bar and ventured into the downpour drenching mid-Manhattan. He headed west toward a small storefront on Forty-third Street, several blocks away.

Thus begins A. Scott Berg's wonderful biography *Max Perkins: Editor of Genius*.

Or consider this one:

At liftoff, Matt Eversmann said a Hail Mary. He was curled into a seat between two helicopter crew chiefs, the knees of his long legs up to his shoulders. Before him, jammed on both sides of the Black Hawk helicopter, was his "chalk," twelve young men in flak vests over tan desert camouflage fatigues.

This is, of course, the opening of Mark Bowden's *Black Hawk Down*. Finally, what about this?

'Twas the darkness that did the trick, black as tar, that and the silence, though how the men contriv'd to clamber their way up the cliff with their musket and seventy rounds on their backs, I'm sure I don't know even though I saw it with my own eyes and did it myself before very long. We stood hushed on the muddy shore of the river, peering up at the volunteers. They looked like a pack of lizards unloosed on the rocks, though not so nimble, bellies hugging the cliff with their rumps wiggling with the effort. We couldn't see much of 'em for they disappeared now and then into the clumps of withered cedar and spruce that hung on the side of the hill. But we could feel the squirming, pulling labour of it all.

This is the opening to historian Simon Schama's narrative nonfiction piece *The Many Deaths of General Wolfe* from his book *Dead Certainties*. It is the shorter of two "novellas" (the second of which is titled *The Death of a*

Harvard Man). His "you are there" approach is interesting, adventurous, and clearly calculated to mimic fiction. The book was a "work of the imagination that chronicles historical events," he said in an afterword.

> The narratives are based on primary sources. In many cases, including some of the most unlikely episodes . . . I have faithfully followed accounts given in letters and journals. . . . Two kinds of passages are purely imagination. In the first kind (as in the soldier's witness of the Battle of Quebec) the narrative has been constructed from a number of contemporary documents. The more fictitious dialogues . . . are worked up from my own understanding of the sources as to how such a scene might have taken place.

He then proceeds to detail the sources he used to write his book. (Indeed, in nearly every case of narrative nonfiction, the authors have gone to pains to detail their source material.)

The *change* of the status quo (at the beginning of the story) into a dynamic, evolving system will give us the story problem and, ultimately, its solution: in other words, the plot. This change, or plot development, comes from asking of your story and its characters the question "Why?" Your story should start at the moment the status quo is about to end.

Once the goal has been achieved, the problem solved, then the story is finished.

The ending is as important as the opening. If the beginning has to push you off the mountain so you can begin your toboggan descent, the ending has to wrap things up satisfactorily so that one comes to a comfortable conclusion to the high-speed ride down the mountain. James B. Stewart, author of *Den of Thieves,* says, "I spend more time on endings than anything else but leads."

An ending has to do two things: bring a satisfactory intellectual culmination to the story and bring the emotional experience to a satisfying conclusion as well. A good example of this is Jonathan Harr's *A Civil Action,* about a lawyer who goes up against two major corporations in order to hold them responsible for the deaths of local children. In the process, the Porsche-driving, high-living lawyer fights the good fight and loses almost everything he once valued.

Endings should be the climax of the narrative, the obvious driving force being a simple answer to the questions "What happened?" and "Why did it happen?" Then there are what can best be described as story-within-a-story endings. Some sort of anecdote is used as a symbol of what the author feels the story is about, and without actually telling the reader what to think, the author tries to lead him there by using the anecdote as a summary. Stewart uses an ending like this in *Den of Thieves*, his book about Michael Milkin and the insider trading scandal of the 1980s. Dava Sobel does something similar in *Longitude,* as we've discussed elsewhere.

An ending, by its nature, has to provide some sort of closure; the one thing you should never do is leave your readers dangling, even with a story that has no conclusion. One should at least hint at the possible conclusions available, and leave the reader with the option of choosing one of them for herself.

Photos

Many narrative nonfiction books are published with photos, and these may even help sell your book. It's worth knowing that all book contracts make getting the photos the author's responsibility. Your agent may well be able to negotiate some sort of modest photo budget for you, but if you're not careful you could end up spending thousands to get permissions.

The best way, and the cheapest, is to take the photos yourself, but that's not likely to work for a variety of reasons, not the least of which is professional quality. Certainly, if you can, take pictures of all the people you interview. Also, ask them for pictures they may have of themselves, of others, of the setting of the story, and so forth.

You may need to track down photos that are in the public domain. You can do this through the Library of Congress, which charges a nominal fee (about $12 as of 2003) for researching each picture.

Newspaper and photo journalism libraries can get pretty expensive—into the hundreds of dollars per picture. Some photographers, depending on their reputation, can charge in the thousands. Usually, you and the editor will discuss the photo situation and what you want versus what you can get and can afford.

The position of the photos in the book will be a decision made between you, your editor, and the book designer. It is common for photos to be lumped together in the middle of the book as an insert. On occasion, however, there is a reason and argument for having the pictures sprinkled throughout the text as illustrations to that text. To do so makes the book much more expensive to produce, however; and if it is not done well, the pictures will not reproduce properly on paper intended to be used only for text, not images.

Interview Releases

The best source for these is entertainment lawyer Jonathan Kirsch's book *Kirsch's Handbook of Publishing Law* (Acrobat Books). It is one of the most readable and one of the best books on publishing law I've come across. Kirsch says in the book that anyone can copy and use the forms he drew up.

Lawyers

For the most part you can leave a legal read to the publisher's lawyer. If you have issues, make sure you get someone who specializes in publishing and entertainment law to read it. In general, however, publishing lawyers are reasonable people who are well versed in First Amendment issues. What they want from a writer, more than anything else, is good, accurate record keeping. Who said what, where, and when? So keep all your notes, tapes, clippings, and the like, if for no other reason than that you will be able to produce them in court should things ever get that far, which is unlikely.

If you're accurate and careful, you should not have a problem with legal readings.

Dramatic License?

· · · · · · · · · · · · · · · · · ·

We all know that Art is not truth. Art is a lie that makes us
realize truth, at least the truth that is given us to understand.
The artist must know the manner whereby to convince others of
the truthfulness of his lies.

PABLO PICASSO

 So, how far can you—and should you—go in re-creating a fictional version of your true story? That is what it is, of course,
as much as you try to make it real. Your story and the events
that constitute it have been deliberately chosen and linked by
placing them in a linear sequence, and shaped and refracted through the
lens of your intellect and prejudices. What began in *real life* as a series of
random acts of mostly cause and effect has now led, in hindsight, to an
emotionally gripping story with a beginning, middle, and end, something
that is not naturally occurring in real life for the most part.

To understand the *why* and *what* of things, we are forced to give them a
coherence they usually lack in the anarchy of everyday reality, and thus we
begin to create art through interpretation and insight. Truth is, even the traditional reporting of a news story is an artificial concoction. (Read two different journalists' accounts of the same event and you'll quickly see what I
mean.) The question becomes, how artificial should one make it? Where is
the boundary between insightful interpretation and fraudulently misleading
the reader?

New Journalism and Real Life

The goal of New Journalism (what we now call narrative nonfiction), Tom Wolfe wrote in his 1973 book *New Journalism,* was to intellectually and emotionally *involve* the reader—to show the reader *real life*—in other words, to help the reader understand the *why* and *what* of subjects that seemed to lack any. I think it no accident that New Journalism sprang up during the turbulent 1960s and 1970s.

Gonzo reporters looked for a way to explain to mainstream America the growing revolutionary subcultures of the 1960s and beyond. They wrote about the hippie drug scene, and the importance and meaning of radical political movements such as the anti–Vietnam War movement, the women's movement, the burgeoning environmental movement, and the Black Panthers. To do this effectively, they looked for a writing technique that would somehow convey the truth of these subjects in a way that conventional reporting did not. The experimental search for the technique that would best capture in print the spirit of their subject and that subject's intent led these reporters, consciously or otherwise, to rediscover the work of an earlier generation of writers, particularly Jack London, Stephen Crane, John Dos Passos, Upton Sinclair, Edith Wharton, George Orwell, and even Charles Dickens, all of whom used their skills as novelists (mostly, but not entirely, in the form of novels) to report true stories of journalistic merit, usually involving social injustice and inequality.

Thus, the New Journalists of the 1960s experimented with re-created dialogue, points of view, and even interior monologue, all in an attempt to get into a subject's head and give us the *why* of a person or situation in the news that to many middle American readers was bewildering and in some cases viewed as threatening to the mainstream way of life.

The Inverted Pyramid

The traditional newspaper-story structure is the inverted pyramid. That is, you state the essence of the story at the top, and expound on it as you progress, thus allowing an editor to cut from the bottom of the story without losing anything vital if the story has to be shortened. The revolution of narrative news reporting has led to what is generally considered a more engaging read. Unlike the inverted pyramid structure, which really just conveys information objectively, though with hooks and élan at its best, the narrative story form gives readers a reward—an emotional denouement—for making it through a story. It's familiar and comforting. Culturally, we use the narrative form to understand, to remember, and to find meaning in our everyday lives.

The problem with using fictional techniques to make a story of facts sexy, however, is that it can seductively lead an inexperienced or lazy writer into believing it's okay to either embellish or shoehorn the facts into a convenient story line that may grossly distort not only what really happened, but also the spirit of the event—the very reason for using the technique in the first place. Turning real life into a narrative carries with it the inherent temptation to sacrifice truth for the sake of effect—usually sentimentalized drama.

In 1981, for example, *Washington Post* reporter Janet Cooke was fired and had her Pulitzer Prize for feature writing rescinded after it was revealed that the eight-year-old drug addict in her column was not a real person, but a composite. Mike Barnicle and Patricia Smith both resigned from the *Boston Globe* after admitting they had fictionalized their columns, as also did *New Republic* associate editor Stephen Glass. All fell afoul of the seductive sirens of narrative nonfiction that lure unsuspecting or ambitious reporters onto the rocks of professional ruin. All made the mistake of believing it's more important and sexy to use sentiment and metaphor in their stories than to research and use verifiable facts.

The Wrong Subject

In general, the narrative nonfiction story is usually told from the perspective of one or more characters. We get to know the innermost thoughts of these characters, but we're not always told how these thoughts were determined by the author, and this can be a problem.

"Sad things can happen when an author chooses the wrong subject: first the author suffers, then the reader, and finally the publisher, all together in a tiny whirlpool of pain," observed the novelist and critic Wilfrid Sheed. This is especially true when, like a lover questioning the faithfulness of a spouse, the reader begins to doubt that an author is treating him honestly, even if the writer appears to be putting all her cards on the table.

An interesting example of this was Edmund Morris's biography of President Ronald Reagan, *Dutch: A Memoir.* Morris was Reagan's official biographer. After years of trying to figure out how to write the book, he resorted to creating a fictionalized version of himself in Reagan's past. The result was a highly questionable memoir rather than a biography, narrated by an Edmund Morris who was several decades older than the real author, who purported to have known Dutch Reagan since the 1920s, and who, among other things, had a son who joined the Weather Underground in the 1960s. Problem was, in a nonfiction biography where one assumes that the facts, above all else, are true, none of these facts were true. Alas, the fictive Morris bore little resemblance to the real Morris, the writer.

This overt mixing of fact and fiction caused a great deal of discussion among critics and readers, most of it unfavorable, and did not do a great deal for Morris's reputation as a writer. In the end, the fictional parts were not that convincing and interfered with the nonfiction parts, forcing the reader to keep track of what was true and what wasn't. Why Morris, clearly frustrated by his subject, didn't simply write a conventional biography is a mystery that may be explained by a writer's technical experimentation in an effort to capture the essence of his subject. However, for the majority of readers the book failed on nearly all counts as a result. For a man who, in

. . . the . . .

the past, had been praised as a graceful and scholarly writer it was a particularly disappointing experiment that in hindsight seemed doomed to failure.

Joe McGinniss's 1993 biography of Massachusetts senator Edward Kennedy, *The Last Brother,* makes up for its lack of verifiable fact by sheer hubris. In some ways, it can be considered the missing link between the traditional biography and Morris's *Dutch.*

McGinniss made a name for himself with several outstanding books earlier in his career, including *Fatal Vision. The Last Brother* is a "speculative biography" of Senator Ted Kennedy (brother of John and Robert, both of whom were assassinated in office). In it, McGinniss speculates on what Ted Kennedy thought or felt about his career, but admits his attempts to interview Kennedy were rebuffed. In a note at the end of the book, McGinniss's response to criticism about this wholesale "supposition" (let us not call it an "invention," please) was that the book was an author's highly personal and interpretive view of his subject. At times, McGinniss said, "a writer must attempt an approach that transcends that of traditional journalism or even, perhaps, of conventional biography."

McGinniss acknowledged using articles and books as a "verifiable source" from which he "distilled an essence." He says quotations in the book "represent in substance what I believe to have been spoken."

Commenting in general on the problems of fictionalizing fact into a story, Farrar, Straus and Giroux editor in chief Jonathan Galassi commented that a "writer (of anything) always has to be aware of how his/her method of narration is affecting the treatment of the subject."

Observing Distorts Reality?

Perhaps the increasing popularity of nonfiction narratives is a reflection of our taste for more *reality*-based entertainment. It's not *real*, of course. Although we can't see them, there's a camera crew present affecting the behavior of the people we're watching. It's almost a visible example of Werner Heisenberg's theory that watching a scientific experiment somehow affects the thing observed, distorting the result.

In *Dutch,* Edmund Morris invented pages of fictitious dialogue, and indeed, fictitious characters, but at least admitted up front he was doing so.

Bob Woodward's book about the Clinton administration, *The Agenda,* while listing sources, is still problematic, I believe. While we're told in the book that the sources of reconstructed dialogue and quotes come from a participant in the reported events, from memos, or from notes or diaries of the participant, we're never told who the participant was. We are forced to take Woodward on trust that everything is kosher, as it probably is, the experiences of Cooke, Glass, Smith, Barnicle, Joe McGinniss, and Edmund Morris notwithstanding.

On the other hand, in *Black Hawk Down,* Mark Bowden went to great lengths to detail the sources for his book, and it shows in the writing. Charlie Spicer, a senior editor at St. Martin's Press, once told my friend Gary Provost, "I worry sometimes where the line is, but frequently I leave it to the lawyers. You can invent a little bit with physical description, but you have to be careful to document everything factual because our lawyers query everything. They want the documentation."

True crime writer Jack Olsen, whose books are models for how to write the genre, in my opinion, was deeply critical of anyone who cheated an audience through deliberate invention. He told Provost in an interview,

> My books take two years to write because I don't invent any details. But I'm not saying it's wrong. If a woman always sits on the floor or the ground with her legs crossed, then I don't think a writer is going very far afield to write something like that in a scene. . . . In your research you develop certain characteristics and physical attributes of people and I suppose you would be justified in slipping one in now and then without knowing for sure that it happened. I probably should do it. I'm not a fanatic. You can't be a fanatic about every single letter of every single word.

Upping the Ethical Ante

Thomas Powers, in the Sunday *New York Times Book Review*, commented on Bob Woodward's *Bush at War*, "What's remarkable about Woodward's book is the same thing that was remarkable about many of his others—extraordinary access to secret documents, like contemporaneous notes of National Security Council meetings, and to high officials, including President Bush."

At one point in the narrative Woodward directly quotes National Security Adviser Condoleezza Rice reproaching Secretary of Defense Donald Rumsfeld in an off-the-record exchange. Powers writes:

> The earlier quotations [in the meeting] might have come from N.S.C. minutes, but what about Rice's chiding of Rumsfeld for being sulky? It would be nice to know who told Woodward that, but more important is whether it is true.
>
> Woodward has been writing books in roughly this way for 20 years, and during that time he has rarely been attacked by his subjects for getting things wrong. . . . The lack of protest [including Rumsfeld's and Rice's, on this occasion] inclines me to trust his account as solid until something else comes along that says different with footnotes.

This is a tough path for Bob Woodward to tread to avoid criticism, though, and it's extremely treacherous for a young (meaning inexperienced) journalist without Woodward's reputation and track record. Just ask Janet Cooke or Mike Barnicle.

"Bob Woodward is the problem," Don Fry, an independent writing coach, said, when asked about the bad-boy reputation narrative writing has earned with some reporters and editors. "He doesn't bother to cite sources and he reads minds. . . . One of the problems with Woodward is he doesn't tell you where he got it," Fry went on. "All the information just floats by."

Readers should be more trusting of his work, Woodward told journalist

Chris Harvey in 1994. "My books are scrupulously reported," he said. For *The Agenda,* for example, he interviewed more than 250 people. "All that's missing is who said it, whose diary it's in, what memo it's in."

Jack Hart, managing editor of the *Oregonian* newspaper, has commented: "Choosing to tell a story in narrative form ups the ethical ante. Plucking a coherent story line from an almost infinite number of possible details is highly subjective. It inevitably reflects the writer's basic beliefs about how the world operates. Narrative writers and editors therefore have extra ethical obligations. As one of our editors puts it: 'Your ethical antenna needs to go up a couple of feet higher if you choose narrative.' " In an interview in late 2002 he added, "The big ethical issue these days revolves around attribution. I'm still struggling with ways to attribute in a nonfiction narrative in a way that doesn't interrupt story flow. And if recent discussion on [the Internet forum] WriterL is any indication, so are a lot of my colleagues."

In *A Perfect Storm* the problem was how to fictionalize a true story with no firsthand sources and still keep it honest. Specifically, Sebastian Junger was faced with dealing with the demise of the crew of a commercial swordfishing boat, the *Andrea Gail,* while not having any possible firsthand evidence of what happened to them, as it is presumed the ship sank with all hands. The author was thus forced to admit he was going to hypothesize parts of his story by using accounts from others who had found themselves in similar (but obviously less fatal) circumstances. He continually draws a picture of supposition based on these sources, at the end of his book giving us a detailed description of what it is like, generically, to drown. It's an adventurous and experimental way to tell a story of fishing and fishermen, against the background of re-creating on the page the rare experience of enduring a terrifying but exquisite "perfect storm" (as weather people describe it).

Jack Hart commented on Junger's book: "*A Perfect Storm* was honest in that it clearly differentiated between fact and speculation. *Sleepers, Midnight in the Garden of Good and Evil,* and much memoir are not. And the opposite of honesty in this business [that is, journalism] is fraud, pure and simple."

Random House executive editor Peter Gethers has a similar but more forgiving attitude:

There are obvious dangers in Junger's technique (although he pulled it off beautifully). There are different types of accuracy, I suppose. One would be technical accuracy—what exactly did this person say and do? Another would be capturing an accurate emotion. This is where technique really comes into play. The best example of this is Junger's description of what it's like to drown. By writing that the way he did, he didn't have to go into the minds of his characters at the moment of their deaths. By showing us the physicality of drowning, he made us know and feel the terror his characters had to have felt.

In Lorenzo Carcaterra's book *Sleepers*, many critics were concerned that too many facts had been changed, so that nothing in the story could really be trusted. Gethers's take on *Sleepers,* however, is quite different. "I was the editor of *Sleepers,* so I know much about it. The controversy was a fake one," he explained.

Carcaterra's narrative is a memoir of a sort about growing up in the tough New York City neighborhood of Hell's Kitchen in the 1960s. Four young men (of whom Carcaterra was one) wound up in a correctional home for boys. There, they were abused, beaten, and raped by the guards. A decade or so later, one of the boys had become a lawyer, and two of the boys had turned into cold-blooded murderers. One night they walk into a bar and run into one of the brutal guards who had forever changed their lives. What happens after that sets a brilliant plan for revenge into motion, the four boys (now men) together again in a scheme to get back at their persecutors in a very public way and expose the horrible wrongs they suffered.

Trouble was, Carcaterra admitted to changing many of the facts in *Sleepers,* so once again we have no touchstone, other than Carcaterra's word, about what is true and what fancy.

Gethers is insistent that

almost all nonfiction books that are about contemporary matters and
people have facts changed—to avoid lawsuits. Names are changed and
descriptions of people are often changed so they're unrecognizable. In
other words, people who do bad things get "saved"—so they don't sue.
All Lorenzo did was change certain things so several good people—the
priest and the young lawyer in the book—would be unrecognizable and
thus not suffer by being recognizable. The media went crazy because
they couldn't find the real people (although they were quite lazy and
probably could have if they were more competent). Along with the Random House lawyers, I oversaw the changes Lorenzo made—they were
nothing out of the ordinary.

Objective Versus Subjective Reporting

I guess I should declare my probably obvious bias at this point. I was trained
in the older traditions of BBC Radio News, and Fleet Street newspapers of the
late 1960s and 1970s, before they fell in the thrall of the tabloid mentality
that is rampant in British journalism today. It was important, my editors in
print journalism and radio insisted, to tell both sides of a story equally, maintaining as best one could an unbiased, objective reporting of the story. If you
have an opinion, get an interview subject to say it for you, retaining at least
the appearance of impartiality. Let readers make up their own minds about
what the events mean, after being given all the relevant facts.

Of course, objective reporting is a near impossibility, because the art of
the print journalist is to pick and choose relevant information from the thousand shards of it either lying around or pried free through incisive interviewing. She then explains to her audience what is happening and what it means.

In other words, objective reporting is dependent on the character, general knowledge, and intellect of the journalist doing the reporting. There is,
at least, an attempt to be objective using this reporting technique, which is
abandoned when writing in the narrative form. So the pressure to be accu-

. . . the . . .

rate in narrative re-creation is stronger because the temptations to get away with invention that captures the spirit of the event (in the reporter's mind) without substantiating facts are greater. *She wore a red dress.* How do you know? *She winced as she sat down, unsteadily easing her aching back.* Who said so? Again, how do you know? Perhaps she flounced. Or did she flop down? Description is not just a visual aid, it is also an indicator of character. Someone flouncing into a seat is very different from someone sitting down carefully so as not to exacerbate a bad backache. You don't have to put the sources into the text of the narrative and break up the flow, but you should have a note at the end of the book detailing information for each chapter where such claims are made.

There is an undeclared, inherent bias on the part of the reporter that is built into her understanding of an event that she has observed or reconstructed and then reported. Only by actively and honestly trying to present both sides of an issue can the reporter hope to balance out her natural bias on an issue and present enough information for readers to make up their own minds independently of the reporter's personal conclusions. Writing a book about an idea or an incident allows the author the luxury—or pitfall, depending on your point of view—to choose a particular viewpoint and write a story through that prism. Yet the best writers, such as Mark Bowden, Tracy Kidder, and John McPhee, do not abandon journalistic integrity in order to contrive a good yarn.

In the best of circumstances, one finds eyewitnesses and experts and people intimately involved with an event who say, in their own words, what it is the reporter feels should be said about an event.

Doctoring the Truth

There's an idea that some teachers put forward that a novelist, or an inexperienced writer of nonfiction, can give himself "permission to lie" in order to write a narrative account. As far as it goes, that's okay, given the exceptions I've noted. It's best, if you're unsure, to have the interviewee verify her quotes, even though to me, as a journalist, that goes against the grain a little because it allows the subject the chance to veto or edit what she said. (Think what might have happened if Trent Lott in early 2003 had been given the chance to edit his remarks at Strom Thurmond's birthday party. Instead of supporting Thurmond, and implicitly his 1948 racist politics, in hindsight, Lott might have been able to remain the majority leader in the Senate.)

It's also okay to tidy up quotes, in effect doctor the truth, in order to make them more readable. People are usually somewhat inarticulate, and yet what they are saying may be profound, if buried amid "um"s and "ah"s. Some people can also be quite profane in their speech and you don't always want to quote them verbatim with every curse word intact. It is fine to reconfirm with the source, if you need to, and as long as you don't change the meaning or sense of what they say when you quote someone, they probably won't even notice that you have tidied up their speech.

Many young reporters use subjective narrative nonfiction techniques as a subterfuge for laziness or willful ignorance of events and their context and history. Emotion (which is often confused with sentimentality) is more important than fact, they argue. Commenting on this, Peter Gethers said that "as with all trends, [I agree that] this one goes too far. The best writing is one that does it all—gets the facts right, tells us what happens, *and* achieves the right level of emotional impact (which I'm all in favor of; I'm not in favor of sentimentality)." He added, "The ultimate value of [narrative nonfiction] . . . is that it lets the author explore the depth and scope of a given situation—and it allows for much more depth than a tabloid piece of journalism, a movie, or a piece of television reporting."

The case of Janet Malcolm and psychoanalyst Jeffrey Masson is instructive of what can happen if the reporter is not careful. Masson was a rising analyst who had been placed in charge of the Freud archives in the Freud house in London. Within a relatively short time he had antagonized his boss, Kurt Eissler (described by journalist Craig Seligman in a *Salon.com* essay as "the high priest of Freudian analysts"), was fired from his job, and was suing his former employers when he met Malcolm.

She is a journalist with a reputation for edgy, uncompromising writing. Still, Masson spent hours talking to her. She encouraged his trust, even putting up him and his girlfriend in her New York home. And then, as Craig Seligman describes it, she "unearthed a frightening talent. [Her book] *In the Freud Archives* is a masterwork of character assassination." And it led to ten years of litigation between Masson and Malcolm, whose major crime was to compress and conjoin quotes from different times to form several long monologues, purportedly by Masson.

Seligman went on:

> It's all but impossible to read Masson's long monologues (many of them, it came out in testimony, cobbled together from more than one interview) without thinking, "What an asshole!" When the articles appeared, their flabbergasted victim howled in shock at the betrayal, and his howl took the form of a libel suit.
>
> The case hinged on five quotations that Masson claimed were fabrications and that Malcolm, embarrassingly, couldn't produce on tape— although, as David Gates pointed out in *Newsweek*, "what Malcolm *does* have on tape—only a few lines are in dispute—is more than enough to make Masson look silly." The suit threaded byzantinely up and down through the courts for years before a jury finally found against Masson in 1994. But for Malcolm the victory was a Pyrrhic one. The public spectacle had been huge and humiliating, her reporting widely criticized and mocked. The lawsuit gained her more notoriety than any of her books ever had; thenceforward everything she wrote would be a target.

Nevertheless, many writers of narrative nonfiction find a way to compress quotes without experiencing the same problems Janet Malcolm suffered. It's as well to be forewarned, however. Masson did not accuse Malcolm of tidying up his quotes, but of *fabricating* quotes. The first jury found for Masson against Malcolm and the *New Yorker,* where the long articles had first appeared. A second jury, however, while finding that two of the passages were fabricated, nevertheless found in Malcolm's favor because in their view neither of the offending passages was libelous.

Poisoned Tales

A serious downside to narrative nonfiction journalism is that it can create an atmosphere where emotionally charged anecdotes force the creation of public policy, driven by a political quick-fix mentality that is a knee-jerk emotional response rather than a rationally considered solution to a problem. It's much easier, for example, for a legislator to vote against a sex-offender-registration law, if he thinks it's too draconian and challenges constitutional notions of civil liberties, if the bill is called a sex-offender-registration law rather than, say, Megan's Law. Suddenly, because of the way the story has been reported, the legislator is voting against a victimized little girl and her grieving family, not a potential threat to our constitutional freedoms.

To survive as an effective, open society we need to be continually and accurately informed of our world and what is happening in it. Many seem to now either dismiss or forget that journalists were once called the fourth estate—unelected, it's true, but nevertheless for the most part imbued with a vocation to keep society honest and equitable by making those in power accountable for their actions through its reporting of what they did and why they did it. If journalists abrogate their responsibilities through lazy, populist, or overtly biased reporting, we head toward ruin as a society if we are not careful. Lazy and cowardly journalism can lead to endorsing government and corporate propaganda rather than questioning it, enhancing ignorance of issues among the voting population, and at the extreme end erode the very foundations of democracy. It allows politicians to steal elections through bully tactics that news corporations, for a variety of reasons, do not expose because the commercial price paid by journalistic institutions is too high if they try to hold the offenders' feet to fire and call them to account for their misdeeds.

There is a reason that any modern government attempting to gain control of a population first silences or muzzles the press, and writers in general, by either shutting off avenues of publication or, in extreme cases, putting writers in jail or killing them.

The reporter is faced with two choices: Take a story and use it to help people understand or think about a larger issue, or take that larger issue and trivialize it by reducing it to an easily digestible though not very accurately reported story.

The art and integrity of reporters has become particularly relevant in recent times, as a debate heats up in the United States following 9/11 over the government's declared need for secrecy and a free hand to jail whomever they want indefinitely to protect the nation from terrorism, which contradicts the Constitution's insistence on a free and open society. "Liberty," said John Adams in an open letter to Thomas Jefferson in 1816, "cannot be preserved without a general knowledge among the people. . . . Power must never be trusted without a check." In an important opinion over the government's attempt to hold hearings and trials in secret, issued in late 2002, Judge Damon J. Keith, of the U.S. Court of Appeals for the Sixth Circuit, wrote: "Democracies die behind closed doors." He went on to say that the people had deputized the press as "guardians of their liberty."

Quoted in the *New York Times* (September 2, 2002), Herschel P. Fink, a lawyer who represents the *Detroit Free Press*, commented on the ruling: "Secrecy is the evil here [not terrorism]." He went on, the government "absolutely" has an obligation to "vigorously" fight terrorism, but excessive secrecy is intolerable. "We just want to watch," he added.

That principle underlines the need for journalists to pay attention not only to what they report but to the thoroughness with which they report it. The evolution of the narrative nonfiction novel is arguably an attempt by some journalists to develop their role in detailing and exploring the important stories of our time. As the pressures of tabloid journalism press writers into more and more superficial accounts of events, reporters can find themselves flirting with writing not news, but propaganda or sentimental, irrelevant pap in a misguided effort to emphasize feeling over relevance because it's more entertaining and less threatening to the powers that be.

What Has All This to Do with Writing Narrative Nonfiction?

Former Grove/Atlantic editor Brendan Cahill commented: "It's hard to have novels that channel into every aspect of American life. In the Age of Information, the sheer amount of fact that is overcoming and overwhelming us day by day instills in us a need for stories to make sense of all the views of our lives."

Lee Gutkind, founder and editor of the magazine *Creative Nonfiction,* an author and editor of numerous articles and books, and professor of English at the University of Pittsburgh, explained that "the world has changed so suddenly over the past few years that now there is nothing that a novel can give us that hasn't already happened in our world. . . . It's hard as hell to compete with our realities of today for nonfiction."

Jack Olsen, I think, summed up the issue of dramatic license pretty well. In his interview with Gary Provost he said,

> Truman Capote, that little, gifted, brilliant son of a bitch, put such pressure on all subsequent true crime writers, especially the ones who can't write as well as he, and that's all of them. He said that all the quotes in *In Cold Blood* were verbatim, but we know he made a lot of them up. He sold the public on the idea of, oh, look folks, at last we have an accurate true crime book. He put such pressure on all the poor slobs that followed

him to do the same thing, even though he hadn't done it himself. To me that is the single biggest outrage ever perpetrated under the name of true crime. If there was a gloomy setting in the courthouse, Capote wouldn't think twice about making it a gloomy day. *In Cold Blood* is a brilliant book, wonderfully written, and fraudulent.

⚫S⚫E⚫V⚫E⚫N⚫

Finding an Agent, or Submitting Directly?

• • • • • • • • • • • • • • • • •

We can't all be heroes, because somebody has to sit on the
curb and applaud when they go by.

WILL ROGERS, AMERICAN HUMORIST

Getting an agent is a profound personal validation for a writer.

DONALD MAASS, *WRITING THE BREAKOUT NOVEL*

Okay, let's start with a confession: I earn a lot of my living as a literary agent (the rest comes from writing), so I have a predisposition when it comes to recommending that writers get themselves an agent. I know it works, because I'm convinced by experience as an author and an agent (and an editor before that) that there is no substitute for a good agent working on your behalf and advising you about your work and your career. Anyone who tells you differently should be instantly suspect.

Simply put, unless you're as talented and driven a personality as, say, Dave Eggers *(A Heartbreaking Work of Staggering Genius)* or a really capable entrepreneur like the authors of *Chicken Soup for the Soul*, the rule of thumb should be: Writers write, editors edit, and agents agent. It's not smart to mix these elements and it's rarely successful. However well you think you'll do on your own, you'll do even better with a good agent.

. . . Telling . . .

I know, I know—good agents are hard to get and bad ones are like bad spouses: You write and you e-mail and you call, all to no avail. What's wrong with these idiots? So what do you do while you're looking and courting?

Publishing is unquestionably one of the more idiosyncratic industries, and from the perspective of someone trying to get published for the first time it can seem painfully whimsical. But it isn't. There are definitive and distinctive things you can do as an author to enhance your chances of being brought into the fold and getting your book represented and then published, which I'll discuss in a minute.

There is a truckload of myths about publishing—even among those who should know better, such as professional journalists. These stories are in some cases driven by misinformation, and in other cases wishful thinking—how publishing *ought* to be, not how it really is. Taken together they have about as much to do with being published in the early twenty-first century as Bronze Age metalwork has to do with constructing Space Lab. There's a common idea, for example, that editors have the time or the inclination to critique material that is sent to them if they aren't going to buy it. Rarely happens.

These days, most of an editor's time is taken up with endless meetings, and producing and moving "product" for their corporate bosses. That's one of the reasons you want an agent. They are more inclined to encourage new writers with promising material, because they have more time to do so—though I should quickly point out that agents don't have a lot more time to develop work with writers who are not their clients than editors. (A fair few of us still do, though.) It's not our job to help you get published—does that shock you? This is a business and it's your job to learn your craft, not mine to teach you. What I want (and what every other editor and agent I know wants) is a writer who has done the work and comes up with a knockout proposal that I can help put the finishing touches to in order to increase his chances of getting published, of launching a career, and then developing that career so that writer and agent both make money.

Do not lose sight of the ball: publishing is a marketplace of ideas. We buy and sell the best and most commercial (in the form of books), which is where the art of writing comes in. It's a heady way to make a living, and all of us in the industry love what we do because of this. But bottom-line, professional writing and publishing is about making money, whether you're a publisher, a writer, or an agent. It's a business and needs to be treated as such.

Do It Yourself

If you want to catch an editor's eye make sure you have an outstanding résumé in your field of expertise. If you're a journalist, for example, with a journalistic story to tell, make sure you've been well published and that you have access to the best sources for your story, ideally previously unpublished ones. You may have already published articles on the subject you want to write a book about. It's even better if you've lectured regularly on it, too. Develop a book that plays to your strengths as a qualified writer and appeals to the broadest audience without becoming too vague. (How do you market to "everyone"?)

Let's say you published an article that might well form the basis for a narrative nonfiction book. As a result of the article being published, not only do a couple of editors get in touch with you, but an agent or two does as well. But while the agent wants you to put together a proposal on spec (speculation), and may not accept your first or even second attempt at the proposal, the editor is ready to give you a book contract on the basis of a phone conversation and the article itself. It's not a big house, the advance is pretty meager, but the editor is really enthusiastic and just loves the book idea and your writing. You'd be mad to turn that down, wouldn't you?

Maybe, maybe not. If one editor is ready to buy something from you basically sight unseen, how do you suppose others might respond if you took the time to actually develop a really good proposal? Yes, it means extra work, but that extra work could pay off in a higher advance. Almost certainly, with more than one editor interested in your project, you'd be able to negotiate a better deal for yourself. What's more, are you sure you want to find yourself writing a book under a ticking contractual deadline that you're not sure you can meet because you haven't done the elementary work of fleshing out the book first? That's a lot of pressure to handle on a first book. What if the editor leaves the house before the book is handed in? What if the house decides to cut back on books being published that year, never mind that you have a contract guaranteeing publication for a certain date? What if you realize you will miss your deadline by six months or more because you're sick, or someone near to you is sick, or you simply can't organize, research, and write the book in the time you agreed to because the material is overwhelming? Disaster is looming.

Help may be relatively near at hand, however.

"Agents? We Don't Need No Stinkin' Agents."

Let's look at that scenario again. The likelihood is, even with a published article, you won't be approached by an editor or agent, though certainly it happens. Nevertheless, you've written a strong article, and it can be a writing sample, and certainly a calling card. You've polished your book proposal and now you're ready to start actively submitting it somewhere.

First question: Do you really need an agent, or can you submit successfully directly to an editor? Indeed, to misquote the bandit in the movie *The Treasure of the Sierra Madre,* "Agents? We don't need no stinkin' agents." Why should you waste 15 percent of your hard-earned money on some interloper?

Among many other qualities (including a keen editorial eye), you get two really important assets with a good agent that you don't get from anyone else: a matchmaker's Rolodex of editors who want and like what you've written, and a canny contract negotiator who likely has already got boilerplate agreements with publishers better than the one a publisher might offer you if you did business with them directly.

So, ideally, you should try and approach an agent before you approach a publisher. However, as we decided earlier, you just aren't having any luck catching an agent's eye with this project. There's no reason you shouldn't approach editors directly if you do it in a professional manner—and that phrase is extremely important. If you don't know what a professional manner is, educate yourself before you start calling and e-mailing.

There's a catch, though. *If too many editors get to see your proposal and reject it, your chances of getting an agent to represent that project diminish exponentially with each rejection you receive.* There are only a finite number of places and people to send a project. Do not be in a hurry to multiply submit something until you're certain it's ready to go out; and if you haven't been published yet, you're not the best judge of your own material. (Neither is your spouse, sibling, child, friend, neighbor, or parent unless they happen to be a professional writer or publishing professional, so it won't help to try and sell an editor or agent on the project by saying, "My mother/brother/sister/auntie/best friend thinks it's the best thing she's ever read, and she/he reads three books a week.")

Do some research on editors who buy the kind of book you're writing. There are lots of books that will help you, such as the *Writer's Digest* guides, or Jeff Herman's *Writer's Guide to Book Editors, Publishers, and Literary Agents,* plus a multitude of frequently asked questions (FAQs) on a number of writers' forums on the Internet. Pick several books that most closely resemble yours, then research which editors (and agents) worked on those books. You can sometimes find this information in the acknowledgments of a book, or reported in the deals info of publisherslunch.com, or in *Publishers Weekly* magazine, the industry journal. Then write a dynamite though not gimmicky three-paragraph (one page max) query letter and proposal.

Next make a preliminary call or send an e-mail to the editor. Using your query letter as a script, pitch your idea in a simple, one- or two-sentence confident manner, and hope they bite and ask to see the material.

Don't leave phone messages that say, "Hi. Ah'm Chuckie from Pine Bluff, Arkansas, and I've written a book that will make a great movie," or, "Hello. Charles Remington here, from Arkansas. My manuscript is just what you've been looking for. Please call me at 555-1212 if you're interested."

Or e-mails that start: "My name is Linguine Z. DePasta. I have recently completed my book and I am currently seeking an agent. I am 32 years old. I grew up in east Boston, MA, and I currently own a home in Revere, MA. I am employed as an accountant for a meatpacking company in Everett, MA. I enjoy writing in my spare time. My book is about cycling around the beautiful United States."

Editors and agents are intrigued by professionals. Let us know up front that you're a freelance writer, or a former editor with *Playboy*, or a professional journalist with the *New York Times*—something that reassures me you won't be wasting my time or that of a colleague.

Now explain what you're writing about: a book about, say, the inside story of what happened at Enron, or being a female firefighter, and that you worked for Enron as an accountant with the CEO, or as a firefighter for however many years. If your project is a reconstruction of the battle for Mogadishu, for example, tell me up front you're a professional journalist working for the *Philadelphia Inquirer*, and that the newspaper ran a series of articles by you on this previously ignored modern battle.

If you decide to e-mail an editor, *do not* assume they want to see your proposal and attach it uninvited. There are too many viruses and weird e-mail things floating around these days, and the odds are great that an e-mail savvy editor will simply delete the material without opening it or reading it.

However, if you intend to send your proposal through the mail it's okay to include a query letter and the proposal if you wish.

If you're lucky enough to be put through to an editor, first of all ask if they have a moment to speak with you. Editors are stunningly busy people, and not every time is a good time to pitch. If the editor says they have the time, make sure you pitch your book idea succinctly and intelligently. Be warm and winning. The editor (or her assistant) will soon enough tell you whether or not she is interested in seeing your project. If she says yes, then say thank you, confirm the correct spelling of her name and get her correct address, and politely ask how long she thinks it will take her to read it.

If you haven't heard by the date the editor suggested, wait a few more days and then call and politely ask how things are progressing.

Some Reasons for Rejection

There are a number of reasons an editor may turn down your project, besides the obvious one of it not being written to a professional standard in the editor's opinion. Here are a few:

- She may have just acquired a book on this subject, or the house may have acquired something similar.
- The editor believes there is too small an audience for the book idea. For example, your book reveals the seamier side of the antiabortion movement's fanatical supporters. Here, while the story would make a great newspaper or magazine article, the wretched truth is that the antiabortion proponents won't want to read the book, and the pro-choice proponents already know as much as they need to about their adversaries. *Could* you write a good book about this subject? Of course. It would have to be a remarkable book and remarkably well done.
- The subject is too local, or too academic for general audiences. Successful true crime stories, for example, tend to be psychosexual or concerned with people who have a national recognition. Why should someone in Texas care what happens to someone in Idaho?
- The subject is too obscure and did not change the way we see and understand the world.
- There are publishing marketing and sales biases, such as that military stories are read by men who are not interested in books

about women in the military (unfair and untrue, but a bias to deal with nevertheless).

- The author does not have the expertise or experience to tell the story successfully.
- Nothing new is being brought to the table; the book is just a rehashing of what has been previously published.

Once Upon a Time . . .

There may well be writers you know who *say* they've represented themselves successfully, but excluding a handful of exceptions (and I mean under five people), I defy anyone to name one successful writer who hasn't improved his or her career by using an agent, a literary lawyer, or some sort of business manager.

Let me tell you story: Once upon a time. . . . my former agent was engaged in what seemed like one of the world's longest divorces, and was not focused on her work.

I saw no reason why my career should stall, however. After all, I was also an agent, I had been an editor, and this was not my first book deal. What could go wrong? So I signed a small book deal with Ms. A., an elderly and experienced editor, with whom I had a good ongoing professional relationship. Indeed, she helped me shape the proposal.

Once I had handed in the manuscript, I learned to my horror that I was being edited not only by Ms. A., but also by Ms. B., a woman in her forties, and Ms. C., who was both opinionated and not long out of college. Someone would request a change, I'd make it, and a couple of weeks later the manuscript would come back with different handwriting asking why I'd made the original change.

"I don't care if I'm edited by Attila the Hun," I cried. "Just pick one person for me to work with!"

I embraced Zen Buddhism and tried to fall asleep to images of sheep bleating, "Better published than not." Things were looking bleak and the deal was falling apart. I wasn't sure what to do to save it because personalities—no, let's be honest, *egos*—were starting to get raw and bruised.

Finally, my agent shook off her lethargy and stumbled back into the picture. When she realized what a nightmare the company was putting me through, she got the original publishers to let me keep the royalty advance and helped move the book to another publisher. It was worth the wait to have the problem resolved so neatly.

The new publisher, John Wiley & Sons, paid me a better royalty advance, changed barely a word of what I'd written, and *The Elements of Storytelling* was published to good reviews. You can still buy it in the stores, and twice a year I get a royalty check. All's well that ends well, but without an agent on the case, the outcome would have been far bleaker.

Sorry—Too Busy

A lot of writers chase agents who are too busy to respond. Successful agents have their hands full just maintaining their regular clientele. The average agent represents about 50 to 70 clients on their roster. However, agents *are* on the lookout for successful, experienced, money-earning writers who know how the game is played and can exploit it to everyone's advantage. So, if you learn your craft and *roll with* the marketplace rather than try to poke it in the eye, your chances of being published are quite high, because the truth is that finding good book projects with strong authors attached is surprisingly difficult. So if you're in that category, like the pretty girl at a ball, all the beaux will notice you and want to take you for a twirl around the floor.

Successful writers are published in magazines and anthologies, have written book reviews for local or national newspapers, have gotten their name in print somewhere, often more than once, and somewhere in the article their byline says something like, "Dobbie Elfen is currently working on a nonfiction book about domestic enslavement."

Successful writers attend writer's conferences and network discreetly. They get their writing noticed by people whose opinion counts and can talk to friends or colleagues in the business about an up-and-coming writer and her work. One of the best ways to get a good agent is to try to find out who is starting up on their own or has just joined an established agency. The news is reported in the industry trades, and on the writer-based chatrooms of the Internet all the time. Editors lose editorial jobs all the time in the volatile economic earthquakes that wrack the publishing industry, and many of these former editors are setting up shop as agents and are on the lookout for new clients. Ask other represented or published writers for recommendations. Try querying members of an organization such as the Association of Authors' Representatives (AAR) though not all good agents are members. AAR has rules about who can qualify to call themselves an agent and has a canon of ethics its members must abide by.

Other good sources are the *Literary Marketplace* (also called the *LMP*), which also has rules about who can be listed as an agent in its pages. Lists of agents can also be found in Jeff Herman's *Guide* and the *Writer's Digest*'s *Guide to Literary Agents*.

Telling a Good Agent from Bad

The wrong agent or a poor agent will not help you at all, and may even hinder you. They'll offer bad advice, make you work hard at the wrong things because they don't have the proper editorial skills, and then not get your work to the best editors.

The right agent will be able to suggest the best audience for your work, and how to polish your submission to appeal to that audience. He'll also know the editors who are looking for the kind of material you've written, and his reputation will definitely carry some weight with editors when it comes to looking at the material seriously and quickly. Perhaps the best indicator of a successful agent is simply that he or she makes a living solely from commissions on sales. (In fact, you can't be a member of AAR, the agents' guild, unless you do.)

If an agent charges a "reading fee" or "editorial fee" my advice is, be very careful. Reputable agents, with one or two notable exceptions, don't charge reading fees, nor do they provide "reader's reports." The whole concept of charging for reading involves a questionable conflict of interest, if you think about it. How can someone give you an unbiased opinion on your work if they're earning money by charging for editorial advice? It leads to authors buying their agent's time and attention with likely little to show for their money at the end of the project except hard lessons learned. (Doesn't work in the dating field either.) The hard truth is that if you can't get an agent interested in your work without paying for some sort of "service," you're almost certainly not ready to be published yet, and you (and they on your behalf) will have a hard time getting a publisher interested. Has the agent actually *read* your book or book proposal, and can he talk about it intelligently? Undoubtedly he will have editorial suggestions about making something clearer or more focused, or more commercially viable, but does he really understand what you're trying to do and sympathize with your efforts? Is he enthusiastic?

Agents look for writers who have put together a terrific project, have paid their dues as professional writers, and are ready to be published. The agent then helps the writer polish the project and sell it, thus beginning, hopefully, a wonderful and enduring partnership.

Catching an Agent's Eye

There are basically three types of literary agents:

- Former editors and editorial types who develop and shape projects with writers.
- Agents who prefer selling to editorial work, and are into the "dance," as a friend of mine calls it. (That's the hard bargaining that can take place during a book deal negotiation—the "I'll go there, and you go here, you give me this, and I'll give you that" kind of discussion.) These agents prefer to represent "one-off" projects (often nonfiction- and high-profile-writer based) that look like commercial successes, and then move on to the next author and the next deal, rather than concern themselves with developing a writer's career.
- Entertainment lawyers who basically just do the deal for the writer. Very successful authors (I'm talking very high six figures or more) sometimes use lawyers because it's cheaper for them to pay an hourly rate than a 15 percent commission. That does not work well for less well paid authors, for obvious reasons.

There's a common misconception that agents spend all their time developing new material and new clients for publishers. Unpublished writers think that if they just take their place in line, agents will get to them eventually. Alas, it's another one of those publishing myths. You have to really catch an agent's attention with good writing and strong ideas.

Agents spend some of their time in the evenings and on weekends reading unsolicited, or "slush," mail, but only after they've finished reading the latest material sent to them by their clients. While they're always on the lookout for good new material by talented writers, they have plenty to do just keeping on top of their existing workload. That means your material has to be really special. If it is, you will attract the attention of agents and editors.

The good news is that narrative nonfiction, if not a hot genre, is well regarded by editors, so the odds of being published, if you do a good job of putting together your nonfiction proposal, are better than average.

Unagented writers don't seem to realize that when an agent takes on a new client, the agent is taking on a negative asset. The client will actually cost the agent money—in time, energy, mailing fees, telephone calls, photocopying proposals, and so forth—before the agent ever sees a dime of the commission they earn from a sale.

What Agents Do

Agents spend a lot of time developing new contacts with editors and publishers and renewing old ones. They pitch projects by clients, write multiple submission queries on behalf of the client, chase editors once the submission has been made to press them for a response, check up on royalty statements, pursue outstanding royalty advances, go through the fine print of contracts, put out "fires," negotiate deals, come up with career plans and tactics to get their clients well published, keep in contact with their foreign agents, and movie and TV agents if they don't handle these rights themselves . . . the list is endless.

Agents also take lunch meetings, attend book parties, speak at writers' conferences, and make it their business to meet and get to know as many publishing house acquiring editors as they can. The essence of the job is matchmaking—putting the right project with the right editor at the best house—so one of the definitions of a good agent is someone who knows the right editor for a project, and that editor's needs, likes, and dislikes. Agents make it their job to keep up with where editors are currently working, what they like and what they are looking for (not necessarily always the same thing), and in certain circumstances actually help to create books for their authors that editors seem keen to acquire.

Each publishing house has its own personality and specialties and is continually reinventing itself in order to gain as large a share of the market as possible. These days editors also move around a lot. Then there are all the mergers and acquisitions that have taken place in the last couple of years and the reshaping of giant companies, such as Bantam Doubleday Dell and its imprints merging with Random House and all its imprints.

You can guarantee that in the next couple of years publishing won't much resemble what it looked like a few years ago. In the face of all this industrial volatility, agents provide a font of cutting-edge knowledge and a haven of stability for authors.

Figuring It Out

As I mentioned earlier, many new agents are not necessarily new to the publishing business. These days, many are former editors or publishing house employees, and while they may not yet have placed many books as agents, they do know the business, how it's conducted, and a lot of the people in it.

If you make repeated calls to an agent and don't get a reply, that's a clue the relationship isn't working, or won't work for you. Most agents will respond within 48 hours.

It is a common misconception that all good agents reside in New York City. While it's true that Manhattan is the heart of American publishing and most of the publishing industry is based there, there are many good agents based outside of the city. Those not based in New York usually make regular trips into the city to meet with editors. However, most of the work is done by phone and fax. Better a good agent outside the city than a mediocre one based in New York.

Anyone can call themselves an agent, take on clients, charge money for this and that, make outrageously optimistic claims, and never get anyone published.

The Association of Authors' Representatives was formed to try to set standards and distinguish good agents from bad. It is a not-for-profit trade organization of literary and dramatic agents. It was formed in 1991 through the merger of the Society of Authors' Representatives, founded in 1928, and the Independent Literary Agents Association, founded in 1977. The association's objectives include keeping agents informed about conditions in publishing, the theater, the motion picture and television industries, and related fields; encouraging cooperation among literary organizations; and assisting agents in representing and defending their authors' interests.

Membership in the AAR is restricted to agents whose primary professional activity for the two years preceding application for membership in the AAR has been as an authors' representative or a playwrights' representative.

To qualify for membership, an applicant must have sold ten different literary properties during the 18-month period preceding application. Member agents must adhere to the AAR's Canon of Ethics, and associate members are full-time employees of a sponsoring agent member.

For the most up-to-date AAR membership list, send $7 (as of this writing, spring 2003) either by check or by money order made payable to AAR. Do not send cash. Include a self-addressed, business-size envelope and write to AAR, 10 Astor Place, 3rd floor, New York, NY 10003. Alternatively, visit the website at www.aar-online.org and get much of the information for free.

The AAR New Agent Questionnaire

AAR publishes a list of questions that you may wish to pose to a new agent when you are contemplating establishing a business relationship. Bear in mind that most agents are not going to bother to take the time to answer these questions unless they've decided to represent you. (The following is reprinted by permission of AAR.)

1. Are you a member of the AAR?
2. How long have you been in business as an agent?

3. Do you have specialists at your agency who handle movie and television rights? Foreign rights?

4. Do you have subagents or corresponding agents in Hollywood and overseas?

5. Who in your agency will actually be handling my work? Will the other staff members be familiar with my work and the status of my business at your agency? Will you oversee or at least keep me apprised of the work that your agency is doing on my behalf?

6. Do you issue an agent-author agreement? May I review the language of the agency clause that appears in contracts you negotiate for your clients?

7. How do you keep your clients informed of your activities on their behalf?

8. Do you consult with your clients on any and all offers?

9. What are your commission rates? What are your procedures and time frames for processing and disbursing client funds? Do you keep different bank accounts separating author funds from agency revenue? What are your policies about charging clients for expenses incurred by your agency? [Commonly these days, book agents charge 15 percent for domestic sales and 20 percent for foreign sales, which are often shared with a foreign subagent. An agent's commission is payable on anything the book earns as long as he or she is the agent of record on that project.]

10. When you issue 1099 tax forms at the end of each year, do you also furnish clients upon request with a detailed account of their financial activity, such as gross income, commissions and other deductions, and net income, for the past year?

11. In the event of your death or disability, what provisions exist for my continued representation?

12. If we should part company, what is your policy about handling any unsold subsidiary rights in my work?

"We'd Like to Make You an Offer."

If someone makes you an offer, tell the editor you're very excited, but you need some time to consider the situation as you're in the process of getting an agent. It's a wise writer who, offer in hand, now returns to his list of dream agents and tells them he has an offer from publisher X. Are they interested in representing him? Most agents will respond quickly and positively to you.

The best way to secure the best deal is to use a reputable agent who has examined and negotiated the offer. This may not be a great deal compared to what other authors may have been offered, but it will be the best deal for you and that book at that moment in time. An agent is in a position to ensure that a contract is honored, saving the writer from pestering the publisher if a problem comes up.

Whether an editor has made the offer to you directly and you've found an agent, or your agent comes back to you with an offer from an editor she showed your proposal to, you've reached a definitive stage in the process.

If your agent is lucky, she may be able to get an auction going, with editors bidding against one another to buy the book. If every editor but one drops out, the agent sometimes has a number of persuasive arguments she can make to get the editor to increase the proposed royalty advance.

Most deals operate from the guiding principles that the editor really wants to buy the book and that the author really wants to be published by that house, and ideally that editor. In speaking to an agent, in an effort to get the best deal for his house, an editor may make the argument that the book he wants to buy may well not be a success despite a belief in the author's talent. He will argue that he's going out on a limb for an untried author, he has colleagues he must convince, and because of this risk the editor needs to get as many rights as possible to try and maximize the opportunities to earn back a royalty advance.

The agent will argue: How can you say the book isn't worth X? Surely, you wouldn't want to publish it unless you saw merit in it, would you? Besides, first-time authors are a better bet in some cases than previously published writers because there are no sales records to impact how many books a bookseller will order. Besides, people know when they are being screwed, and it is not a wise move to treat an author poorly from the outset; give them some respect so that the relationship can grow in a healthy manner to many books with you. The principle that an author should be allowed to reap the benefits of his or her work if the book performs well is one that good editors have no problem honoring. The success of a book should be everyone's success. Give us this; show some good faith so that the author will really know how important her or she is to the company. And so on.

Of course, if there is a good sales track record, then an agent will argue that very strongly as well; the author has proven herself already and should be treated accordingly.

Having negotiated the deal in broad measure, once the publishing contract arrives the agent now turns into a paralegal and examines the contract closely. She'll discuss technical details with the editor as well as the publishing company's contract staff in an effort to get the client the best deal possible, taking care of contingency disasters that almost certainly will never happen, but nevertheless need to be prepared for.

When Things Go Wrong

Publishing relationships between agent and writer and between editor and writer suffer many of the same problems that romantic relationships collapse under: unrealistic expectations of what an agent can or should do; poor communication; writers (or agents) who are inconsiderate and disrespectful of each other, forgetting to say thank you occasionally, and so on. Remember, everyone has other demands put on their time and resources. Respect each other's need for privacy but also expect that your agent will respond quickly if there is a problem that needs to be fixed. Learn to trust each other.

Your agent will often be someone you like, but he or she is not your friend, nor is that a good basis for a business relationship. We agents are not shrinks, or a source of emotional or psychological support, or even a personal editor. A good agent may exhibit some or all of these abilities because it is a job that involves nurturing, but don't expect it and don't ask for it, especially at the beginning. If you have personal problems, figure them out before you get together with your agent. Her job, remember, is to sell your work. If you have nothing to sell there isn't much she can do for you.

A major area of conflict that can arise is over editorial revision. Many agents these days have editorial backgrounds (many were editors at one time in their career), and in publishing the onus of editorial work on a manuscript has fallen more on the agent's shoulders. Alas, many editors are not as skilled at line editing as they once were because they lack the mentors, and they also don't have the time to work on manuscripts the way they once could. Consequently, they're looking for manuscripts that are in near-perfect condition. Of course that's rarely the case, but agents know that in order to stand any chance of getting published, a book needs to be in good shape editorially.

However, there's no point making editorial changes to your manuscript just because someone says you should make those changes, regardless of whether or not those editorial comments are insightful. If the changes don't make sense to you, don't make them. You'll never please anyone if you can't please yourself first. But that is not the same thing as saying you shouldn't try to develop as objective a view as possible of your work, particularly when it comes to genre and structure. You've got to figure that whatever you're trying to do in your manuscript isn't working. The suggested solutions may not be right, but there's clearly some kind of problem, and it needs a solution.

10 Reasons Why You Should Get a Good Agent

Here are ten reasons why you should get yourself an agent rather than try and represent yourself.

1. Your agent's enthusiasm and professional reputation will count for something in selling your book. An agent is well versed in the tools of getting a book out into the marketplace, including the best timing for a submission and developing a little industry buzz about your book.

2. It's an agent's job to know which editor at which house is interested in projects like yours, or is looking for projects like yours. If you have gone to the wrong editor for your book, you may well have closed a door at that house you can't reopen.

3. An agent commonly submits a project to several editors at the same time (called multiple submissions). Editors accept this, but don't like authors trying to do the same thing.

4. Until you're published, you're not the best judge of your own work. An editor knows that if the agent sees something commercially viable in your work, he or she should pay attention to that submission.

5. An agent can nearly always get a better deal for your book than you can, even if the initial contact is yours.

6. Even if you're a lawyer, unless you know publishing law, publishing contracts can be a pain to understand and negotiate. Agents earn their commission just by negotiating good contracts with publishers for their clients. Many agents have already won changes in publishing houses' boilerplate contracts because of previous deals they've cut for other clients at that house.

7. The agent makes money when you make money, so your interests are intertwined. Agents will get you the best deal, and their subagents may be able to earn you extra money through foreign and translation markets, and the movie and TV arena.

8. An agent can run interference for you with a troublesome editor or publishing house employee. If you don't think this means much now, wait until you learn your editor was fired, and your new editor is too busy or too cavalier to pay attention to you when the proof-

reader rewrites your book just as it is going into galleys. (This really happened to a client of mine.)

9. Your agent keeps track of who owes you money, how much, and when it's due to be paid.

10. A good agent will be a career manager and adviser and will encourage and guide you in your literary endeavors.

Marketing and Promotion: Who Do You Know? What Can You Do?

• • • • • • • • • • • • • • • • • •

The market came with the dawn of civilization and it is not an invention of capitalism. . . . If it leads to improving the well-being of the people there is no contradiction with socialism.

MIKHAIL GORBACHEV, SOVIET POLITICAL LEADER

Writing ought either to be the manufacture of stories for which there is a market demand—a business as safe and commendable as making soap or breakfast foods—or it should be an art, which is always a search for something for which there is no market demand.

WILLA CATHER, "ON THE ART OF FICTION"

 For the moment let's not even worry about what format your book is published in, be it hardcover, trade paperback, or mass market original. Answer this question, and be brutally honest with yourself: Do I honestly believe that 10,000 people will buy my book over the course of a year?

If the answer is no, then the odds of your book being published by a reputable established publisher diminish considerably—maybe to one in five. If, prior to publication, a book is expected to sell 8,000–10,000 copies, we enter the realm of university presses and regional presses, which tend to offer small advances and stringent publishing contracts. I made up that statistic based on my 20 years of experience in book publishing as an editor, writer, and agent, but before you throw away this book in outrage for not being more sensitive to your aspirations and efforts as a writer, consider this: You may quite rightly believe that *someone else*—say, a publishing marketing-and-sales professional—*should* be able to sell 10,000 copies of your book. But how many could *you* sell, if you had to? What if the publishing company professional assigned to your book, for whatever reason—perhaps overwork, perhaps incompetence, perhaps exhaustion, perhaps indifference to your book's subject—screws up the promotion and marketing of your book? How do you fix that? Your career as a writer of books is ultimately dependent on two things: sales figures and review acclaim, in that order.

The truth is, these days the most successful authors aren't necessarily the best at writing or even the most creative—but they are the most effective in finding and developing an audience for their work, and helping to move their product off the shelves.

Most of us who try to make a living in the arts are faced with balancing this difficult dilemma: We want to be the best writers, actors, singers, whatever, *and* sell well. We soldier on, ever the optimists, pulling the handle of the great slot machine of life, believing that next time those three spinning wheels will line up three perfectly matching fruits, and our reward will come chug-chugging out of the slot as bells ring and lights flash. And for some of us, staying power, growing confidence in and command of our craft, good advisers, and increasingly maturing and improving choice of material means that we create books with "legs" (that is, slightly higher sales each time), so that our careers progress forward, if not as flamboyantly as we might like sometimes.

A writer friend of mine, for example, who is pretty successful in his own right, is still stuck in the low- to mid-six-figure range of advances despite writing five relatively successful novels and a couple of screenplays. Not so long ago, a writer friend of his got a million dollars for his new book.

"Okay," my friend John said to Jeff, with both admiration and some professional frustration at his lack of similar success, "now I'm officially jealous."

"Wait a minute," Jeff said. "This is my seventeenth book. I've paid my dues."

And he was right. Jeff had labored hard for 20 years or so, not just as a writer who improved his books with each one published, but also at helping to promote those books. And he'd also been a little lucky. Hollywood had finally come knocking, and that had helped to tip him over the edge.

The fact is, authors these days must embrace not just the Holy Grail–like quest of profound creativity and mastery of craft, but also dance with Mammon without falling under his corrosive spell. That's a tough balancing act to pull off.

Taking Advantage of Trends

Writers sometimes think that rushing books into print on a topical subject is a way to fame and fortune. This confuses magazine publishing with book publishing. The big problem with trends in book publishing is that by the time you've responded to them, it's too late. Here's a crude timetable to give you some idea of how things work in book publishing:

- From idea to research to book proposal: three months
- From book proposal to literary agent: three months
- From agent to editor and book contract: three months (if you're lucky)
- From contract to delivery of manuscript to editor: six months
- From transmission by editor to finished book on the shelves: nine months

Total time: Two years

You might think from this that you could go straight to the editor and gain some time, but the truth is, an agent knows exactly who in a publishing house is looking for material and what his or her tastes are, so the agent will probably shorten the time it takes to get an editor to accept the book. They can also send to more than one editor at a time. It's tougher for an author to do that. Your proposal could languish in an editorial slush pile for months before it gets rejected, and you have to start the process all over again.

Part of the problem with rushing a book is that publishers have monthly slots for books, and sometimes it takes a while for a slot to open up. If a publisher publishes a book early, then someone else's book is going to be bumped from its allotted publishing slot. Meanwhile, the sales and marketing process for that book is already under way and suffers if it is tampered with, while the sales and marketing for your book may not have yet begun and you'll be published into a void, with little or no attention from reviewers and others who need books at least three months ahead of pub date.

Audience, Audience, Audience

Okay, so your book has been sold, written, accepted, and it's coming out soon. Your job is now to focus on what to do to help it become a success.

Apart from the obvious need to make us care about the characters in a story, whether they are the doomed sailors of *A Perfect Storm* or the unhappy children of *Angela's Ashes,* narrative nonfiction books also need, in order to sell well, to touch some sort of cultural nerve. Of course, divining what that communal nerve will be is guesswork based on honed intuition, objective observations of the culture, experience studying the topic you want to write about, and the kinds of books this audience has previously been attracted to. Nevertheless, catching a reader's attention isn't just a function of how well you write your proposal or your book. It's about somehow making sure your story is told in such an emotionally gripping way it will appeal to as wide an audience as possible beyond your core audience.

At the beginning of this book, I spoke about the need to be aware of the audience appeal of your book. It is a defining aspect of whether or not an idea you feel passionate about can be written in a commercially successful way. Does the area you want to write about have a fan base? A subculture? Could you tap into that base somehow?

You should objectively compare your idea against what is already published on the subject. For example, why another book of military history? Can you really re-create another *Black Hawk Down*? If so, the odds are high you have a winner. Is there really room for another biography of Ben Franklin? What does your book add to the field? If it's only your thoughts and philosophies, unless you're an expert whose opinion is sought by colleagues in your field, the likelihood is your book might be a tough sell. If, however, you know your subject well enough that you realize there's a "hole" (something that hasn't been written about much yet), you're probably onto a good thing. Now, before your book hits the stores, is the time to start working all these leads.

We come to the big question: What will my publisher do to promote and market my book? The short answer is, not much. However, a publisher will usually follow where you lead.

Mining Resources

As each new season of books moves toward publication, publicity and marketing teams create plans to get their companies' books noticed—and sold. Publishing is an innately creative and inventive industry, so these plans can include not only traditional ways of pitching titles, but also targeted campaigns to reach niche audiences. At presales and launch meetings, sales, publicity, and marketing get together with editorial staff to explore ways to maximize the books' sales potential.

"One of the challenges at a big house is making choices about which books will receive an extra push," Tracy van Straaten, director of publicity at Simon & Schuster Children's Publishing, told *Publishers Weekly*. "Usually, the list [of books for that season] tells us what to do; many publicity and marketing opportunities just present themselves. But it's also fun to come up with creative things to do."

A publisher's anticipation of how a book will perform is determined by the print run and the popularity and sales history of an author. Each season's list contains clear choices for which book will get niche treatment, and publicity and marketing staff must be careful how they allot limited financial resources on targeted campaigns. To help with that decision, they research markets, do targeted mailings, and talk with sales reps around the country who can tap into potential outlets. While the success of targeted campaigns is hard to measure, they can deliver incremental sales for a book. The numbers may not be overwhelming—but water dripping into a cup eventually fills it up. Everything helps, particularly over the long term.

Van Straaten added, "Sometimes an author is our best resource. If they are knowledgeable enough about a topic to write a book on it, chances are they have great contacts."

Lissa Warren is senior director of publicity at Cambridge's Perseus Publishing and the author of *Book It: A Publicist's Guide for Authors*. Commenting on what authors can do to help publicize their books, she said,

> The sad truth is that most editors, reporters, and producers do not like to be approached by authors directly. Some of them will humor you. Many of them will be rude to your face or hang up on you. Even if they take the bait and decide to interview you, your book is less likely to get a mention if you approach the media directly (they'll just use you for your expertise; if the publicist books it, they'll feel like they owe her a mention of the book). So it's far better for you to let your in-house or freelance publicist approach the media on your behalf. But if that's not an option, by all means you should do it.

But what does an author do if he or she is approached directly by the media? "My instinct is to say, [talk to my] publicist," said Warren.

However, if the reporter is on deadline or the producer is pressing you for a commitment, forwarding them to your publicist could jeopardize the booking. So use your best judgment. If you do decide to handle it yourself right then and there, be sure to notify your publicist as soon as possible so that they can e-mail press material to media contacts and get a book right off to them. That will increase the chances that they'll mention it.

The most common method publishing house publicists use when niche marketing is to cold-mail the book to a specialized media list. Each publisher will have a database of sources and will also use resources like Bacon's Media Directories as well as other mailing-list services. Books that appeal to a particular culture, such as Asian, African-American, or Hispanic, will be mailed to special-interest magazines and newspapers with review or features departments so they can let their readers know a new book that may appeal to them is about to be published.

At some of the larger publishing houses, the marketing departments create brochures or newsletters that are mailed out to reviewers, teachers, librarians, veterans, amateur and professional associations—anyone, in fact, who may be interested in knowing the book is coming out.

Authors Are the Best Resource

With established authors, or writers with a column and a following in a magazine, fan mail can be very useful. The simple answer to selling books is publicity—as much as you can get for yourself and your book. Start with local publicity, and then expand to regional, and finally national. How many people live in your town, your county, your state? What organizations are interested in your book? How many members do they have? What's the best way to reach them?

If you can sell 5,000 copies regionally you're already beating the odds big-time and getting the system to work for you. Remember, even though all 5,000 were sold in the Barnes & Noble in and around your town in the north, a B&N in Florida or Texas consults the computer and sees total figures nationwide. With some encouragement, if a book looks like it's moving, they may well want to get on the bandwagon and provide a hot property for their customers.

It's helpful to ask what the publishing company's publicity and marketing plans for your book will be. Ask if they intend to tour you. It's not likely, but you should be prepared in case they say yes. Find out who's going to pay for it, at least in terms of hotel and traveling expenses, and make sure it's them. If you do go on tour, make a space in your schedule to accommodate your publisher's plans. Any problems, get your agent involved. It's okay to ask the publicist for a copy of the press release before it's sent out. You need to make sure your book is being represented accurately and well.

"Just keep in mind that it's the publicist's name that goes at the top of that release, and she needs to feel comfortable with it too," cautioned Warren. "Besides, she knows the media's likes and dislikes better than you do, and sometimes a publicist can lend a healthy perspective—one that's quite different from your own."

You can also ask how many galleys (prepublication copies) she's sending out. "The more review-driven your book, the more galleys that need to be sent out. . . . Biographies, memoirs, novels, short-story collections, and poetry are very review-driven," Warren said.

Be aware that some publicists prefer not to share their media lists, considering their Rolodexes proprietary information. "A publicist's greatest asset is her contacts, after all, so you can understand why she may be a bit hesitant to share them," Warren added.

If it's possible—and certainly after you've had a couple of books published that give you a decent track record (say, sales of 20,000 copies or more)—try and choose a publisher who is known for selling and marketing well books like yours. Check bookstores, the Internet, writers' conferences, and so forth. You should also develop your own marketing plan (obviously, it needs to be down-to-earth and practical), suggesting how best to market your book. Can the book be marketed directly to your audience? What contacts do you have that you can exploit?

Niche marketing can be more effective than aiming for national coverage. However, the big problem with niche marketing and publicity is that it is very time-consuming. Publicity departments are often small and overworked, they have limited and finite resources, and those resources are generally earmarked for the books that a committee has determined will benefit the company's bottom line most. The publicity department will get out copies of your book to reviewers and others who can help in the promotion of the book. They'll also help you get local signings, and maybe make follow-up calls, and if appropriate arrange interviews. After that you may well find yourself on your own.

The Seasonal Lists

Until the 1990s, most bookstore business in the United States was done through independently owned and operated stores that were served by a publishing house sales force that ranged in size from about ten to thirty sales representatives. Each rep would attend to an account personally, like a door-to-door salesman, needing perhaps four months' lead time to service the store. The reps in turn needed sales kits to present new titles to their accounts, so this meant that a publishing house had to create a predictable cycle for the introduction of new material through catalogues and other sales materials.

Several times a year sales reps for the company touch base with bookstore accounts. Some reps have large geographic areas, such as New England or the Pacific Northwest, and others have large-volume clients such as large chain stores. The larger publishing companies have full-time sales forces, while the smaller houses use commissioned reps.

The problem with commissioned reps is that they often represent more than one publisher at a time, and earn money only on the books they place. The inherent problems of the system are obvious. If the rep is selling your first book at the same time that she's promoting Bob Woodward or Richard Preston's new book, guess who's going to get the short end of the stick?

Sales conferences take place two or three times each year in order to give the sales reps the information and materials they need to sell the upcoming titles. These sales conferences have become the central organizing force behind book marketing.

Book production deadlines are created by working backward from the sales conference date. As a result, the editorial and publicity-and-marketing staffs know when a manuscript has to be delivered, when catalogue copy, flap copy, and publicity material has to be written, and so forth, so that a list can be closed in preparation for the sales conference. If you miss your deadline, you mess with the schedules and your book will be bumped to the next list, or get very little attention from sales and marketing at the sales conference.

Publishers try hard to have just the right number of big books in a list, often separating into different seasons books that might otherwise compete for shelf space with one another. As the door-to-door salesman has been replaced with the telemarketer, so too, the larger book chains have replaced the independents. While the sales reps continue to service accounts, accounts are also sold by sales staff working from the publisher's home office who present titles in monthly rather than seasonal groupings. The problem with the list system these days is that it forces publishers to rush or delay the publication of a book for no other reason than to hit a particular list. Some publishers are more laid-back than others about this. Nevertheless, the focus on making the lists means that a book won't get any formal marketing involvement until the book's list comes up. This means that guerrilla marketing (such as interactive marketing on the Internet), from a publisher's perspective, is frowned upon, or at least ignored. This is where an author can be most effective. The Internet takes time to develop an audience, and is a grassroots medium. Many publicists don't have the time or the resources to exploit these factors properly. But authors do.

The best way to try and combat this is to develop the "ripple in a pond" strategy. Drop a pebble in water and watch the ripples, ever more, ever wider, move out from a central point. The central point of your marketing and sales strategy, the point where the pebble hits the water so to speak, should be local stores and local media outlets. If you can get local bookstores to stock your book with the help of your publisher, and if you can imaginatively get the book to the attention of a local audience, through, say, the local newspaper and local radio and TV (the story would be both what the book is about and the fact that you are a local personality), then its success will soon cause statewide interest and, as the ripples move out and widen, regional interest and eventually national interest.

One of the big problems with huge superstores elbowing out independent bookstores is that the superstore book buyer is often based in a headquarters far from the point of contact with customers on the bookstore sales floor. The superstore buyer is responsible for buying books for a number of stores in the chain, but is not often interested in addressing or appealing to local interests. He's more interested in promoting a handful of name-brand authors and homogenizing his customers' taste.

The buyer for an independent store is often the store's owner, and she very often reads voraciously, loves to meet authors, and hand sells books in her store to customers, who often ask her advice on what to read next.

The chains seem to carry a wide variety of books. In fact, they often buy fewer titles overall than would several smaller independent stores, each with its own buyer reflecting his tastes and those of his customer base. Several independents catering to customers in the same location will buy a broader range of titles though stock fewer copies of each title, while the chains may keep books on the shelves longer and stock more copies of individual titles. It becomes a battle between volume of books and quantity of titles.

Here's an interesting dilemma: Who knows better about what will sell?

The author, who wrote the book and is considered an expert? The publisher, who's taken the gamble to create and promote the book because they believe it's a valuable addition to the genre, or may even revitalize it? Or the guy who deals every day with the book-buying public?

The truth is, the buyers for the chains rarely meet their customers, unlike the owners and staff of an independent. But the mechanics of big business, obsessed as it is with the bottom line, can seriously impact the number of copies your book could sell. The local large chain store, for example, may not order many copies of your book because it's perceived as too niche. In some cases, a book buyer based miles away will make determinations on books to be sold in a store that have little to do with local dynamics, despite a local store manager's recommendations.

Bookstores also make money these days by charging publishers for prime placement in their store. For several thousand dollars, a publisher can get a particular book placed near the front of the store. In many cases, bookstores also charge the publisher thousands of dollars to have their books included in the store's mail order or book club catalogues. What can an author do about this? "Publishers have to pay—handsomely—for that kind of 'real estate,' " said Lissa Warren.

And, even if your publisher is willing to pay, the buyer won't offer them the option unless they feel your book would be appropriate for this kind of treatment. Amazon.com has a similar program, but it's for space on their home pages rather than table space. The best thing you can do is speak with your marketing manager about all of this. The good news is, for the independents, front table placement is at each store's discretion—which means it's something you can influence by contacting the store yourself.

The small guys are at a disadvantage. The big publishers won't usually bother to spend this kind of money on your book unless you're seen as a new Tom Wolfe, Jon Krakauer, Tracy Kidder, or whoever. Even if it is written into a publishing contract, authors have little control over what a publisher decides to spend their money on, or if they will spend any money at all on your book beyond publishing it. Yes, it may be a breach of contract—but what can you do about it in any real sense if they "forget" to honor that clause? Get into a legal fight? Get a reputation for being litigious? Not stand up for yourself? Who will want to publish your next book if you have that kind of reputation and if you also have weak sales figures? These are tough questions to deal with.

Once all the advance orders are in, the publisher will have the warehouse ship the books to the stores. These days, publishers try to keep print runs low (a print run is the number of books a publisher prints in total when the book is published). With narrative nonfiction this is often perhaps 10,000–15,000 copies on average, with restock by going back to press more than once as demand merits. Returns (that is, unsold books shipped back to the publisher by the bookstore) will also end up in the warehouse, so publishers may wait critical marketing periods if they think a book will return, and then redistribute returned copies, rather than print more immediately. This can all affect the dynamics of book sales.

Self-Aggrandizement, or Publicity?

Publicity is one of the most effective things an author can do on her own behalf, especially if she works in conjunction with her publisher. It's not about telling everyone how wonderful and fabulous you are, but letting them know you have something to say that might interest them.

It's almost never too soon to start working on publicity for your book—with this proviso: If you get people excited about the book before it's available in the stores, you will lose the momentum you began, and will have to work twice as hard to get it back later on. Timing in publicity is critical.

Once your manuscript is completed and handed in, draw up two lists. The first is of half a dozen people whom you can approach to ask for a quote, or blurb, once they've read the book. They should be both well known and relevant to your endeavors. The second list should be a wish list of famous people (obviously, they must all still be alive and approachable) whom your agent or editor might be able to help you reach, with the same objective—get a quote. These should be writers or experts in the field you've chosen to write about whose work you genuinely admire. With the backing of a publishing contract, many authors will say, "Send me something when it's ready."

It's your job to ask, and their job to say yes or no. But it's business, so don't take rejection personally. Many authors have their own deadlines to meet, and many are simply burnt out from the process of being asked for quotes based on their celebrity.

Your publisher's publicity department will promote your book for about three months before they move on to another author. If you ask nicely they may give you a copy of their marketing plan, and a copy of the press kit they used for the book. If you have a problem getting hold of these, ask your editor or your agent to get them for you. No marketing plan? There's an answer for you right there.

In general, advertising an unknown book by an unknown author is expensive and achieves little. Adverts for books work in only two ways: They boast of a book's success in prizes and sales, essentially telling its audience, "Don't miss out on this hot property everyone else has read!"; and they tell the eager fans of famous authors (or those interested in the specific things the book is about) that the author's next book is imminent. Tracy Kidder's fans, or Mark Bowden's, eagerly await the next book, and the adverts tell them it's on the way.

Hiring a freelance publicist can be expensive, and a gamble. You can spend $3,000 or more and end up with a couple of reviews and not much else after three months of effort. On the other hand, you can avoid getting a publicist; your book can start to generate some interest; and by relying solely on the good offices of the publishing company's publicist, you may find that you have lost a number of opportunities to promote yourself and

. . . the . . .

your book because the publicist was just too overworked to do a thorough job for you.

Before you decide to hire a freelance publicist, make sure you can take advantage of anything she or he puts your way. A good publicist is expensive, and a bad or mediocre one probably can't do much more than you can do for yourself. Far better to learn the lesson of the *Blair Witch Project* filmmakers and use the power of the Internet to target your ideal audience.

A great deal of publicity and promotion is knocking on doors and getting them politely slammed in your face. What you get with a good publicist is her Rolodex of sources, whom she knows personally and whom she can call up and often talk into giving you an interview. That means she will be picky about the book and author she takes on, because her credibility is riding on your ability to come across with the goods for her contact.

If you're going to do interviews you have to learn how to get your point across quickly and succinctly and, well, sexily. I'm not referring to overt sexuality, but making sure that you know what it is about your book that's going to whet people's appetites to hear more, and get them to go out and pick up a copy next time they're in their local bookstore.

Learning to Become Media Savvy

The best way to become media savvy if you have no experience at all is to take an evening class in media communications. Media trainers are available, but they're expensive, although worth considering if you're in a pinch and you can find a good one. You need to develop an ability to think fast on your feet.

Before you start doing interviews, jot down on a "cheat sheet" (a three-by-four-inch index card, ideally) what you want to get across. Come up with at least four major points of conversation. Always, if you're able, turn a question into something that will allow you to promote your book.

Acquire a small library of witty stories and practice using them. Even if your topic is deadly serious, be a fun, energized guest. If you can accomplish this, then you'll help a potential publicist by giving them someone that TV and radio talk show hosts and their producers will want to have on their shows, regardless of the book you've written.

Before you cringe at the thought, consider this: What's more important to remember—the title of one book, or the name of an author who may have written several books that are available?

It's good to get comfortable with this fact: Marketing and publicity are not about art, they're about selling. You need to learn to get strangers to pay attention to you and your book, despite the noise and chaos of their lives, and then *fork out money* to read it. We watch interviews with authors not to hear them talk about their latest book, but because they are interesting *thinkers* and witty raconteurs.

How Can I Get Myself on TV?

If you want to get on TV or radio, start locally, and convince producers you've got something interesting to say, and that you'll be an entertaining guest. Study and research what works on camera and what doesn't. You need to learn how to sit, how to make the camera like you, because it can be a pretty cruel instrument. Think about the image you want to project. Make sure it doesn't detract from your ability to talk seriously about the topic you've been asked to discuss.

In much the same way that you got yourself an agent and a book deal, you need to sell yourself to TV producers when you contact them. Send them a photo to demonstrate how photogenic you are, plus a list of topics that they could base shows on, and a suggested list of thought-provoking and "sexy" questions they might want to talk with you about. Is there something in the news, some current event, that you can tie into? Can you take questions from the audience or your interviewer that test your knowledge of your subject in an entertaining way?

Don't expect anyone other than maybe a research assistant to actually read your book. Use every opportunity to promote and sell your book, from an on-air display, if that's possible, to setting up your own local bookstores' signings ahead of time when you fly into a new town to give your interview. Make sure they know you're going to be a "celebrity" on local or regional or national TV. Milk it, sell books.

Some Things to Do to Help Publicize Your Book

- Several months before your book is due to be published, your publisher will usually send you an author questionnaire. This is usually several pages long and, once you've filled it out, provides your publisher with basic background information about you and your book. It also gives you a chance to mention any ideas you have about promoting your book. The publicist will be particularly interested in any media contacts you've got. Try to provide as much information as possible, including whether they've covered your work in the past, and when.
- Push to meet your publicist, perhaps over lunch or drinks. Try to develop a good working relationship, so that you're up on what's going on and in a position to pick up any slack.
- Try to create some sort of book tour for yourself if the publisher isn't going to, even if it's only local and unfunded. Timing is important, because bookstore calendars fill up fast.
- Ask to see, and try to help craft, press material. No one knows your book and your accomplishments better than you. Come up with some provocative, newsy questions an interviewer might want to ask you.
- Consider hiring a freelance publicist. Sometimes publishers will do that on their own for books that, for one reason or another, require more time or attention than in-house staff can give. It's a major decision and a major investment but can be worth it in the case of

nonfiction. You can try and get the cost of a freelance publicist written into your contract, or at the least, try to have your publisher cover half the cost.

- Write an op-ed, newspaper, or magazine article that's tied to your book and mention it in your bio.
- Ask other authors about the publicists they've used and what they thought of them, and search the Web for information.
- Consider hiring someone to create a Web campaign for your book. Check with your publicist first because some publishers include Web campaigns in their promotional efforts. There's no point in your paying for something that the publisher is already doing.
- For three months or so around the publication date of your book, keep yourself available to promote your book.
- Try to be generous with your time and gracious to your interviewers. Most interviewers will probably not read your book and may ask you foolish questions or misrepresent what you've written. Deal with it. Politely, and with self-deprecating humor if you can, correct them. The point is not to worry about whether or not they have done their job properly, but to come across as a nice guy who has written an interesting book. Take advantage of reaching the audience you are being presented with, for free. Who knows who may be tuned in to the show?
- When you call someone, first of all ask them if they have time to talk, don't just launch in with your pitch.
- Make it easy for your publicist to contact you. That way you're not likely to miss an opportunity for coverage of your book.
- Be prepared to research likely media for your publicist. Help her help you.
- Get your photos scanned in digitally as bitmaps (.bmp), jpegs (.jpg), or tif (.tif) files so that you can e-mail them as attachments to whoever wants them.
- Put together a tape of any previous TV interviews you've done.

- Send low-key, "Just checking in, did you get the book?" follow-up e-mails to everyone who got a galley or finished copy. Remember, quotes on this book may not make it to the cover, but they will help in selling and promoting the next book.
- Don't burn bridges, if you can avoid it. This is a networking business, and you never know who knows who, or what they will say about you, so try and keep things as professional, positive, and upbeat as possible regardless of how frustrated you sometimes feel. "Publishing" and "frustrating" can sometimes seem synonyms for each other.

Writing a Book Proposal

● ● ● ● ● ● ● ● ● ● ● ● ● ● ● ● ● ●

The secret of success would seem to be to choose something
that no one has ever thought about for long enough to write a
book proposal [about] without dropping into a sudden
narcolepsy. Once you have discovered a subject so obscure that
no other publisher has come across it before, all that remains
is to prove that it holds the key to universal understanding.

ANDREW BROWN, REVIEWING *UNIVERSAL FOAM: THE STORY OF BUBBLES FROM*

CAPPUCCINO TO THE COSMOS BY SIDNEY PERKOWITZ

 I've left the chapter on how to write a book proposal to last,
because it's really a separate task and skill from writing the
book. They are related, of course, and the proposal comes first,
but the proposal is a description of and sample of a proposed
book. It's primarily a sales and marketing tool—for you and for your book. It
needs to be focused, accompanied by supporting materials, and above all
dynamic. You need to impress the editor and the sales and marketing staff,
make them feel they must have your book at all costs—but do it without
being too cute, or arrogantly obnoxious, or obviously trying to make a silk
purse (the proposal) out of a sow's ear (the subject of the proposal).

You should start with these four thoughts in mind:

- What's the book about?
- What's so important and special about this book? Why should a

publisher want to publish it? (Aren't there enough books out there already without adding another to the pile?)

- Why are you the best person to write this book?
- Who's the core audience for the book, and why will they care about it?

Are we back to audience, audience, audience? Afraid so, and I make no apologies for it.

Jim Srodes said,

The book proposal is a separate item from the book. You can't be too enthusiastic in a book proposal, you can't gush enough to an agent or a prospective editor, because if you don't show your enthusiasm, why should they? I [once] lost a sale because an agent was diffident with what I thought was a great proposal. It doesn't really matter (all you agents close your ears now, and all you editors also) if it looks anything like the final book. Sell the book, then write the book.

Proposals, Not Manuscripts

Almost all nonfiction books are sold on proposal. It's unusual for a nonfiction book to be written on spec and then sold, and for that reason crafting a proposal requires a skill that is separate from, but not independent of, your ability to write the book. You may think that the work you've begun on your book should be enough to sell it—but publishing, as you've probably gleaned by now, is a cooperative venture between author and publisher, and your job as author is to provide an editor with the ammunition he needs, at least initially, to get this book into the marketplace and sell the hell out of it.

The upside is that the more you become involved in this process, the more control you can exert on how well—or how poorly—you'll eventually be published. A word of warning: The more you rely on your belief that your skill as a writer alone should be enough to get you that book contract, the more you put yourself in the position of being just another pretty face in a lineup of many other pretty faces. If you refuse to take the time to practice your audition pieces and do the equivalent of stepping forward from the line to sing, dance, act, and otherwise demonstrate what you have to offer, you are unlikely to successfully grasp the brass ring—be it a role in a play or movie or a book contract.

This may sound harsh, because many authors tend to struggle with the concept and principles of writing a book proposal. It seems unnatural, false, a con job in some way. Nothing could be further from the truth. No proposal is, or should be, cast in stone, but you would not consider building a house without blueprints, or prepare a particular dish without a recipe that you can refer to from time to time in order to keep yourself focused and on track. So a book proposal, in part, is the blueprint of the book.

There's a common argument I hear from authors who are unhappy about beefing up a usually meager proposal for their book: "How can I commit to paper something I won't know about until I've done the research? It'll obviously change as I start writing it, so won't I be misleading the editor? Cheating her in some way?"

Editors hear this all the time, and it's not something they worry about unduly. Most editors expect a book to change as you write it. Books are, after all, organic creatures. Editors form and maintain a confidence in a writer based on the strength of his or her proposal regardless of difficulties the author may have during the writing process. An editor anticipates problems. It's part of their job, as it is part of the agent's to help fix these problems. However, a book will *improve* from the original proposed idea, not deviate completely. If you get into trouble you always have your blueprint to fall back on. In a worst-case scenario, you and your agent and the editor can discuss writing another book and abandoning the one they bought on proposal. But it will be a joint decision, based on discussion of a better, more commercial idea and the difficulties you're having with this book, not a unilateral decision on your part; and the new book will still need to have an outline and description for you to work from.

What's more, the better the proposal, the more likely you are to get a higher royalty advance. The reason is obvious: The more something is an unknown quantity, and therefore more of a gamble on a publisher's behalf, the smaller the amount of money they are going to risk on the project, if they decide to risk any money at all.

Publishers long for authors who write well, and who have strong concepts that the author knows what to do with. They will pay much more for that author than for one who may have more innate talent but is less confident about what he is selling and his ability to produce it. That is not to suggest you need to fake it—it is to suggest that you get enough of a grasp on your material that you become so confident of your mastery of it and its appeal that editors immediately pick up on the fact. When an editor picks up a proposal and is immediately drawn in, you can bet your bottom dollar he realizes that other editors seeing that same proposal will no doubt feel the same way.

Brendan Cahill, then a senior editor at Grove/Atlantic, was asked how it was possible for a writer to create an effective proposal that would lead to a book contract. "There are essential things that need to be in any proposal," he said.

Generally it's got to be about a topic that's broad enough for a general readership. The writer needs to be, if not expert, then well informed about the given topic, and to have done the initial thought work, legwork, that it takes to be able to render that experience in a thoughtful and intelligent way. And also to have the narrative techniques, skills, and be able to express the story in a way that will appeal to readers. There are books out there on how to write a book proposal that hone in on the specifics, but generally, once you have some sort of journalistic bylines under your belt, use the people who you know: agents, friends, friends of friends; and try to get your proposal into the hands of the right people who will be interested in it. Look at the books of the writers you admire, see who publishes them, find out who their editors and agents are. Find them and try to pitch them.

The basic philosophy behind writing a book proposal is to describe to the editor the book you want to write, and provide the editor with sufficient facts and figures that will give her enough ammunition at an editorial board meeting to convince colleagues, both in editorial and in sales and marketing, that this proposed book is not only a quality piece of work, it will make money for the publishing company.

What I'm going to do is outline some basic principles you should apply to writing a book proposal. Obviously, each proposal should convey the uniqueness of the particular book it's representing, so there is no formula that can or should be applied.

One of the things writing the proposal can do is help a writer focus and organize a book idea. It should have the form of a story or narrative, and be between 20 and 40 pages, no longer, depending on the sample material included.

A commonly accepted structure for a nonfiction book proposal broadly follows this outline:

Page 1	Title Page. Name of book, name and contact info for the author.
Page 2	A one-paragraph, in-a-nutshell description of the project or idea—that is, the project in a hook format.
Page 3	A one- to two-page overview of the project in a dynamic narrative style.
Page 5	A marketing analysis of perhaps half a page, explaining who the audience is for the book and why the book will appeal to them.
Page 6	A brief description of competing books, with emphasis on recent commercially successful books in the field (if there are any), and why your book fills a need not currently filled in this field.

Page 7	A half-page biography of the writer, emphasizing writing experience, any expertise on the proposed subject, and why he or she is the best person to write that book.
Page 8	A table of contents (TOC) that is quite literally a list of chapters and their subheadings (in other words, an at-a-glance description of the book).
Page 9	A half-page or one-page narrative description of each chapter listed in the TOC.
Page 18 (approximately)	A sample chapter or two from the book.
Finally	Accompanying material, such as reviews of previous books, supporting documentation for the book, copies of photos that might be used in the book.

Make sure that every page of the proposal is bylined and tagged in some fashion and easily recognizable, with continuous numbering (except for the first page). If an editorial assistant drops the pages by accident, he or she should be easily able to reconstruct the proposal. Keep pictures and graphics to a minimum and don't include them if the quality is poor.

The structure of a proposal can be divided into two broad categories: features and benefits. Simply put, *features* are concerned with what an object is; *benefits* are concerned with why you need it. Many writers put together proposals filled with features, but they forget to include any of the benefits. To be effective, a proposal should be balanced with both.

The Features Part of a Proposal (the *What*)

The Cover Letter. This should be brief, warm, and probably contain the "hook," ideally a one- or two-sentence summation of your story and why it's so compelling. It should include your address and phone numbers, along with relevant information such as that you're a prize-winning writer, a member of this or that group, an expert in the topic you propose, that you were referred by or mentored by someone significant—whatever. Mention the book's title and what kind of book it is, then let the proposal do the rest of the work.

Always include a stamped self-addressed envelope.

The Title Page. Center your title and the subtitle of the book proposal. Under that add your name, address, e-mail, telephone number, and voice and fax if you have those. Make yourself easy to reach. Does your answering machine work? Is there a professional message on the machine when an editor or agent does get through? All these things count.

The Table of Contents. A TOC provides an at-a-glance guide to the book's content and organization, and perhaps a glimpse of the wit or seriousness you intend to bring to the project through your subtitling of each listed chapter. (Chapter 1: "I Am Miserable and Broke." Chapter 2: "I Meet Elvis, the Man Who Will Change My Life." Chapter 3: "I Attend Astronaut School." Chapter 4: "Elvis Is Accused of Murdering My Sister.") At least 75 percent of a book proposal's success lies in its organization. You may have a great idea, but if you present it poorly, that shows not only a poor writing ability but also poor thought processes. In nonfiction, beyond the originality of the idea in question, what you're offering is a logical exploration and understanding of the importance of your subject. Agents and editors look for books that are logical, well written, and organized. It's a good idea to work on the TOC early on. As you develop the proposal you'll find you'll continually revise it, but it will provide an excellent overall map to the project while you're working, as well as a guide to its final form when completed.

Chapter by Chapter Descriptions. Once you've nailed down the overall structure of your book in the TOC, you should write at least a couple of paragraphs, if not more, expanding on what you plan to cover in each chapter. The key here, as throughout the proposal, is your ability to write succinctly yet dynamically about your subject.

Sample Chapters. This is pretty self-explanatory. A nonfiction book needs a mixture of narrative, emotion, and logic to work well. It doesn't matter what chapters you include, but you should aim at a sample of about 15–20 pages. No more than two chapters need to be included. If you use partial chapters, make sure everyone knows they are not the complete versions of the chapters.

Author Biography. Who you are is important in selling the project. Why are you the best person to write this book? It's less true in narrative nonfiction, but worth bearing in mind, that it's better to be an expert on something, or work in collaboration with one, than not, because you will be competing with others who are experts even if their books aren't very good. Establishing your credibility may mean getting articles published in magazines on the subject you propose before you start querying editors and agents with your book idea. Try and write this bio in the third person, rather than first person, unless you have a life experience that makes your view particularly valid.

The Benefits Part of a Proposal (the *Why*)

The Hook Overview. The hook should be a one- or two-sentence, in-a-nutshell description of the book that nails it. (In fiction, this can often be determined by thinking, *What if . . .* or, *Suppose . . .*). It helps the editor sell the book to colleagues in 30 seconds or less. Down the line it may end up helping the sales rep sell your book to a bookstore buyer. In general, make sure that, as in your overview, your passion and interest for your subject come through. An effective second-person voice can work here: "Have you ever thought about how you would survive if you were attacked by modern-day pirates and set adrift at sea? Joe Bloggs didn't, until it was almost too late. And it cost him his family, and a leg."

The Larger Overview. This overview is an expansion of the first. If, after hearing the hook, colleagues say, "That sounds interesting, tell us more," you can now provide the editor with broad facts and figures (if applicable) and a general overview of the project. This overview is a much stronger sales tool than your manuscript because it allows you to state not only what the book is about (features), but also why it's important (benefits).

Here are some general things to think about in an overview:

- What's the book about?
- Why is there a need for this book? What's the hole in a genre or topic that this book can fill?
- Who's going to read it?
- How will your readers be entertained by this book? State your case as dramatically as you can without being overly sensational. Startle us from the outset and make us consider your topic with fresh eyes.
- How is your book different from others in the field?
- Why are you the best person to write this book?
- How long will the manuscript be, and how long will it take you to write it?

Don't answer these questions with hype or rhetoric. Nobody's interested in your opinion on how great this book idea is; what you have to do is convince them with solid content summed up in a paragraph or two.

Close your overview with something that sums up the benefits or merits of the book, reminding the reader of the book's importance.

Try and do all this in no more than four double-spaced pages, and ideally two.

Marketing Analysis. In this section you need to explain who the audience is for your book—that is, who's going to go into a store and plunk down $7 for a paperback (or $14 for a trade paperback, or $25 for a hardcover) version of your book. What evidence can you offer that your assessment is accurate? Use facts and figures you have researched here. How many people belong to organizations or subscribe to magazines that deal with this topic? What other books out there have proven there is a successful and eager audience for your proposed book? Why will these people still be interested in reading about your topic in two years' time, or five years' time (what publishers call a book's backlist life). Give us statistics about groups who may be interested in buying copies of the book. It won't help to be sloppy or too general in your assessment. If you have experience or knowledge in selling, marketing, or promoting, mention that here. Do you have a seminar that you take around from place to place, or do you lecture to groups of people regularly? What can you do to translate your experiences into book sales? Are you a member of organizations that will help publicize your book and, ideally, buy lots of copies? Could you help sell bulk quantities of your book to organizations that might want to give them away as gifts to members? Do you have a connection to well-known people who might endorse your book and help increase book sales that way? A strong marketing plan accompanying a book proposal will go a long way in helping to sell it.

Competing Books. What I mean is a list of a half dozen or so of the most successful and most recent books published in the field or on the topic you propose to write about. Nothing breeds success like success, particularly if you have a new take on a successful idea. When listing the books, give title, author, year of publication, publisher, a one- or two-sentence description, and a line pointing out the difference between your book and the published book. Every competing book gives you an opportunity to make a new point about your book idea, so take advantage of the opportunity. Use the library and the Internet for your research. Browse the bookstores in your area; befriend bookstore owners; chat with book people in general. If there's nothing in the field to compare with your book, make certain you convince editors and agents that there really is a market for the book, and you're just the first person to have spotted a hole and decided to fill it.

Some Closing Thoughts on Writing a Book Proposal

It's worth remembering that on average it can take perhaps two years from a nonfiction book contract's being signed to the book's appearing on the shelves, so your book idea must be appealing enough that in two or three years' time, people will still be excited about it.

Your proposal should be tightly written, with style and verve. It should offer just enough information in an accessible and (hopefully) entertaining manner to convince an editor you know your subject and can write well about it. It should also be well organized in a logical progression of ideas and facts, and ideally reflect the tone and style of the final book.

Research the competing books section as soon as possible because what you discover may save you a lot of work, disappointment, and aggravation if there's no viable market for the book for one reason or another (for example, someone with better credentials has just published a book exactly like the one you propose).

The fact that another book has recently been published on your subject may not necessarily be a fatal blow to your book idea, because you may find, once you've read the published book, that the author treats the subject differently than you intend to treat it. It is very useful, however, to apprise editors and agents of the fact that you know this other book is in the marketplace and why it won't be a problem for your book idea. If an editor, in ignorance of this other book because you failed to mention it in your proposal, puts forward your idea in an editorial meeting and someone around the table says, "But so-and-so just published a book exactly like this," that editor will have been made to look foolish and ill prepared. Your chances of getting published just plummeted.

Propose one idea at a time. Don't inundate an editor or agent with a shopping list of ideas at one time, on the basis of "If you don't like this, then try that." It's unprofessional, and shows a lack of commitment and passion to the project.

Included below are two sample book proposals from clients of mine, along with some thoughts they had about the proposals and the books they subsequently wrote.

These proposals were sold in auction to major houses and represent two quite different types of narrative nonfiction. It should be clear that while they follow in principle the outline of writing a proposal, each author has interpreted that outline as they feel best represents the book.

The First Proposal

In crafting his proposal for *Heart So Hungry: The Story of Leonidas and Mina Hubbard and the Mapping of Labrador* (Knopf Canada, 2003), Randall Silvis said that the idea came to him a few years ago, after a trip to the Arctic Circle for the Discovery Channel. In an interview in the fall of 2002, he told me:

> Upon my return home, I was talking about the trip with an acquaintance who had also been to Alaska. He mentioned another trip he had made, this one to Labrador. He made the place sound so interesting that I did a bit of Internet research, and there came across the stories of Leonidas and Mina Hubbard.
>
> After I had done a fair measure of research I came to the conclusion that a part of this story had never been adequately told—Mina's "internal" story, that is, the psychology behind her expedition. To me it was the most intriguing aspect of the Hubbards' story, because I like nothing better than to examine the demons and desires that drive an individual. This story contained love, tragedy, adventure, and revenge—how could I pass it up?

After I came across the Hubbards' story, every reference led me to an article or other publication. Each of these in turn led me to others. Like any good hunting dog, a writer has to first find the scent. Then just keep your nose to the ground all the way. The biggest difficulty I faced turning the research into a narrative with a beginning, middle, and end was that my task was to intertwine three separate expeditions—one in 1903 and two in 1905—into a single narrative. It's like trying to force together a thousand pieces of a jigsaw puzzle into a straight line. Fortunately my book is a hybrid of fact and fiction, which allows me to extrapolate certain connections; by re-creating Mina's thoughts and conversations, I can use them to draw the story away from and then back to the main narrative. The trick is not to be arbitrary in this device, and not to stray from what I perceive to be Mina's essential character.

The hard part for writers tackling narrative nonfiction is finding the story. Sometimes a good one will drop into your lap, but this is rare. A writer has to be vigilant—reading, talking, listening, traveling—in order to come across a story worth telling. The rest, assuming one possesses the proper storytelling skills for language, characterization, dialogue, and so forth, is all a matter of structure.

Here is his proposal as we submitted it to editors.

. . . the . . .

HEART SO HUNGRY

• • • • • • • • • • • • • • • • • •

A Proposal for a Nonfiction Book
by Randall Silvis

Stars so beautiful. Heart so hungry, so hungry, oh so hungry.
FROM THE DIARY OF MINA HUBBARD

PROLOGUE

In 1953, at 83 years of age, Mina Hubbard is a small woman,
not frail but petite, an expatriate American living in a small
village in England, a quiet village of neat homes with hedge-
rowed yards and well-tended gardens. Even now there is evidence, in the quickness of her gait and in the angle, not quite
imperious, at which she holds her chin, of a certain brashness
of character, a headlong spirit. When she crosses one of the
narrow streets, for example, she does not pause to study the
traffic; she strides on, eyes straight ahead, arms extended to
hold the cars at bay. Her eccentricities are well known by the
locals, and accommodated with affection, because Mina herself
is an affectionate and generous woman, notwithstanding her
unyielding attitude toward traffic. Moreover, she is not merely
a local character but a woman of international reputation. The
car and lorry drivers are happy to slow or swerve to let Mina
Hubbard pass.

But a locomotive is not as maneuverable as an automobile.

A train cannot swerve to avoid an unswerving woman. And when Mina Hubbard strides across the local railroad tracks, she is confronted, for the first and last time in her life, with an opponent that her own strength of will cannot deter.

Or could it be that Mina has been waiting most of her life for just such an unswerving opponent? Has she, possibly, been trying for half a century to silence the awful memory of her husband's final days, been hoping for relief from that memory every time she stepped headlong onto a busy street? Has she, all along, been challenging those cars and lorries and buses, and finally a train, to bring her peace at last?

It seems unlikely that Mina Hubbard could have failed to hear the train rumbling toward her. Unlikely too that, even if she failed to hear it or failed to glimpse it looming into the corner of her vision, she would have failed to feel it, so close, shaking the earth beneath her feet.

On the other hand, Mina Hubbard lived a very unlikely life indeed. Her own small footsteps caused a fair amount of earth shaking. So maybe she *had* fully expected that train to get out of her way.

And maybe she hoped it would not.

Who was this woman who remained headstrong and heedless to the very end? She was not always so obdurate. By all accounts, this stubborn streak did not show itself in Mina Hubbard until the unfortunate year of 1903, the worst year of her life, the year her beloved husband died of starvation in the frozen wilderness of Labrador. That was the year her determination was hardened in the forges of grief and was later alloyed with outrage. That was the year an unflinching devotion to her husband's memory began to transform Mina Hubbard into the most celebrated female explorer of her time.

THE STORY

1902: In the Staten Island Hospital, the young Leonidas Hubbard Jr., recuperating from typhoid, restlessly wanders the hall. He encounters another young man, a stranger named Dillon Wallace who has been visiting the hospital daily, where his bride of one year, a patient there, is dying of consumption. Hubbard strikes up a conversation with Wallace. In their shared miseries—Hubbard has lost a good job as a journalist because of his illness, and he worries how he will provide for his own young wife—they find some comfort, and in the fondness they share for hunting and fishing.

After the death of Wallace's wife, Wallace relies more and more on Hubbard's friendship. On one of their many hikes together, Hubbard reveals that he has talked his new employer, the editor of New York City's prestigious *Outing Magazine,* into sponsoring a canoe expedition into Labrador to chart 500 miles of the last unexplored wilderness in North America. Hubbard is desperate to make a name for himself, to secure his and Mina's future by joining the ranks of men like Peary and Roosevelt and Amundsen, whose recent exploits have spawned a national fervor for exploration. Indeed, there is more to his proposal than a desire for financial security.

"I am haunted by a craving for adventure, Dil. By a desperate need to see what has never before been seen. To walk where no white man has ever walked. Few such places remain."

Wallace is reluctant. It would not be easy, he says. Not like one of their fishing trips.

"But you are haunted too, Dillon, you know you are. We are both of us haunted men. Come with me into Labrador. We will confront our ghosts together."

Despite his misgivings, Wallace eventually agrees.

• • • • • • • • • •

From this point on in the proposed book, *Heart So Hungry* becomes a two-pronged narrative. The principal narrative begins in 1904, when Mina Hubbard is living quietly in Massachusetts, a grieving widow. To those who know her, her life seems over already, a woman only thirty-four, petite and pretty. She has attempted to distract herself from grief by returning to high school, completing her degree, and by starting her training as a nurse. Even so, it seems to Mina Hubbard that there can never again be laughter and sunlight in her small cottage, no room for any emotion but despair.

But then the book arrives—*The Lure of the Labrador Wild* by Dillon Wallace, her husband's best friend and fellow explorer. The book contains several photographs of her loving husband, Laddie, so dashing and young, so full of life. Seeing them, she is reminded of how it had all started—how, with the brightest of hopes, the tragedy had begun. . . .

And now we flash back to the preparations for Leonidas Hubbard's 1903 expedition. Despite numerous setbacks, Hubbard is unflinchingly optimistic—too optimistic, in the view of Dillon Wallace. But in every argument, Hubbard's eagerness carries the day. He is responsible for outfitting and planning the expedition. Unfortunately his preparations mirror his editor's notion that a canoe trip into unknown Labrador will be hardly more demanding than a picnic in the Catskills. As a result, the expedition is poorly provisioned; Hubbard expects to find plentiful game all along the journey. But he fails to pack a shotgun. Nor does he deem it necessary to secure a reliable set of maps. And when he can convince no local guide to lead them into the wild, Hubbard hires a Canadian named George

Elson, a quiet, half-breed Scot–Cree Indian who has never been to Labrador.

In the summer of 1903, these three men, accompanied by Mina, sail by freighter from New York City to Halifax. It is already mid-July, and far too late to start a journey into the northern latitudes. Perhaps because of her sense of foreboding, Mina finds the crossing dismal, her accommodations cramped, the ship tossed by storms and plagued by icebergs. The only thing that keeps her spirits elevated is her husband's boyish enthusiasm. He enjoys every miserable moment of the trip.

"What great fun this is!"

On the bleak Labrador coastline, where not a glimpse of tree or bush can be seen, nothing but a boggy and wind-scoured flatness, Mina bids her husband godspeed and sends him off to his adventure.

• • • • • • • • • • •

A year later, as Mina reads Dillon Wallace's chronicle of the expedition, she comes to a passage that causes her to feel something other than the numbing chill of grief that has been her only emotion since the previous October. She reads, not once but several times throughout the book, Wallace's implication that the expedition failed because of Hubbard's incompetence, that if Wallace had been the expedition leader, success would have been guaranteed.

How, she wonders, could Wallace say such a thing? And why? For mere self-aggrandizement? She was well aware of the drama with which he played up his own brush with death, his almost miraculous survival. But she had never expected that he would stoop so low as to blame the tragedy on her husband, his own best friend. Were it not for Leonidas Hubbard's vision and ambition, Wallace would not now be enjoying such fame as a speaker and writer. Nor would Mina have moved there to Massachusetts, to the village next to Wallace's, so as to help him with that odious book!

For days Mina strides around town seething, unsure of what to do with all this outrage. The only thing she knows for sure is that she cannot let this insult to her husband go unanswered.

Then, the final humiliation: Wallace announces that he will undertake the expedition again, ostensibly in memory of his friend. Mina knows better. She knows that, with his own success, Wallace intends to establish her husband as a fool.

She cannot allow this to happen. And the only way to prevent it is to humiliate Wallace himself. This she will accomplish by mounting her own expedition and beating Wallace to the finish line. But of course she must keep her plans secret. She would be laughed at and ridiculed, discouraged at every turn.

There is only one man she can trust—the half-breed George Elson, who always spoke with great affection for her husband. She asks Elson to guide her into the wilderness. He considers the scheme harebrained and impossible. But ever since he left Hubbard alone in a tent in 1903, Elson has been wracked with guilt. And so, he agrees to guide Mina, if only to prevent her from a fate similar to her husband's.

Months later, in the summer of 1905, Mina Hubbard and George Elson journey to Halifax. As far as the public knows, Mina intends only to investigate the details of her husband's earlier expedition. She seeks out the three men who, in 1903, rescued Dillon Wallace. Their stories strengthen her conviction that Wallace had failed to do his utmost to save her husband.

Before Mina departs Halifax, word gets out that she suspects Wallace of hastening, if not precipitating, her husband's death. Wallace hears the gossip and notes in his journal that he intends to have Mina Hubbard arrested for slander. The controversy is reported in the New York City newspapers, and passions are soon inflamed. Nearly all sentiment, however, including that of Hubbard's own family, is aligned against Mina.

In the midst of this animus, the rival expeditions are forced to share the steamship *Harlow* as they sail up the Labrador coast to the Northwest River Post, where they will take to their canoes.

Aboard ship, Mina and Wallace have only one brief and tense encounter. Otherwise they do their best to avoid each other.

At the Northwest River Post, Elson recruits two young Eskimos to accompany Mina Hubbard's expedition. There are five men in Wallace's party. Neither team wastes any time launching their canoes on Grand Lake. And on the night of June 27, 1905, the teams camp on opposite sides of the lake.

Wallace's team appears organized and professional; Mina's seems little more than a ragtag band of ne'er-do-wells led by an inexperienced woman. But Mina is relentless, haunted by the spirit of her husband, driven by love. When, on the Naskapi River at the northern end of Grand Lake, Wallace's team pulls out to portage around a rough spot in the river, Mina's team remains in the water, and thereby gains its first advantage.

This early lead is Mina's first small victory, but it brings her no joy, for it comes at the site of her husband's first mistake. It was here, in 1903, that Leonidas Hubbard mistook the mouth of the Susan River for the Naskapi, and consequently directed his team up the wrong river. When the Susan narrowed to a stream, barely navigable, Hubbard was forced to dump some of their provisions. Next day, their canoes capsized, and even more provisions were lost. Still, they forged ahead. Unfortunately, the game they had thought would be bountiful was hard to find, and since Hubbard had failed to bring along a shotgun, even harder to shoot. They had no reliable maps of even chartered territory, and, once they entered uncharted land, they could only wander aimlessly, using up their precious provisions and losing too much time. . . .

● ● ● ● ● ● ● ● ● ●

Each of these incidents and the many to follow from the 1903 expedition will be juxtaposed against those of the principal narrative of Mina Hubbard's expedition. Mina's ordeal is far less dangerous than her husband's, far less demanding. Aided by George Elson's unflagging loyalty and the admiration they come to feel for each other, she is able to find moments of joy in the wilderness that so delighted her husband. But every day also brings another painful memory. Sometimes she notices something in the landscape that reminds her of an entry from her husband's journal, and this catapults us back to a recreation of that moment during her husband's trip. Sometimes the flashback is triggered by a comment from George Elson, the unifying factor in both Hubbard expeditions. Dramatic tension is maintained by occasionally looking at Dillon Wallace's journey as he and his team race to beat Mina to the finish line.

Wallace's expedition, by comparison to Mina's, is beset by pitfalls. They capsize and lose provisions; they get lost; Wallace injures himself with an axe.

The real poignancy, however, is captured as we watch Mina experience, through her own expedition, the agonies faced by her husband during his.

The early Labrador winter of 1903 closes in on Hubbard and Wallace and Elson. Tensions rise, fears increase. Hubbard falls ill. Finally, when only some 33 miles short of Lake Michikamau, the midpoint of their journey, Wallace and Elson turn back to get help for Hubbard, who is dangerously ill and incapable of travel.

Hubbard spends the next few days alone in his tent as the snow accumulates around him. On Sunday, October 18, 1903, he writes a hopeful entry in his journal:

"Yesterday at an old camp we found the end we had cut from an old flour bag. It had a bit of flour sticking in it. We boiled it with our old caribou bones. . . .

"The boys have only tea and one half pound pea meal. Our parting was most affecting. George said, 'The Lord help us, Hubbard. With his help I'll save you if I can get out.' Then he cried. So did Wallace. Wallace stooped and kissed my cheek with his poor, sunken, bearded lips, and I kissed his. George did the same, and I kissed his cheek. Then they went away.

"Tonight or tomorrow perhaps the weather will improve so I can build a fire, eat the rest of my moccasins and have some bone broth. Then I can boil my belt and a pair of cowhide mittens. They ought to help some. I am not suffering. The acute pangs of hunger have given way to indifference. I am sleepy. But let no one suppose that I expect it. . . . I think the boys will be able with the Lord's help to save me."

Eventually Elson and Wallace make their separate ways to civilization. Wallace, who started the trip at 170 pounds, now weighs 90. Rescuers are sent for Hubbard, but too late; he has died of starvation. As soon as they are able, Wallace and Elson, in the dead of a Labrador winter, return for their friend's body.

• • • • • • • • • • •

On August 1, 1905, George Elson and Mina Hubbard leave the river to climb a wooded hill. From that hill they see Lake

Michikamau, which her husband never reached. Mina is well ahead of schedule and has had a fairly easy time of it. But she cannot find much pleasure in her accomplishment. She wonders if, for the sake of her husband's memory, it wouldn't be better if she does *not* succeed where he had failed. Wouldn't it be better if, somewhere along the way, she should be killed "by heat and flies and effort and most of all thoughts"?

Despite reservations, Mina holds to her plans. And on August 10 she reaps the reward of an encounter with the Montagnais Indians who live along the coast. The Indians are initially frightened of Mina's party, and especially of the first white woman they have ever seen, but they soon invite the explorers to stay and feast with them. Mrs. Hubbard is inclined to accept this invitation until the men in her party are extended the hospitality of "many fine wives until you leave." Mina then deems it appropriate that they should leave at once.

Farther north, on August 20, Mina's party encounters the Naskapis, the elusive Barren Ground Indians. From them George learns some wonderful news: Ungava Bay, their endpoint, lies a mere 200 miles north.

To Mina's eyes the Naskapis are in a wretched state, in short supply of provisions and with a long, hard winter looming. So, before taking to the river again, she has forty pounds of her own supplies unloaded for the Naskapis.

Again on the water. Mile after mile of thunderous rapids are braved and left behind. Mina begins to contemplate success:

"I dread going back. . . . But I mean to try to face the other life as bravely as I can and in a way that will honor the one I loved more than all the world and who loved me with such a generous love. Only what am I going to do? I don't know. . . .

"I might possibly get back and get my story and some of

my pictures in print before Wallace is ever heard from, and that would be the thing for me."

As for Dillon Wallace, his expedition continues to be troubled. Whereas Mina's party encounters so much game that she is sometimes forced to forbid the men from shooting or else the meat will go to waste, Wallace's team suffers so severely from dwindling provisions that he is forced to send three of his party back. Only he and Clifford Easton continue. But this makes their journey no easier.

On the unpredictable George River north of Michikamau, their canoe capsizes in whitewater, and thirty minutes pass before the men can drag themselves out of the frigid water. Both men are hypothermic. Their struggle to build the fire that will save them is every bit as dramatic as Jack London's fictional tale.

But Wallace and Easton do survive, and on October 14 they manage to reach the Post at Ungava Bay, only to find Mina Hubbard and her party already there, having arrived not days but a full month and a half before Wallace.

• • • • • • • • • • •

Unfortunately, the triumph brings Mina Hubbard no lasting peace. Though she later marries again, the marriage does not last, for she remains haunted by the memories of her beloved Laddie. Though heralded as an explorer, she finds little satisfaction, as indicated by this entry in her diary: "Had to laugh a good many times and very heartily, but when laughing hardest was hardest to keep from crying. . . ."

Morever, it is as if her husband's restless and impetuous spirit has come to possess Mina, for although she lives a long life, she moves back and forth between England and America, always searching for something that no longer exists . . . until, at the age of 83, headstrong to the end, she strides across the railroad tracks in an English village and is struck down by the train.

SOURCES

This story would draw its information from the unpublished diary of George Elson, the unpublished diary of Leonidas Hubbard, and the unpublished diary of Mina Hubbard (all available on microfilm from the Public Archives in Ottawa), the unpublished diary of Dillon Wallace (held privately in Beacon, New York), as well as from any additional correspondence or unpublished materials that can be discovered. Further, there exist three excellent accounts of the explorations written and published by the principals: first, the book that so inflamed Mina Hubbard's passions, *The Lure of the Labrador Wild* by Dillon Wallace, published in 1905 by Fleming Revell; Mina's account of her subsequent expedition, *A Woman's Way Through Unknown Labrador*, published in 1908 by McClure Company; and Wallace's account of his second expedition, *The Long Labrador Trail,* from the Outing Publishing Company in 1907.

Additional insights into the character of Leonidas Hubbard, his preparations for the expedition, and on the harshness of Labrador itself will be gathered from William Brooks Cabot's book *Labrador*, published in 1920, as well as from Cabot's private journal, slides, and lecture notes, all held at the Smithsonian Institution.

A more recent account of the Hubbard-Wallace adventure also exists: *Great Heart* by James Davidson and John Rugge. This book was published by Viking Penguin in 1988, but although Mina Hubbard's expedition is recounted in the second half of the book, it is told primarily from the point of view of her guide, George Elson. What I propose is a narrative told from Mina's point of view, the drama of how this small, indomitable woman was driven by love to become the first Caucasian to traverse the wild heart of Labrador. It is, unlike her husband's ill-fated and romantic adventure, very much a love story—a tragic love story, yes, but one that lifted Mina Hubbard and George Elson into the realms of human greatness.

STYLE AND APPROACH

By making use of the aforementioned sources, it will be possible to assemble a complete if skeletal chronology of the three separate expeditions to be related here. We know, for example, that Mina Hubbard met with Wallace after reading the manuscript of his book, and that her reaction to this manuscript was the genesis for her own expedition. What we do not know is what Mina and Wallace said to each other at that meeting, whether the conversation was heated or restrained, if Wallace fidgeted in his chair as Mina pointed out the traitorous passages, or if Mina spoke in a timid whisper and could scarcely bring herself to look at him.

Yet these unknown details are the very essence of human drama. Without them we have no story, only a dry delineation of facts.

In the tradition of Capote's *In Cold Blood* and Mailer's *The Executioner's Song,* I will use the tools of creative nonfiction to give life to this drama by re-creating dialogue, setting, nuances of a character's movements and body language, all the while striving to remain well within the truth of the real character and the actual events.

ABOUT THE AUTHOR

Randall Silvis is the author of seven books of fiction to date. His novel *On Night's Shore* (Thomas Dunne/St. Martin's Minotaur, January 2001), a historical thriller featuring Edgar Allan Poe, received a starred review from *Booklist*. Historical novelist Maan Meyers said of *On Night's Shore:* "Move over, Caleb Carr. Randall Silvis's writing is exquisite and true." The *New York Times Book Review,* in a glowing review of *On Night's Shore,* praised its "vibrant panorama" and "pungent impressions," while the *New York Post* said, "Silvis has created an evocative backdrop, brilliantly capturing the sights and sounds of 19th century Manhattan. . . . *On Night's Shore* drips with descriptive power."

Silvis's eighth novel, *Disquiet Heart,* also a historical thriller featuring Poe, was released in 2002.

Randall Silvis's first book of fiction was chosen by Joyce Carol Oates to win the prestigious Drue Heinz Literature Prize. He has been a Thurber House Writer-in-Residence, a Fulbright Scholar, a finalist for the Hammett Prize for Literary Excellence in Crime Writing, and the recipient of two fellowship awards from the National Endowment for the Arts.

As a writer of nonfiction, his work includes numerous cover stories and feature articles for *Destination Discovery,* the magazine of the Discovery Channel. His historical features include nonfiction narratives about Blackbeard, Tecumseh, and the Alaskan Highway. His two-part series about the real Pocahontas was used to launch the Discovery Channel Online.

Randall Silvis will bring to *Heart So Hungry* the stylistic and dramatic skills of an acclaimed novelist and award-winning playwright, plus the impeccable research skills of a historian.

SALES AND MARKETING

Audience

Heart So Hungry will be directed at the same mainstream audience that has enthusiastically supported numerous best-selling nonfiction narratives of personal adventure, such as *Into Thin Air* and *The Perfect Storm,* in which man battles against the forces of nature. It will appeal as well to readers of historical adventures such as the Alexander and Hurley chronicle of Shackleton's *Endurance,* Niven's *The Ice Master,* and the forthcoming history of the Iditarod, which garnered an advance of $500,000. It will find another eager audience among readers of historical biography, such as Dava Sobel's *Longitude* and Alison Weir's *Eleanor of Aquitaine.*

All of these are fine books that have enjoyed widespread success. But nonfiction books in which intriguing moments of history are illuminated in a series of highly dramatic incidents, books in which compelling and endearing characters are pitted against nature *and* against one another, books in which the hero or heroine is willing to risk even life itself in the pursuit of an ideal, these books are rare. Indeed, the kind of people we discover in them are rare.

Heart So Hungry will slip neatly into each of three subgenres of nonfiction: the biography, the historical re-creation, and the personal adventure narrative. As the story of a grand and dangerous adventure it will appeal to armchair explorers of both genders. But *Heart So Hungry* will distinguish itself in two important ways. First, it is the story of a *woman's* triumph, of an ordeal voluntarily undertaken in the name of love—the story of a woman who triumphed where men could not, and in a pursuit that was, and for the most part still is, considered wholly masculine. As such, it is an inspirational story that resonates with deep emotional impact.

Secondly, *Heart So Hungry* is first and foremost a love story. The adventure, the challenge, and the danger all grow out of the love. A woman risks everything, including her own life, for one reason only—to prevent the memory of her beloved if impetuous husband from being besmirched. Love, loyalty, tragedy, personal danger and sacrifice, and triumph—all with a woman as central character.

For these reasons *Heart So Hungry* will hold a special appeal for female readers.

Marketing Points

Heart So Hungry will exemplify the qualities of human drama, perseverance, and triumph that appeal to television talk shows, from Oprah and Rosie and Leeza to Larry King, as well as to magazine-format shows, radio talk shows, and popular print publications.

The author has made extensive public appearances to promote his previous seven books, and is comfortable in all the aforementioned formats; he is prepared to undertake a promotional tour of readings and book signings upon the publication of *Heart So Hungry.*

A SAMPLE CHAPTER

June 21, 1905, aboard the Harlow, *steaming west across Groswater Bay out of Rigolet.*

There would be no avoiding Dillon Wallace now. Of course Mina could remain in her cabin all the way to Kenemesh if she wished, she could claim to be ill, say she had caught whatever it was that laid Joe Iserhoff low. George would take care of her, bring her meals, see that she stayed warm.

Nor would it be an outright lie to make such a claim, because anyone could tell just by looking at her that she was ill, truly ill, sick in her heart. The news, brought by George Elson just hours earlier, that the *Virginia Lake,* with Wallace aboard, had docked at Rigolet with only minutes to spare before the *Harlow* set sail, had struck her like a poison. One minute her skin was on fire, eyes burning, breath coming in gasps, and the next minute she felt chilled to the core, trembling as if naked in the icy North Atlantic. And every time she thought of Wallace's gear piled above her on the foredeck— George had told her exactly where the gear was located, told her how many men accompanied Wallace, how fit or unfit each man appeared—every time she envisioned that pile of traitorous gear a wave of nausea washed through her, violent and sudden, a sickening lurch that either left her feeling so scalded by anger that everything she looked at seemed bathed in the red of flames, or so chilled by grief that all the world seemed encased in blue ice.

But to hide in her cabin was to give Dillon Wallace a power over her, and that Mina could not allow. She would not take her meals in the cabin, would not cower below as if he, the latecomer, the interloper, now owned the deck.

For Laddie, she thought as she laced up her boots. It would become her mantra, her prayer of strength each time a difficult choice confronted her. *I must do this for Laddie.*

And no, she would not change out of her black mourning clothes, not yet. She had read the looks that met her all along the way, she knew the thoughts behind those looks. How dare anyone question her? Who knew better than she how long

Laddie had been gone? Who else on this entire ship, the entire planet, lived each moment with an image in her head that would never go away, the image of Laddie's last hour, of Laddie trying to write in his diary, chewing on an old flour sack, starving to death in a tent half-buried in snow?

Out into the corridor she went, up onto the deck. She would go wherever she pleased on this ship. Let anyone try to stop her. Maybe Wallace *had* caught up with her in Rigolet, erasing her slim early lead, but what difference did it make? Neither he nor the gossipmongers nor the icebergs nor an army of judgmental looks would deter her. Because Laddie was with her. He would show her the way.

A pewter sky, a chilling blast of air. She stood at the rail and could feel the cold rising up off black water. But the air was bracing as well. The scent of the frigid sea stripped the nausea out of her. Such bleakness wherever she looked, such desolation. Still, there was something exciting about the challenge of the place, something elemental, almost primeval, that gave her strength. Maybe that was why Laddie had been so drawn to the wild. Challenge and risk brought out the best in him. She was determined that it would do the same for her.

She turned and started walking. It seemed inevitable, preordained, that Wallace would be coming toward her. She knew it was him even before they drew close enough in the gray light to recognize one another. And at the first sight of his face, a sudden flutter in her stomach, a weakening. She almost jerked away. But no, she would not, she must not. Her face hardened, her eyes narrowed. Her gait stiffened, but she would not let it slow, would not turn away by so much as an inch. She walked on, marched toward him, her eyes locked on his now but seeing nothing, only gray all around.

When they were but steps apart he wet his lips, was about to speak. A hand came up toward his hat. Mina's gaze drilled into him. And at the final moment he looked away, he averted his head as they passed.

She continued on a few more paces. Then slowed, put a hand to the rail, paused for a moment, closed her eyes, drew in a slow full breath.

She opened her eyes then and looked out across the black water, the darkening sky. No, Wallace would not stop her. Nothing would stop her. *Nothing*.

· · · · · · · · · · ·

The ragged coastline of Labrador again coming into view, materializing out of the gray mist. A jumble of rocks and little else. A hard and silent nakedness. It was as if God, when He finished constructing the Pyrenees and the Rockies, when He tired of shaping the New England coast and the high cliffs of Scotland, had looked around for a place to dump his leftover materials, saw a vast empty spot where the North Atlantic carved into Canada, and unloaded His pockets there.

Such a bleak and barren place, so colorless. Yet Mina was excited to be here at last. And how different were her emotions from those of the first time she had laid eyes on Labrador!

That time, two years earlier, she had been aboard the *Virginia Lake*, no less rust-eaten a bucket than now, and only slightly more cramped and stinking than the *Harlow*. But that had been Laddie's expedition and she had done her best to share his enthusiasm, the boyish thrill each time he spotted an iceberg, the way he loved to stand with his face to the freezing wind, his eyes bright with the anticipation of adventure.

For Laddie's sake she had done her best to keep the trepidations to herself. But a foreboding sat heavy in her chest. She heard a warning in every conversation.

Somebody remarked that it was late in the season, wasn't it, it was July already, too late to be embarking on a canoe expedition.

We have every confidence in our schedule, Laddie had said.

The summers are short up here. You hardly notice them at all.

We have taken all necessary precautions.

You'll be lucky even now to see a day in the forties. Them northeast winds can bring snow anytime.

We are not concerned.

Five hundred miles by canoe before the river freezes over? Through unexplored land? Just asking for trouble, that's what it sounds like t'me.

But Laddie had waved it all aside, even when William Cabot questioned him. Cabot, the Boston engineer and explorer, was the very individual who, eighteen months earlier, had first suggested to Laddie that he make a name for himself by charting the Labrador interior, one of the last unexplored wilderness areas in North America. He was aboard the *Virginia Lake* now with his own canoe, on his way to a solitary paddle up the Labrador coast, where he hoped to encounter a few members of the elusive Naskapi tribe.

The moment they saw each other on the *Virginia Lake,* Laddie invited Cabot to join the expedition inland. Cabot neither accepted nor declined the invitation, but over the next few days, his every conversation with Laddie had been peppered with questions.

What firearms have you packed? he wanted to know.

Laddie named the rifles and sidearms.

No shotgun?

Too heavy, Laddie had told him. The ammunition alone would slow us down.

Rifles are fine for caribou, but what about the geese? What about rabbits and the other small game? You won't pick them out of the bush with a deer rifle.

But the ammunition . . . , Laddie said.

You should have brought a small-bore shotgun at least. You could have lightened the load with reduced shot charges.

Laddie's eyebrows went up. A small-bore shotgun was not something he had considered.

Your canoe is an eighteen-footer, Cabot pointed out.

It is. Same as yours.

But I'll be on my own. You've got two other men with you. Three men plus all your gear in one canoe?

We'll be fine, Laddie told him.

Not if you capsize you won't. You'll have all your eggs in the one basket.

We'll get along fine.

What size gill net have you brought?

Laddie answered that he intended to pick up a gill net at the Northwest River Post. The locals could advise him on the size of the Naskapi River fish.

But you've written ahead to have the net ready, haven't you? You surely don't expect to wait there while it's made for you, late as it is already?

Laddie only laughed and told him, Yes, yes, you're absolutely right but we'll be fine, we're going to have a smashing good time of it.

George Elson had stood by quietly, as solid as a stone and twice as loyal. But what of Dillon Wallace? Had he ever once backed up his partner? Had he ever once told Cabot not to worry, Hubbard has it all planned out, we have every confidence in our man Hubbard here? Nor had he bothered, as far as Mina knew, to whisper to Laddie in a private moment, When we get to the Post, Leon, let's look into that matter of a shotgun. Let's see about another canoe.

And Mina, she kept her fears to herself. They accumulated in her chest and in the pit of her stomach, small ice-crusted stones. They made her tremble when she lay against her husband in the narrow bunk each night. Made her cling to him as they strolled the deck in the nightly fog, Laddie filling his lungs with the salt breeze, Mina cringing each time Captain Parson's "Halloo!" rang out in an attempt to locate icebergs by the way they bounced his echo back to him.

Then came Battle Harbor and the Labrador coast. She could not believe how bleak it was, no grass or greenery of any kind, nothing but rock and more rock, jagged cliffs and patches of old snow. Here she would be put ashore to await the next southbound ship, while Laddie and George and Wallace sailed north another thousand miles, another world away to an even harder desolation, there to set out in a single canoe, no shotgun, no accurate maps, maybe no gill net—with nothing but Laddie's enthusiasm to guide them.

Laddie took her into his arms to say good-bye. And she could not help herself, the fears welled up in her suddenly, the sobs exploded. He stroked her hair and whispered that he loved her, he adored her. And please don't worry, my beloved, it's just a little canoe trip, three men in a boat, rub-a-dub-dub. I will be safely at home with you well before Thanksgiving.

She was helped into the jolly boat, she was rowed ashore. There to stand on the slippery black rock, sobbing uncontrollably, feeling such emptiness, such ache worse than death, worse than dying herself, while the *Virginia Lake* drifted away with Laddie at the rail, waving, blowing kisses, and grinning from ear to ear.

ENDS

The Second Proposal

When I interviewed Amy Yarsinske (in fall 2002) about her proposal for her book *No One Left Behind: The Lt. Comdr. Michael Scott Speicher Story,* she had spent close to ten years investigating his case. Her devotion to Speicher's cause and her desire to see justice done for him inspired a passion in the proposal, and the book that was subsequently published, that is obvious.

She said about writing the proposal:

The Speicher book was fatefully a marriage of author to subject from the beginning. I follow a subject (in this case Scott Speicher's initial loss in January 1991), and if it keeps returning to me again and again as a powerful subject and one that requires the unique abilities I have as an investigator and writer, and I adjudge that I can handle it, I'll press on and do the book.

In this very unique circumstance, however, I had far greater parameters and reasons for doing the book than to write Scott Speicher's story; I wanted to bring him home or at minimum have a hand in that process. To this day, I think that wanting to account for Scott Speicher remains the driving force in my continuing to work on the case behind the scenes.

The obstacles were primarily the sensitivities of some people in the military and intelligence communities who were uncomfortable with my investigation of Speicher's disappearance. This is understandable, though not always easy to navigate.

Fortunately, I had the military background for the task. You have to have an intuitive sense of your subject and where it is going to be a successful narrative nonfiction author. I believe that to have a strong beginning, middle, and end, particularly with story movement that transfixes the reader, you have to come out powerfully from page one.

Sometimes this means letting go of tedious detail and letting the story communicate the importance of the subject. Nonfiction writers display a proclivity for drowning the reader in details in the narrative they can just as easily present in an appendix section. Narrative nonfiction writers must maintain "forward motion" in their stories. Their manuscripts have to walk the line with impeccable detail gleaned from thorough research while telling a story. To me, narrative nonfiction is ultimately the marriage of fact told in the style of a riveting fiction.

Here is the proposal we submitted to editors.

NO ONE LEFT BEHIND

• • • • • • • • • • • • • • • • • •

The Lt. Comdr. Michael Scott Speicher Story
by Amy Waters Yarsinske

Potential endorsers I am able to contact who are willing to look at the book with a view to giving a quote:

Ambassador Richard Butler, former executive chairman, UNSCOM Iraq; fellow, Council on Foreign Relations; and author, *The Greatest Threat—Iraq, Weapons of Mass Destruction, and the Growing Crisis of Global Security*.

Admiral Stanley R. Arthur, former vice chief of naval operations and president, Lockheed-Martin Fire Control Systems.

Former secretary of defense William Cohen.

Judith Miller, *New York Times* columnist and expert on Iraq and the Middle East.

General Norman Schwarzkopf, former battle commander, Operation Desert Storm.

Senator Bob Smith, R-New Hampshire, Senate Select Committee on Intelligence.

Commodore Tony Albano, Lt. Commander Speicher's best friend.

OVERVIEW

Shortly after the Desert Storm cease-fire in 1991, Iraq repatriated all captured coalition personnel—all, that is, except Lt.

Commander Michael Scott Speicher, the first American casualty of the action.

Lt. Commander Speicher was the only U.S. serviceman lost over land during Operation Desert Storm whose status remained killed in action/body not recovered (KIA/BNR)—until January 11, 2001, when his status was changed to missing in action (MIA). He is the only American serviceman whose status the Department of Defense has ever changed.

The story of how Lt. Commander Speicher was lost over the desert on the first night of the Persian Gulf air war, and remained unrescued, unclaimed, and seemingly unwanted, has haunted all who flew with him, and those who still serve in the armed forces and have heard his name. Why was he forgotten? Is he still alive, held for over a decade in a Baghdad prison? Why won't the U.S. government be more forthcoming about the fate of Lt. Commander Scott Speicher, even now?

In 2000, the U.S. Senate Select Committee on Intelligence asked the intelligence community to assess Lt. Commander Speicher's fate. That assessment concluded that Iraq can absolutely account for Lt. Commander Speicher, but has deliberately concealed his whereabouts.

During the Persian Gulf War claims were made by all intelligence agencies that the precise nature of Lt. Commander Speicher's shootdown were unknown. But postwar analysis has now determined that his Hornet was shot down by an Iraqi MiG-25PDS Foxbat E and went down on the wadi west of Baghdad.

The question that remains—what happened next?

In *No One Left Behind* . . . Amy Waters Yarsinske will set out to answer these questions. Through exclusive interviews and dogged research she tells the remarkable—and disturbing—story of what happened to Lt. Commander Speicher, and why he is not at home today with his wife and children.

When Mark Bowden wrote *Black Hawk Down,* his 19-part series in the *Philadelphia Inquirer* came first. Similarly, Yarsinske has done the same for Lt. Commander Scott Speicher's saga. Her book is a detailed and gripping expansion of the story that will begin in November with her five-part series in the *Virginian-Pilot*—home to the nation's largest navy readership—surrounding the loss of Lt. Commander Speicher. It is expected to keep the community of 1.5 million people in Hampton Roads on the edge of their seats as each day's article draws them further into Lt. Commander Speicher's fate.

It all comes down to what happened in the wee hours of 17 January 1991 . . .

Through her interviews Yarsinske is able to take us from the White House situation room to the ready room aboard the aircraft carrier USS *Saratoga,* where Lt. Commander Scott Speicher spent his last few hours in the company of fellow navy pilots before walking out to the flight deck to climb aboard his Hornet. Her research puts us in the cockpit with Lt. Commander Speicher as an enemy MiG blows him out of the sky.

Through years of research, Yarsinske, a former naval intelligence officer and now a professional writer, was granted access to key, previously classified documents, photographs, and films. In piecing together and solving the mystery of what happened to Lt. Commander Michael Scott Speicher—and why—she interviewed and worked closely with U.S. government officials, military flag officers, intelligence agency heads, ambassadors and military attachés, as well as former American and British prisoners of war and British Special Air Service (SAS) personnel. Interviews with three former United

Nations Special Commission (Iraq) chief inspectors proved enormously revealing in the Lt. Commander Speicher case and shed light on the Iraqi economy of violence and production of weapons of mass destruction.

At some risk to herself, she sought out the assistance of sheikhs, ambassadors, and informants in the Middle East emirates. One of her sources is a sheikh who continues to be a contract agent for the Central Intelligence Agency, while another is an Egyptian doctor who fled an Iraqi hospital after 100 cases of inhalation anthrax exposure came rushing through his door, 50 soldiers dying immediately.

Yarsinske is able to answer the question—is Lt. Commander Speicher still alive? Alas, no, he is not. By all accounts, he was a victim of the chemical and biological soup where he parachuted into Iraq that first night of the air war. He gasped his last breaths in a dank and lonely hospital room—an Iraqi medical team's opportunistic experiment—in An Nasiriyah, where he'd been taken in anticipation of the POW/MIA exchange in the first week of March. It was a pitiful and painful death.

Other interviews were more personal—Lt. Commander Speicher's wife, Joanne, and his cousins, aunt, and sister, his best man, best friend, fellow pilots, and his squadron commander, Michael T. "Spock" Anderson. None have ever spoken publicly of their loss.

"No one is ever going to pay attention to Lt. Commander Speicher's case," said a former navy air wing commander, "until someone writes a book like *Black Hawk Down*. . . ." Yarsinske is doing just that.

THE LT. COMMANDER SPEICHER REVELATIONS— THE PREVIOUSLY UNTOLD STORY

The situation room in the White House was rung with tension the night of 17 January 1991 as coalition forces were within moments of launching the first air strike of the Persian Gulf War. The targets in Iraq that night included several chemical and biological weapon storage and production facilities.

Lt. Commander Scott Speicher was two minutes from his target when an Iraqi MiG-25PDS firing an AA-6 Acrid missile tipped with a chemical/biological warhead shot him down.

What no one told coalition pilots flying missions that night off Saudi Arabian airfields and U.S. Navy aircraft carriers was that there would be no combat search and rescue into a "hot zone" soup of blazing, damaged chemical and biological weapons targets struck by the first wave of aircraft that included Lt. Commander Scott Speicher's Hornet.

Less than an hour after he was downed, Lt. Commander Speicher's combat search and rescue mission was called off from the situation room of the White House. Exposing a Delta or SEAL team to anthrax or VX—present around Lt. Commander Speicher's last coordinates—would have meant risking the death of the rescue team, at least 8–10 more people. At the morning's Pentagon briefing, when then Secretary of Defense Dick Cheney was asked about aircraft losses, he said tersely, "We lost an F/A-18." Turning to his military advisers, Cheney continued, "And it was a fatality."

But Lt. Commander Speicher did not die immediately. He was fine for nearly 18 hours, laying down an escape and evasion symbol before capture by Bedouins. He escaped his captors, but not before the inhalation of anthrax and chemicals began to work on his lungs, slowly filling them with fluid and breaking down his tissue.

Captured again by Iraqi troops, his hands secured behind him, Lt. Commander Scott Speicher was stripped, intimidated, and beaten by his captors before they realized how sick he really was. Carted off to a nearby hospital, he was put in a room down a hallway now filled with injured British airmen and U.S. Navy lieutenant Bob Wetzel, who called upon his Iraqi doctor on two occasions to help "the heavy breather." But the Iraqis refused, saying that they knew about Lt. Commander Speicher (although the Iraqis never identified him by name), but there was nothing they could do. The "heavy breather" breathed his last breath in the early morning hours of January 22, 1991—or did he?

The Pentagon is still not ready to admit its newest fighter was shot down in an air-to-air engagement, especially by a far less advanced MiG of another era. To make matters worse, Secretary of Defense Cheney had considerable stock interest (in his wife's name) in McDonnell Douglas, the Hornet's manufacturer, a fact not revealed until much later. He chastised one admiral who, while lecturing to an applied physics seminar at Johns Hopkins shortly after the war, mentioned the circumstances of the Iraqis' only air-to-air kill (Lt. Commander Speicher's aircraft).

One of the purported physicists turned out to be a *New York Times* reporter who wrote a short piece about the admiral's revelation. An irate Cheney called the admiral at home, admonishing him never to say anything more publicly about the MiG. The same admiral later wrote the top secret intelligence report on the Lt. Commander Speicher incident—and he covered the MiG in detail.

Lt. Commander Scott Speicher was the victim of twisted circumstances—and considerable vanity. The U.S. would not go looking for him; the Iraqis would not return him or his remains. The United States did not want to publicly admit that one of their latest and greatest fighters had been shot down by a lucky Iraqi MiG-25PDS pilot. No one wanted to admit that the fears of taking on a dictator like Saddam Hussein, with his stockpiles of chemical and biological weapons he threatened to use, had been borne out.

Using previously classified documentation and interviews with the key players in covert operations, Yarsinske has reconstructed a chilling and compelling story.

●●●●●●●●●●●

Has it all been told in the newspaper articles? Not by a long shot. Items that the newspaper articles won't deal with include:

1. The chemical and biological warfare angle.
2. Interviews with the Iraqi medical team who may have treated Lt. Commander Speicher for exposure—or experimented on him, depending on which side of the medical equation one falls.
3. Interviews with the big players—such as former presidents Bush and Clinton, cabinet officials, former secretaries of defense, the navy, chiefs of naval operations, and Joanne Speicher.
4. The big questions regarding how Lt. Commander Speicher was shot down.
5. Significant documentation for the story from the offices of the secretary of defense, the navy, the Defense Prisoner of War and Missing in Action Office (DPMO), the Defense Intelligence Agency, and the Central Intelligence Agency that did not make declassification in time for the newspaper articles.

6. And lastly, the ultimate question: "Where is he?" which is not going to be answered in the articles in the *Virginian-Pilot*. The editors are concerned only with the factual elements of the Lt. Commander Speicher "mystery" that could be proven as the newspaper went to press, not what actually happened to him.

COMPETING BOOKS

No One Left Behind . . . will be written in a similar style to, and appeal to the audiences for such strong sellers as:

Black Hawk Down: A Story of Modern War (Atlantic Monthly Press), Mark Bowden.

In Harm's Way: The Sinking of the USS Indianapolis and the Extraordinary Story of Its Survivors (Henry Holt), Doug Stanton.

Ghost Soldiers: The Forgotten Epic Story of WWII's Most Dramatic Mission (Doubleday), Hampton Sides.

Delta Force: The Army's Elite Counterterrorist Unit (Avon), Charlie Beckwith, Donald Knox.

Killing Pablo: The Hunt for the World's Greatest Outlaw (Atlantic Monthly Press), Mark Bowden.

THE MARKETING ANALYSIS

There are United States senators and congressmen asking for the truth of what happened to Lt. Commander Scott Speicher.

Similarly, past and present members of the armed forces, who number in the millions, who know of or have heard of the Lt. Commander Speicher story, are keenly interested in reading what happened. Because of the inherent risks involved with small conflict engagements between U.S. forces and others using chemical and biological weapons, the true story of Lt. Commander Scott Speicher is of paramount interest and importance. His case represents an embarrassment to the U.S. government that failed to account for him, to bring him home; and to the Iraqis, concealing his captivity and possible death well after he should have been repatriated. Lt. Commander Speicher's story is one of human survival, and if another Lt. Commander Speicher debacle is to be avoided in the future, this is a story that must be told for ourselves and those we put in harm's way.

The story has already been introduced to millions of viewers in two somewhat superficial *60 Minutes II* segments, and bantered about by news agencies and magazines for over a decade as "an unsolved mystery." It has been called by some, in fact, "the greatest mystery in naval aviation for the last ten years"—what happened to Lt. Commander Scott Speicher?

Amy Waters Yarsinske is a member of the Association of Naval Aviation—the flag organization of naval aviators; the Naval Order of the United States—the nation's oldest and most prestigious historical and fraternal naval group; the Naval Aviation Museum Foundation—the organization behind the National Museum of Naval Aviation, the world's second most trafficked aviation museum; Battleship Wisconsin Foundation; USS Wisconsin Foundation; and the U.S. Naval Institute.

Though the Department of Defense cannot officially endorse a book, they eventually put out a "recommended reading" message to the joint services that goes down the chain of command to every soldier, sailor, marine, and airman—essentially having the same effect. Reviews and recommendations by major figures in the Lt. Commander Speicher case, from the

White House leadership who oversaw the case, the defense officials who executed various actions, to the foreign leaders who had a hand in it, are anticipated.

THE AUTHOR

Amy Waters Yarsinske has published some 21 books with a variety of presses and contributed to the success of others, including Constance Rosenblum's critically acclaimed *Gold Digger*. Yarsinske is today recognized not only for her well-honed writing skills and expertise in military subject matter, but also the exceptional research that goes into making her books so compelling. On the subject of this proposal—Lt. Commander Scott Speicher—she has no peer outside the Pentagon. Her television credits include contributions to *Modern Marvels: Air Shows*, an Actuality Productions one-hour program.

Yarsinske is considered "family" to the U.S. Navy and military in general. She is a former naval intelligence officer and married to a former active-duty, now reserve naval aviator and Gulf War veteran. Yarsinske is considered an expert in contemporary and historical naval aviation and is the author of several books pertaining to military aviation and navy subjects.

Yarsinske has a strong background in public relations and marketing. She is a frequent television and radio show guest and has actually hosted one- to two-hour radio segments on previous books, spun newspaper and magazine series off her books, and has an excellent relationship with booksellers and distributors.

The author has two bachelor of arts degrees and a master's degree, and in addition to her memberships in numerous naval and community organizations, Yarsinske is a member of the Authors Guild and the Virginia Authors Room in the Virginia

Center for the Book. She is represented by Peter Rubie, of the Peter Rubie Literary Agency in New York City.

Table of Contents

• • • • • • • • • • •

No One Left Behind is divided into sections rather than traditional chapters. Each section is broken out further into subsections indicating shifts in the story from different witness perspectives or known accounts. This tack keeps the narrative moving. The book will be around 350 pages and take six to nine months to complete, with photographs provided by the family (which has not provided any images to the media over the past decade, but will do so for the book), the Navy Department, various news organizations, as well as previously untapped sources being used by the author.

Part 1: Vanishing over Iraq

On January 17, 1991, in the early hours of the Persian Gulf War, Lt. Commander Michael Scott Speicher was shot down in a dogfight with an Iraqi MiG-25PDS Foxbat E while flying a suppression of enemy air defense mission west of Baghdad—bodyguard for the bombers, in effect.

Two hours into the flight and a few minutes from target, the coalition force's first air strike of roughly 500 planes bore down on Baghdad. Divided into five-plane formations, the *Saratoga*'s two F/A-18 squadrons focused on their mission that night, suppressing surface-to-air missile sites. Though they could hear the air force AWACS running air intercepts and vectoring for bogeys (friendly aircraft) and bandits (enemy aircraft), Commander Michael "Spock" Anderson's five Hornet pilots spoke only to each another on their own frequency, unable to communicate with other squadrons' pilots in the strike formation. Battle planners had placed stringent guidelines on radio communications in order to maintain discipline among all the aircraft on the strike.

As hard-core as Speicher had been about being on the first wave of air strikes, the emotions of all the *Saratoga*'s air crews that night were a mix of excitement and fear. Speicher was no exception. Though he high-fived his best friend, Tony Albano, as the two walked up to the airplanes, Speicher's mouth felt parched and his pallor was ashen—but so was everyone else's. This was for real. They were going to war. Speicher catapulted off the *Saratoga*'s deck, checked in on ship comms, and headed for combat. For the remainder of the flight he, like his squadron mates, observed radio silence. That is, until the MiG made its appearance in the VFA-81 *Sunliners*' formation.

The *Sunliners* were on the ingress into Baghdad when Skipper Spock Anderson saw the MiG come off the Iraqi airfield at Al Asad, right below him. A dogfight ensued between Anderson and the MiG. Eventually, fellow *Sunliners* pilot Barry Hull joined in the hunt for the MiG, but he couldn't get a lock on it and headed for the *Sunliners*' target over Baghdad, about two minutes away.

In a dark, small piece of sky, Spock Anderson went head to

head with the Iraqi MiG. "This is Quicksand 0-1 . . . *Sunliner 401*," said Anderson, calling the AWACS flying command center somewhere above him. "I've got a fast mover (at close range) on my nose, he's hot." If the AWACS called the MiG a bandit, Spock could shoot him down. Without it, the rules of engagement kept him from doing so. But Anderson persisted. "I've got a fast mover, on my nose. He's hot." The call came back from the AWACS operator: "NEGATIVE, NEGATIVE BANDIT. CONFIRM BOGEY."

Meanwhile, Speicher, focused on his head-up display, was concentrating on his suppression of enemy air defense mission. He could hear Spock's pursuit of the MiG, but as he focused on possible ground-to-air problems, ignoring for the moment possible air-to-air threats, a predator set his sights on Spike's Hornet. The predator was the Iraqi MiG (Foxbat E) that air controllers thought had gone "cold"—and which the AWACS operator had repeatedly refused to call a bandit. "Who would have guessed that a MiG-25 would circle back around behind us?" said Hull, one of Speicher's squadron mates. "I mean, you just think about it, when you meet at the merge, when you've got over 1,700 knots of closure and somebody goes 'whhhhhh-hewwww' past you . . ."

Such was the turmoil in the fast-moving dogfight above the Iraqi desert that night. The Foxbat pilot fired from Lt. Commander Speicher's "six" (Speicher's six-o-clock position, directly behind the aircraft), his air-to-air missile grazing the underbelly of the Hornet and possibly clipping the starboard wing as it hurtled past and detonated. The sky lit up in a glow. Lt. Commander Speicher jettisoned the canopy and ejected into the darkness over the Iraqi desert, but no one knew it yet.

As the air wing completed their mission and turned back toward the *Saratoga*, the pilots checked in over the radio. Speicher did not check in. No verbal radio calls were received but his survival radio did emit its beacon for approximately five minutes. No other signals were immediately observed—it was nighttime. He had dropped off the face of the earth and no one had made the correlation between the explosion witnessed by VFA-83 executive officer (the *Sunliners*' sister squadron) Commander Bob Stumpf and Speicher vanishing. The pilots on Speicher's strike mission returned to the *Saratoga* just before dawn without him.

Combat search and rescue (CSAR) forces were not officially notified of Speicher's radio beacon nor were they notified of the specifics of his case. Divert airfields were contacted with negative results, according to a memorandum issued on July 19, 1999, by Deputy Assistant Secretary of Defense Robert L. Jones. But an actual search and rescue was never executed.

During their intelligence debriefings on the ship, David Renaud, who for a long time was thought to have been the closest pilot to Speicher, reported seeing explosions five miles away, in Speicher's direction, at the same time Stumpf had witnessed a blast in the sky. Renaud even drew a little circle on his map where he calculated he had last seen the fireball. Admiral Stanley R. Arthur, then commander of all allied naval forces in the Persian Gulf, and later vice chief of naval operations, has gone on record regarding this incident. "The first report was 'airplane disintegrated on impact; no contact with the pilot; we really don't believe that anyone was able to survive the impact.' "

A few hours after the first mission had returned to the ships, Secretary of Defense Dick Cheney held a news conference in Washington, D.C. On the basis of one account of a flash in the night sky and twelve hours of radio silence, Cheney declared Speicher dead. To Stumpf and others on the *Saratoga*, Cheney's pronouncement was premature. There was no evidence to suggest Speicher was dead, but Cheney declined to comment further, thus igniting speculation that Speicher could be alive.

However, the captain of the *Saratoga*, Joseph E. Mobley, a former Vietnam-era prisoner of war himself, personally told Joanne Speicher from the moment Speicher went missing until the end of the war that "every effort continues to be made to locate Scott." A week after his initial loss, Lt. Commander Speicher's commanding officer reiterated this message, noting to a terrified Joanne: "All, repeat, all theater combat search and rescue efforts were mobilized." But this was far from the truth. Lieutenant Commander Speicher's crash site was not located before the end of Operation Desert Storm. But then again, no one looked either—not in an "official" capacity.

Part 2: Iron Hand

Lt. Commander Scott Speicher caught his last glimpse of American soil as he looked over the wing of his F/A-18 Hornet after takeoff from Naval Air Station Jacksonville, Florida, the morning of August 7, 1990. It was, not unlike his departure for other cruises, a sad day. But the sadness was compounded by the ache of leaving Joanne with two small children in her arms—Meghan, age 3, and Michael, 18 months. As he winged out toward open sea and the *Saratoga*, fear, sadness, and anticipation no doubt filled his heart and his mind. The United States was edging ever closer to armed confrontation with Saddam Hussein and his Iraqi air and ground forces. The *Saratoga* and its carrier air wing would be square in the middle of it.

For four months the *Saratoga* remained on station in the Persian Gulf region. Near Christmas in December 1990, the aircraft carrier pulled into Haifa, Israel, for a much-needed liberty call—but disaster soon marred the occasion. Sailors overcrowded a liberty boat carrying them back to the ship and it capsized, drowning twenty-one people on board. Speicher wrote home to his grandmother in Jacksonville, Florida, about his good fortune in not having been on that particular liberty boat. He hoped good luck would repeat itself in the face of the rising tensions in the Persian Gulf. "We'll see what the coming year will bring."

The new year brought war. The *Saratoga*'s some 2,500 airmen snapped into action the night of January 17, 1991, and many of them, like Lt. Commander Speicher, participated in the first strikes over Baghdad. Iron Hand, a mission designed to suppress the enemy's surface-to-air missile (SAM) threat, had been planned weeks in advance of the first wave of air strikes that night. Spock Anderson, Spike's commanding officer, was strike leader. Lt. Commander Speicher's mission was supposed to be an Iron Hand mission and when he launched from *Saratoga* in the early hours of January 17, he was armed with anti-SAM missiles and detection equipment; no one figured he wouldn't come back.

When John Webb heard the news that an American pilot had been shot down the first night of the air war over Iraq, he got an uneasy feeling, one, in fact, that left him unable to get it off his mind. "The odds were awfully long," Webb, then a University of Florida track coach, kept telling himself, that the navy pilot was his longtime friend and former college roommate Lt. Commander Scott Speicher. But as he heard more news coming out of the Pentagon, his uneasy feeling began to come true. "It was Scott—and my heart sunk."

Webb grew up with Lt. Commander Speicher in Jacksonville. They graduated together from Forrest High School and were roommates at Florida State University. Scott had been the best man at Webb's wedding—and vice versa—and the two men had remained close friends all their lives. At Christmastime, Lt. Commander Speicher sent Webb a letter that began: "Merry Christmas from the Red Sea. We're just floating around waiting for the fireworks."

•••••••••••

The concept for this chapter is to discuss the circumstances—a road map, per se—surrounding events as they unfold before Lt. Commander Speicher's disappearance the night of January 17, 1991. The facts, as they are known, make compelling reading. This is also the juncture to flesh out more of Lt. Commander Speicher's words in letters home and to friends such as Webb; to learn more about what he was really thinking in the days and weeks before hostilities erupted. Interestingly, Lt. Commander Speicher, one of the best pilots on the *Saratoga,* was not supposed to fly the first mission of the war, but he refused to be left behind. "When it just came down to flying the airplane, there was nobody like Spike," recalled Barry Hull, another pilot in Lt. Commander Speicher's squadron. Other pilots, like then Commander Bob Stumpf and Lieutenant Commander Tony Albano, would say the same. The *Sunliners* were supposed to suppress enemy air defenses west of Baghdad. It was a very dangerous mission. Stumpf was later the first to say that he thought it odd Lt. Commander Speicher would be declared dead so quickly—without a search and rescue.

Part 3: The Hunting Party

Lt. Commander Scott Speicher was last heard from on his radio, feet dry over Iraq, flying northeast toward Baghdad. Though there had been two eyewitness accounts of an explosion where his F/A-18 Hornet had last been sighted, there was still no hard evidence that he died in the blast. Shortly after the end of the Persian Gulf War, on March 7, 1991, Pentagon spokesman Pete Williams guaranteed the American public that the military would continue to search for the country's missing soldiers and airmen. When allied prisoners were released at the end of the war, Tony Albano, who had been Lt. Commander Speicher's roommate aboard the *Saratoga,* was dispatched to Saudi Arabia in the event Scott was among the prisoners being freed. Albano did not spot Lt. Commander Speicher, but weeks later, the Iraqis did the unconscionable and sent a pound and a half of human flesh to the Americans, claiming it was the remains of a pilot named "Mickel." Blood and DNA analysis determined that the remains were not that of Lt. Commander Speicher.

Almost immediately, U.S. government agencies involved in the Lt. Commander Speicher case speculated whether Saddam Hussein and high-placed Iraqi ministers were trying to conceal Lt. Commander Speicher's fate—or had they simply made an egregious mistake? There had been no evidence that Iraq kept prisoners or failed to return allied remains when the war ended. But apparently, no one bothered to ask which was true—collusion or mistake? Where they hiding anything? If so, what was the U.S. government keeping quiet? On May 7, the navy started the process to officially declare Lt. Commander Speicher killed in action/body not recovered (KIA/BNR). Victor Weedn, the forensic pathologist who tested the flesh sent to the Americans, remarked that the test did not show that Lt. Commander Speicher was dead. (He also wrote a fascinating report about the same, which will be exposed in the book.) Joanne Speicher was asked by the navy to sign off on their decision to declare her husband dead. Since she was under the impression all search and rescue efforts had been expended, she agreed.

While most of the United States celebrated victory in the

Persian Gulf, the Speicher family held a private—and excruci-
atingly painful—memorial service in Arlington National Ceme-
tery. Without a body to lay to rest, there were lingering
questions and an open emotional wound for Scott's family—one
that has not healed. But Lt. Commander Speicher's case was
closed—killed in action/body not recovered.

• • • • • • • • • • •

Just as Lt. Commander Scott Speicher's family was beginning
to mend and Americans had since turned their attentions to
the war in the Balkans, the unexpected occurred. In December
1993 Sheikh Hamad bin-Abdullah al-Thani, then Qatar's minister of defense, entered Iraq's western desert roughly 150 miles
southwest of Baghdad. He and his party went into the Iraqi
desert under the guise of hunting with the sheikh's rare fal-
cons at the behest of U.S. intelligence, which sent him looking
for the Bedouins selling the parts of an American F/A-18 Hornet in their souks. Sheikh Hamad asked them to guide him to
the crash site, which they did. Sheikh Hamad soon appeared at
the American embassy in Doha, Qatar, with startling news—his
"hunting party" had made an important find.

The Qatari minister brought home photographs of the aircraft's canopy, a metal shard with serial numbers, and memories of seeing an ejection seat. He gave all the evidence to
American embassy officials in Doha, whose defense attaché
forwarded the items to the Pentagon for analysis. From the
photographs, the condition of the Hornet's nose suggested the
jet had not disintegrated in the air. Pieces of the plane, including a part of the radar assembly, and pictures were forwarded
to Washington, D.C. The serial numbers on the shard and information on the radar assembly proved it was Lt. Commander
Speicher's F/A-18 strike fighter.

The Pentagon stirred. Almost three years after the war ended, Lt. Commander Scott Speicher's Hornet had finally been located. But questions had already arisen as to why American forces had not looked for the aircraft sooner. The Pentagon diverted one of its spy satellites over the downed aircraft's coordinates to confirm its location. Then, the Department of Defense went back and checked the imagery it had used to track Iraqi Scud launches during the war. It found the crash site—with the outlines of a jet in the sand—exactly where Spike's friend David "Frenchy" Renaud had indicated it would be.

The satellite footage showed something else—something much more disturbing than Lt. Commander Speicher's ejection seat far from the wreckage of the plane's fuselage. Located on the ground a short distance from the crash site, analysts found the image of a two-letter escape and evasion (E&E) symbol used by downed pilots to indicate they are alive and want to be rescued. Without a working radio, this would have been the only way for Lt. Commander Speicher to signal for help.

Pentagon officials then checked classified debriefs of other pilots who had been shot down, captured, and later released by Iraq. One aviator said his captors told him that "the guy in the F/A-18 shot down on the first day is on the run and we're going to catch him." But as retired admiral Stanley R. Arthur says of this whole situation: "You get this sinking feeling that there's something really wrong here, that you missed something." Arthur was right—much was missed, and how much was yet to be fully revealed.

Part 4: "The Heavy Breather"

Lt. Commander Scott Speicher ejected from his stricken Hornet, landing moments later on the desert floor below. This chapter takes readers through those agonizing hours leading up to his capture by Bedouins, escape, and the onset of anthrax and chemical exposure on his tissue and lungs. Newly released reports provide a window into the scenario as it is known at this time, coupled with information the author has obtained from her own sources.

Weakened by fast-working biological and chemical agents, Lt. Commander Speicher was an easy capture for the Iraqi Republican Guard who came upon him. Realizing how ill he was, they transported him to a nearby hospital, where he was deposited in a room at the end of a ward with other recently captured British and American airmen, including Lieutenant Bob Wetzel, a fellow airman off the USS *Saratoga,* who first described "the heavy breather." "I was in and out of consciousness," Wetzel recalled recently, "but I first heard this guy breathing hard maybe the night of the 18th. You have to understand . . . I was probably three rooms away, but it got so bad, I asked one of the Iraqi doctors (a couple of times) if they could go help him. But he said something to the effect, 'Yeah, we know about him, but there's nothing we can do to help.' The guy's breathing got worse and worse." In the wee hours of January 22, according to Wetzel, he stopped hearing the heavy breather. Wetzel believes the heavy breather was moved, laid in the back of a panel truck, and taken away.

The fate of the heavy breather, the medical team being sought by the U.S. intelligence network, and the frightening details of the chemical and biological agents unleashed that first night (and subsequent ones) of the airstrikes will be explored—as will their ramifications to the U.S. and Middle East. This is one of the most compelling elements of the book. Witnesses and documentation now point to the employment of chemical/biological agents in the Lt. Commander Speicher case, one of the primary reasons Lt. Commander Speicher's fate was later buried—quite literally. The Iraqis could not return remains tainted with agent, and the U.S. could not send in a team to retrieve an airman it knew would soon be dead from exposure—the "old bones" that Chairman of the Joint Chiefs of Staff John M. Shalikashvili later calls Lt. Commander Speicher in his rejection of a covert operation to retrieve him in 1995. How else would Shalikashvili know he'd be nothing more than bones without overt evidence of death? That is, unless the general knew Lt. Commander Speicher was going to be a dead man from the outset? This chapter confirms the many "dark thoughts" of Pentagon insiders who long felt there were colleagues knowledgeable of Lt. Commander Speicher's fate, but hid it—and hid it well.

Part 5: Promises Kept

Senior officers, such as Admiral Stanley Arthur, felt mounting evidence strongly suggested Lt. Commander Speicher survived the crash. The U.S. Navy's premier operational intelligence unit—SPEAR—commenced a black operation on the Lt. Commander Speicher case in 1993; the State Department did the same, calling their version a black-box project. Arthur wanted to launch a covert mission into Iraq to check out the crash site. The site was so remote, where was the risk? But a strong faction in the Pentagon was more concerned about policy than one pilot. General John M. Shalikashvili, then chairman of the Joint Chiefs of Staff, scrubbed the plan, saying: "I do not want to have to write the parents and tell them that their son or daughter died looking for old bones," according to Timothy G. Connolly, then principal assistant deputy secretary of defense for special operations, and other senior officers who witnessed the general's statement in December 1994. But what they did not realize then was that Shalikashvili was merely executing the orders of his commander in chief—President William J. Clinton.

Advocates of the covert mission were stunned, not only by Shalikashvili's statement, but by their hands being tied so tightly. Shalikashvili's comment essentially breached the warrior's code. "You lose one of your own, you go back and find him," said Arthur. "The more modern concept was that you can't take the risk of a loss." For Arthur, the issue has always been clear: "Did we or did we not have a lost pilot?" He said he believed there was a chance that Lt. Commander Speicher had ejected successfully and survived. "We know there was an ejection attempt," he stated in December 1997. "I thought he bailed out. I was adamant that we get back in there."

But for six months, the nation's top military leaders sat on what they knew—and they knew a lot more than they let on— or did they? Two days before Christmas, on December 23, 1994, Secretary of Defense William Perry, General Shalikashvili, Timothy Connolly, and at least four other Pentagon officials, including Frederick C. Smith, the assistant secretary for international security affairs, looked at the options. Connolly and all parties to the meeting but Shalikashvili, Perry, and Smith voted to send in a covert military mission. The risk assessment was decidedly in favor of it; the chances of failure were minimal, but the success factor was exceptionally high. Recall the remoteness of the crash site from Iraq's human population—it was in a part of the desert where no one typically ventured. The plan, as later described for publication, involved four helicopters carrying a special operations team that would cross the Iraqi border from Saudi Arabia at night. The team would return with everything it could find—black boxes, bones (if there were any), wiring from the cockpit, fragments of metal, and any other evidence at the site. The rest of the Hornet would be blown up.

Smith preferred the diplomatic route—openly approaching Baghdad through the International Committee of the Red Cross. The Red Cross, he argued, would seek Iraqi permission to go to the crash site with a forensic team from the Pentagon. But Connolly was adamant in his objection. "You don't preserve your options when you essentially announce to the Iraqi government that you know that you found a crash site, and you found something at the crash site that might lead you to conclude the pilot is alive," said Connolly later. "Because if, in fact, the pilot is alive and being held by the Iraqis, the pilot isn't alive anymore." On January 4, 1995, Defense Secretary Perry instructed Secretary of State Warren M. Christopher to ask the Red Cross for assistance. Eleven months later, in December 1995, Operation Promise Kept alighted in the Iraqi desert.

By March 1, 1995, the Red Cross communicated to the Pentagon that the Iraqis would be willing to cooperate with American plans to excavate Lt. Commander Speicher's crash site. But the Iraqis had also taken good notes. "Conceivably," said Assistant Secretary of Defense Frederick Smith, "the mission was prepared to leave the following week"; it was named Operation Promise Kept. Yet the operation architects, as well rehearsed as they were, had naively not taken into account the bureaucratic problems and purposeful delays presented by the Iraqi government as the team sent communications that it was prepared to march into the desert on its fact-finding mission. In the meantime, the Pentagon had its spy satellite photograph the crash site every three days. Each time analysts interpreted the film, the site appeared undisturbed. But then things changed. The Iraqis moved in and began dismantling the crash site as U.S. analysts sat back and watched. It would be nearly nine more months before the team went into Iraq in search of clues, and much would happen to the site during the delay.

In December 1995, two years after the Qatari minister's initial "discovery" of the Lt. Commander Speicher wreckage and one full year after General Shalikashvili's decision to nix the covert operation, Operation Promise Kept went looking for clues in the Iraqi desert. Upon arrival, the team found that the crash site had undergone a complete and thorough excavation. Gone were the ejection seat, the cockpit section of the fuselage, and other pertinent parts of the aircraft. More important, however, there were no bones—not even a shard. But stranger still, the team did find Lt. Commander Speicher's flight suit near the site in a condition that suggested, upon analysis, that it had been exposed to minimal weathering and minimal adherent soil. The team also discovered pilot life-support equipment (that had been cut off the pilot) and a 20-millimeter shell roughly one kilometer east of the flight suit. The condition of the flight suit and pilot-related materials, the method in which they were found, and the presence of the 20-millimeter shell (a shell from the gun in the nose of Lt. Commander Speicher's F/A-18) indicate that these items did not originate where they were recovered. Evidence had clearly been planted for the team to find. (A copy of Bruce Trenholm's report on the flight suit and several interviews with him—and other members of the team—reveal several key pieces that led to an understanding of Lt. Commander Speicher's real fate.)

Material analysis of the aircraft wreckage indicated a catastrophic event occurred in the forward part of the aircraft, resulting in a power loss and a short duration fire. Indications are that Lt. Commander Scott Speicher then jettisoned the canopy during the ejection sequence. Further team analysis indicated that the flight suit and life support equipment had been cut off the pilot. An officer familiar with the team's findings said that it recovered one of the plane's data recorders from the Bedouins. "The evidence showed the pilot successfully ejected from the aircraft," he said. The survival rate on ejection from an F/A-18 Hornet is 85 percent, with a 70 percent chance of minor injury. The Hornet is considered one of the safest aircraft on ejection.

Of the team's findings, Tim Connolly recently remarked: "I don't believe we have any evidence that he's dead." But the question that lingers on everyone's mind harks back to the events before Lt. Commander Speicher ever takes off from the *Saratoga* on January 17. Details of that night may explain why Lt. Commander Speicher never called for help once on the ground. Pilots are repeatedly grilled about the importance of keeping their survival radios with them at all times. It is the key in crash scenarios for getting rescued. Speicher held on to his radio, setting off one cycle of his distress beacon before being overcome by the Bedouins. More about this and other revelations regarding Combat Search and Rescue assets who were never contacted to pick up Speicher will be discussed.

"No one knows whether Lt. Commander Speicher lost his radio or not," said VADM Thomas R. Wilson, head of the Defense Intelligence Agency. "It could have been taken from him just as easily as it could have been lost." Other pilots had the same radio and ejected with it without difficult while those with the older radios, a couple of whom were prisoners of war, lost them in the ejection sequence. There is little validity to the theory Speicher lost his radio.

After the perplexing mission to the desert in 1995, around

mid-1996, General Shalikashvili penned a letter to the Central Intelligence Agency expressing his misgivings about the Lt. Commander Speicher case. While Lt. Commander Speicher was still listed KIA/BNR, mounting evidence that he survived the crash, and without any evidence that he died, compelled American intelligence agencies to launch a new search. Is he dead, or alive? The question seemed to lean toward "alive" when U.S. intelligence operatives in the Middle East say an Iraqi defector who escaped to Jordan informed them that in the first days of the war, his vehicle had been commandeered by two Iraqi soldiers who made him drive them and an American pilot from the desert to Baghdad and the military authorities. The pilot, the informant claims (an indigenous Bedouin), was alive, alert, and wearing a flight suit. The defector picked Lt. Commander Speicher out of a photo lineup, and passed two lie detector tests. Other Iraqis fleeing to Jordan and other friendly Middle East countries corroborated the defector's story and some were positive Lt. Commander Speicher was being held in an underground detention center in Baghdad. The Defense Intelligence Agency's most reliable defector is in a witness protection program in the United States. "We have him protected because Hussein doesn't let a defector live long," said VADM Wilson.

But there was strong evidence of Lt. Commander Speicher's capture before the December 1995 Red Cross mission to the crash site. Congressionals on Capitol Hill had already begun trading key information in their respective armed services and intelligence committees. Iraqi defectors who got out of the country well in advance of their comrade in Jordan have told how they were present in Iraqi field headquarters when reports of a live pilot on the ground came in and units were dispatched to find him. The National Security Agency purportedly has the transcripts of enemy radio transmissions describing the live capture of Lt. Commander Speicher. The Pentagon now readily admits they have the imagery of Lt. Commander Speicher's authenticator code and escape and evasion (E&E) marked on the ground right next to his ejection seat, which was in perfect condition. He was alive after the ejection, capable of crafting his authenticator code, and he evaded the enemy for a short time before finally succumbing to exposure from a chemical/biological agent. But where is he? Where are his remains? This chapter will answer these tough questions as well as address the geopolitical issues that have long consumed this case. More important, this chapter will put an end to the mystery of Lt. Commander Michael Scott Speicher.

SAMPLE CHAPTER (EXTRACT)

Part 1: Vanishing over Iraq

On January 17, 1991, in the early hours of the Persian Gulf War, Lt. Commander Michael Scott Speicher was shot down by an Iraqi MiG-25PDS Foxbat E while flying a suppression of enemy air defense mission west of Baghdad—bodyguard for the bombers, in effect.

Two hours into the flight and a few minutes from target, the coalition force's first air strike of roughly 500 planes bore down on Baghdad. Divided into five-plane formations, the *Saratoga*'s two F/A-18 squadrons focused on their mission that night, suppressing surface-to-air missile sites. Though they could hear the air force AWACS running air intercepts and vectoring for bogeys (friendly aircraft) and bandits (enemy aircraft), Commander Michael "Spock" Anderson's five Hornet pilots, including Anderson himself, spoke only to each other on their own frequency, unable to communicate with other squadrons' pilots in the strike formation. But there was one exception—the *Saratoga*'s E-2C Hawkeye flying "the box" over Saudi Arabia, an invisible grid in the airspace over Saudi's northeast desert bordering Iraq where they would essentially "sideline coach" the U.S. aircraft heading into battle.

Battle planners had placed stringent guidelines on radio communications in order to maintain discipline among all the aircraft on the strike. The *Tigertails* of VAW-125 and their E-2C Hawkeye were not a necessity on the strike, but since everyone wanted a piece of the action, they put up a Hawkeye anyway, its mission limited to Saudi airspace. *Tigertail* executive officer Commander Mark Sullivan piloted the plane. Wanted or not by air force planners, the *Tigertails*' role that night would extend further than flying around in "the box."

It was serious business above the skies of Baghdad that night. The mood was set from the moment the *Saratoga*'s pilots sat in their ready room chairs and listened somberly as the *Saratoga* battle group commander recited words of encouragement to his pilots.

"Gentlemen, George Bush has called on us to do our duty, to liberate Kuwait, and that liberation is going to start tonight. There are several types of people back in the United States right now, who will be watching as your bombs start dropping over Baghdad. It's going to be just about time for the evening news back home. There's going to be a guy sitting in a bar with long hair and a beard, an old hippie type, who is drinking beer and watching TV and he's going to go, 'Fucking A, those are my boys, goddamned U.S.' There are going to be Moms out there that are crying and saying, 'That's my boy.' They are going to be watching you, you need to do this well. This will be with you for the rest of your lives. You will remember this night forever, so you want to do the best job you possibly can because if you don't, you will regret it until you die." That said, *Sunliner* pilot Lieutenant Barry "Skull" Hull felt his mouth go bone dry.

"The very first thing we did was get a time hack so we're all on exact time," Hull later remembered. "We're synchronized. In 30 seconds it's going to be 24 after the hour, then 10, 9, 8, and then he goes, 'Hack!' " The atmosphere in the room turned somber. There was little chatter and the mass briefing seemed to take forever. Then the squadrons went to their own ready rooms for individual mission briefs.

"God, I need a drink of water," said Hull as he stood in the paraloft suiting up in his flight gear before heading up to the flight deck on the escalator. I must be more nervous than I think I am, he thought, because my mouth is so dry. Then he remembered the Diet Coke and apple he'd packed in his pockets for the flight. "These missions are so long." Forty aircraft flew off the *Saratoga* that night in a span of 20 minutes. Every 30 seconds an aircraft was shot off the deck into total darkness.

As hard-core as Lt. Commander Speicher had been about being on the first wave of air strikes, the emotions of all the *Saratoga*'s air crews that night were a mix of excitement and fear. Lt. Commander Speicher was no exception. Though he high-fived his best friend, Tony Albano, as the two walked up to the airplanes, Lt. Commander Speicher's mouth felt parched and his pallor was ashen—but so was everyone else's. They were going to war. Lt. Commander Speicher catapulted off the *Saratoga*'s deck, checked in on ship comms, and headed for combat. For the remainder of the flight he, like his squadron mates, observed radio silence—well, almost.

Saratoga's Hornets headed to their rendezvous point over Saudi Arabia and joined up with their tanker, call sign "Gopher." The tankers flew a big circle in the sky, filling up the Hornets. But Gopher didn't stay on the job long. At the prescribed time, Gopher and the other tankers headed off to the Iraqi border to supply other aircraft. Hornets, fully topped off or not, began peeling off the tankers. Since he had a fairly long track yet to go on his mission, Hull hung around with the tanker as long as possible. "We were at the left side of the tanker moving in. I came off the basket and to the right side of the tanker. I pulled my plane up 20 or 30 feet and looked down at this guy below me, tanking. I could look into his cockpit and see this glow of the instruments and the green formation lights and I thought, Man, this is so cool." He also remembered thinking that that was one of his squadron mates, but he didn't know who it was—at least not at that moment. No one was talking. Piecing it together on board the ship later, asking around with the other pilots on the strike, he realized he was looking down into Lt. Commander Speicher's cockpit.

"We were called HARM shooters—high-speed anti-radiation missile," said Hull. "The HARM missile is an extremely sophisticated, deadly weapon. I love those things; they're about a million bucks a pop, I think." They were all HARM shooters that night. Their job was to knock out enemy air defenses with the HARM missiles. Sent out on a SEAD (suppression of enemy air defenses) mission, the *Sunliners* and their sister squadron, the VFA-83 *Rampagers,* led in by their executive officer, Commander Bob "Ripper" Stumpf, rolled into their target area. They were to hit radar facilities, command and control centers, and surface-to-air missile (SAM) sites.

But as the *Sunliners* rolled into the target that night, just as Anderson's pilots began firing their HARM missiles, a lone MiG-25 made its appearance in the VFA-81 formation. The *Sunliners* were on their way to Baghdad when Skipper "Spock" Anderson saw the MiG come off the Iraqi airfield at Al Asad, right below him. At first no one got too excited. The greater threat seemed to be the Iraqi SAM sites on the ground—the fixed SA-2 and mobile SA-6 sites that dotted the landscape below. The *Sunliners* bore down on the target with the help of their air controller—their air wing Hawkeye—who came up on the radio and said: "*Sunliner 401* (Anderson), I've got a (encoded) and that's an SA-6."

"You do not want to fly through the envelope of an SA-6; it'll shoot you down," Hull iterated. "It's one of those things they haul around on 18-wheelers." Hull got a pop up—an SA-6—on the coordinates. When Anderson didn't answer with latitude/longitude on the mobile SAM, Hull got on the radio and yelled, "God damn it! Give me the coordinates!" Spock read them off again and Hull wrote them down on his kneeboard. Another guy on the flight chimed in, "Ah, no bother, no worries." But it turned out he wasn't in Hull's piece of sky. Hull got a sinking feeling. "Oh God, no!" The SA-6 was right below him and he didn't know what to do. As he pressed on, it wasn't until later that he remembers thinking, It was that damn SA-6 that got Spike. It was only later that he figured out it was a MiG-25.

The F/A-18C Hornet carries radar homing and warning (RHAW) gear to detect against missiles. "The gear gives us a warning, audio and visual cues in the airplane. You get these chirps, like 'deedle, deedle,' and that's your warning. The more extreme the threat, you hear 'deedle, deedle, deedle,'" said Hull, recounting the events of that night. As the *Sunliners* flew into the target, they experienced high-pitched "deedle, deedle, deedle, deedle," the RHAW gear gauges set off by the plethora of Iraqi missile sites and antiaircraft fire lighting up the nighttime sky. "I'm looking down at my gauge," he continued, "it's so covered up I can't make any sense out of it." Overwhelmed by the incessant chirping of the RHAW gear, Hull said, "Screw it," and turned it off. It's too much, he thought to himself, and I can't make this information out. I'm going to do what the guys in Vietnam did and I'm going to look outside the cockpit. The few old-timers he'd talked to had told Hull that if you see the telephone pole (SAM) coming at you, don't worry because it's going to trail off behind you. It was the ones coming up in front of you that were going to get you. Looking into the darkness around him, Hull pondered the old-timers' advice, occasionally glancing at the RHAW gear gauge and saying to himself, I'm going to die looking at this gauge.

The *Saratoga*'s Hornet pilots thought they were seeing an optical illusion as they edged closer to Baghdad. They didn't know what it was. At first it looked like the Northern Lights because there was a greenish glow to the night sky. The whole landscape was lit up with an intense glow in the distance. Until they flew over the middle of it, Iraqi antiaircraft fire shot up like Fourth of July sparklers, illuminating the night and blanketing the ground. It was an unbelievable sight to see the tracers and bullets snaking up into the sky. When the realization of what it was sunk in, it was like being gut punched. "It was all around me," recalled Hull, "360 degrees, and I just remember being terrified." Trapping aboard the ship later, Hull climbed down from his cockpit to clamoring plane captains and deck crew—young enlisted men—who wanted to know what it was like over Baghdad. They peppered him with questions. The first thing he said to his own plane captain was: "You know, if they hadn't been shooting at me and if I hadn't known they were shooting at me, it was actually kind of pretty."

In the cockpit of his *Rampager* F/A-18C, Commander Bob Stumpf was surprised to see the light show that began as they crossed from Saudi into Iraqi airspace. "We didn't really expect this but pretty much as soon as we entered Iraqi airspace there was antiaircraft fire, missiles and AAA. The terrain was rough right along the border between Iraq and Saudi Arabia. We really didn't expect to see that until we got much closer to our target area." It was hard to tell how far away the Iraqis were firing their barrage. Though he never felt absolutely targeted that night, Stumpf knew there were missiles fired close enough to get him. He started some vertical maneuvers, changing altitude rapidly—up and down—to make it hard for antiaircraft crews on the ground to target him. "That was a violation of the plan because there were so many airplanes over Iraq that night that each person was assigned a certain route and a certain altitude and you were supposed to stick to it," he recalled later. "If everybody did what I did, they would deconflict, kind of like the FAA does. But I figured the chances of getting hit by a missile were much greater than getting hit by some other airplane I couldn't see." Meanwhile, the air force AWACS was painting the air-to-air picture for the *Sunliners* and *Rampagers* on its frequency with *Saratoga* pilots, adding to the one already set in motion by the *Tigertails'* E-2C Hawkeye, which could be heard breaking into the air-to-air action that soon followed.

As they moved over the border, Stumpf was more concerned that his pilots got their fuel, got off the tanker in time, and went on their mission. Stumpf had a difficult time getting gas off the tanker, in fact not getting enough, because the A-6E Intruder in front of him didn't plug up to the tanker at the end and he ran out of time getting to Stumpf. Low on gas weighed heavily on his mind. Then, it was almost like somebody had flipped a switch and the mission went from routine to high stress. Stumpf went from confident and experienced fighter pilot to the unsettling thought *Holy shit, I think I'm going to die.* It seemed like it took "all day" for Stumpf to calm the terror of what was going on visually all around him.

A dogfight ensued between Anderson and the MiG. Eventually, Barry Hull joined in the hunt for the MiG, but he couldn't get a lock on it and he continued pressing home his mission over Baghdad. "I thought the MiG-25 had just blown on through. But he circled back around and came up our tailpipes." In a dark, small piece of sky, Spock Anderson went head to head with the Iraqi MiG. "This is Quicksand O-1 . . . *Sunliner 401*," said Anderson, calling out to the AWACS flying command center somewhere above him. "I've got a fast mover (at close range) on my nose, he's hot." If the AWACS or E-2C called the MiG a bandit, Spock could shoot him down. Without it, the rules of engagement kept him from doing so. But Anderson persisted. "I've got a fast mover on my nose. He's hot." The call came back from Cougar, the AWACS: "NEGATIVE, NEGATIVE BANDIT. CONFIRM BOGEY."

Meanwhile, Lt. Commander Speicher, focused on his head-up display (HUD), was concentrating on his suppression of enemy air defense mission. He could hear Spock's pursuit of the MiG, but as he focused on possible ground-to-air problems, ignoring for the moment possible air-to-air threats, a predator set his sights on Spike's Hornet. The predator was the Iraqi MiG (Foxbat E) that AWACS thought had gone "cold" and the E-2C couldn't get a clear picture of—and which Cougar had repeatedly refused to call a bandit. "Who would have guessed that a MiG-25 would circle back around behind us?" said Hull. "I mean, you just think about it, when you meet at the merge, when you've got over 1700 knots of closure and somebody goes 'whhhhhhhewwww' past you . . ."

Hull was already in air-to-ground mode to fire his HARM missiles when Spock Anderson came up on the radio, talking to the controller—the E-2C Hawkeye, which had drifted north over the Saudi border into Iraqi airspace. "*Tigertail . . . Sun-*

liner 401, I've got a fast mover [he gives the range], on my nose, he's hot." The range made the hairs on the back of Hull's neck stand up as he went back into air-to-air mode. Then he thought, Oh my God, what was I thinking?!?! How stupid was I to be in air to ground. And then he saw the MiG, too. "Oh my God, oh jeez—oh, shit!" Hull had always wanted to be a fighter pilot. "I just thought it would be cool." Now there were bad guys out there and they wanted him dead. Hull had the MiG on radar. In a questioning tone, he asks the *Tigertails*, "CONFIRM BANDIT?" But the response was "NEGATIVE, NEGATIVE BANDIT, CONFIRM BOGEY." The radio calls between Anderson and the air controllers became plaintive, urgent.

Anderson wanted the controllers to call the MiG a bandit but the AWACS and Hawkeye simply would not do it. Spock persisted. The AWACS operator came back at Spock, "NEGATIVE BOGEY, NEGATIVE BOGEY." Spock retorted: "CONFIRM BANDIT." The AWACS shot back: "NEGATIVE BANDIT, DECLARE BOGEY," which meant the operator was absolutely refusing to declare the MiG a bandit. Spock tried the *Tigertails* again. *Tigertails* refused.

Such was the turmoil in the fast-moving dogfight above the Iraqi desert that night. The Foxbat pilot fired from Lt. Commander Speicher's "six," his air-to-air missile grazing the underbelly of the Hornet and clipping the starboard wing as it hurtled past and detonated. The sky lit up in a glow. Lt. Commander Speicher jettisoned the canopy and ejected into the darkness over the Iraqi desert, but no one knew it yet. His fellow pilots were too mesmerized by the burst of the Acrid missile—it looked like a small sun breaking apart.

As the air wing completed their mission and turned back toward the *Saratoga*, the pilots checked in over the radio. Lt. Commander Speicher did not check in via voice communication

. . . the . . .

on his survival radio, but the radio did emit its beacon for up
to five minutes after Lt. Commander Speicher ejected—just as
it was supposed to do—but no one responded to the coordinate.
Spike had dropped off the face of the earth and no one had
made the correlation between the explosion witnessed by two
VFA-83 *Rampager* pilots, his radio beacon going off, and Lt.
Commander Speicher vanishing. The pilots on Lt. Commander
Speicher's strike mission returned to the *Saratoga* just before
dawn without him.

Combat search and rescue (CSAR) forces were alerted that
an American pilot was down—but not employed—and possible
divert airfields contacted with negative results, according to a
memorandum issued on July 19, 1999, by Deputy Assistant
Secretary of Defense Robert L. Jones. But an actual search and
rescue was never executed. This was confirmed by message
traffic—or the lack thereof—between the *Saratoga*'s intelligence officer and personnel recovery assets at Special Operations Command Center (SOCCENT) at Riyadh.

During their intelligence debriefings on the ship, Lieutenant
David Renaud, who for a long time was thought to have been
the closest pilot to Lt. Commander Speicher, reported seeing
explosions five miles away, in Lt. Commander Speicher's direction, at the same time Stumpf had witnessed a blast in the sky.
Renaud even drew a little circle on his map where he calculated he had last seen the fireball. Admiral Stanley R. Arthur,
then commander of all allied naval forces in the Persian Gulf,
and later vice chief of naval operations, has gone on record
regarding this incident. "The first report was 'airplane disintegrated on impact; no contact with the pilot; we really don't
believe that anyone was able to survive the impact.' "

A few hours after the first mission had returned to the
ships, then Secretary of Defense Dick Cheney held a news con-

ference in Washington, D.C. On the basis of one account of a flash in the night sky and twelve hours of radio silence, Cheney declared Lt. Commander Speicher dead. To Stumpf and others on the *Saratoga,* Cheney's pronouncement was premature. There was no evidence to suggest Lt. Commander Speicher was dead, but Cheney declined to comment further, thus igniting speculation that Lt. Commander Speicher could be alive.

However, the captain of the *Saratoga*, Joseph E. Mobley, a former Vietnam-era prisoner of war himself, personally told Joanne Speicher that "every effort continues to be made to locate Scott." A week later, Lt. Commander Speicher's commanding officer reiterated this message, noting to a terrified Joanne: "All, repeat, all, theater combat search and rescue efforts were mobilized." But this was far from the truth. Lt. Commander Speicher's crash site was not located before the end of Operation Desert Storm. But then again, no one looked either—not in an "official" capacity.

ENDS

.S.O.U.R.C.E.S.

. . . .

The quotes and interviews in this book come from four essential sources:

- Interviews I carried out for the book
- Public discussion panels I was on
- Research in LexisNexis
- Remarks by authors in their books about how and why they wrote the way that they did

In most instances, I have cited in the text where the information quoted came from. When I say "in an interview in fall 2002," the interviewer was myself unless otherwise stated. However, I thought it appropriate to also annotate here the source material for the comments quoted in each chapter—practicing, I hope, what I preach.

Introduction

Opening quote: http://www.brainyquote.com/quotes/quotes/t/q110841.html.
Kirn: "The State of Narrative Nonfiction Writing," *Nieman Reports,* fall 2000.
Dickson: Washington Independent Writers conference, May 17–18, 2002,
   Washington, D.C., National Press Club taped roundtable on narrative
   nonfiction.

Chapter 1

Opening quote: http://www.brainyquote.com/quotes/quotes/t/q111095.html.

Vare: "The State of Narrative Nonfiction Writing," *Nieman Reports,* fall 2000.

Gethers: Interview with Peter Rubie, fall 2002.

Galassi: Interview with Peter Rubie, fall 2002.

John: Quoted in "Science Mania: Read All About It" by David Lister, *The Inde-pendent* (London), March 10, 1999.

Gibson: Interview with Peter Rubie, fall 2002.

Hart: Interview with Peter Rubie, fall 2002.

Dunow: Quoted in "A Dark First Novel Suddenly Soars to the Top" by Bill Goldstein, *New York Times,* October 21, 2002.

Rabiner: *Thinking Like Your Editor* by Susan Rabiner and Alfred Fortunato.

Goodwin: http://www.brainyquote.com/quotes/quotes/d/q113581.html.

Krakauer: *Into Thin Air* by Jon Krakauer.

Winder: Quoted in "Books: Too True" by Blake Morrison, *The Independent* (London), April 12, 1998.

Spicer: Quoted in *Editors on Editing,* edited by Gerry Gross.

Chapter 2

Opening quotes: *The Columbia World of Quotations* (1996).

Galassi: Interview with Peter Rubie, fall 2002.

Krakauer: *Into Thin Air* by Jon Krakauer.

Conaway: Interview with Peter Rubie, fall 2002.

Gethers: Interview with Peter Rubie, fall 2002.

Gibson: Interview with Peter Rubie, fall 2002.

Twain: Quoted by science reporter James Burke in a lecture at the Smithsonian Institution, June 28, 1999 (http://smithsonianassociates.org/programs/burke/burke.htm).

Hart: Interview with Peter Rubie, fall 2002.

Beavan: "First Success: Colin Beavan," *Writer's Digest,* May 2001.

Bowden: *Black Hawk Down* by Mark Bowden.

Dickson: Washington Independent Writers conference, May 17–18, 2002, Washington, D.C., National Press Club taped roundtable on narrative nonfiction.

Srodes: Ibid.

Ehrenreich: "PW Talks with Barbara Ehrenreich," *Publishers Weekly,* May 14, 2001.

Chapter 3

Opening quote: *The Columbia World of Quotations* (1996).

Krakauer: *Into Thin Air* by Jon Krakauer.

Chang: *The Rape of Nanking* by Iris Chang.

Rhodes: *How to Write* by Richard Rhodes.

Eichenwald: "Rewriting the Rules of Nonfiction" by Kurt Eichenwald, published on booksense.com, January/February 2001.

Burke thumbnail: Adapted from his lecture at the Smithsonian Institution, June 28, 1999 (http://smithsonianassociates.org/programs/burke/burke.htm).

Junger: *The Perfect Storm* by Sebastian Junger.

Srodes: Washington Independent Writers conference, May 17–18, 2002, Washington, D.C., National Press Club taped roundtable on narrative nonfiction.

Kidder: Quoted in *How to Write* by Richard Rhodes.

Conot: *Rivers of Blood, Years of Darkness* by Robert Conot.

Howarth: *The John McPhee Reader,* edited by William Howarth.

Bowden: *Black Hawk Down* by Mark Bowden.

Chapter 4

Opening quote: *The Columbia World of Quotations* (1996).

Krakauer: *Into Thin Air* by Jon Krakauer.

Burnham: Quoted in "The Talk of the Book World Still Can't Sell" by Warren St. John, *New York Times,* May 20, 2002.

Coady: Ibid.

Cahill: "The Age of Creative Nonfiction," *nidus* Roundtable Discussion, 2001 (http://www.pitt.edu/~nidus/archives/fall2001/rt1.html).

Conot: *Rivers of Blood, Years of Darkness* by Robert Conot.

Eichenwald: "Rewriting the Rules of Nonfiction" by Kurt Eichenwald, published on booksense.com, January/February 2001.

Rabiner: *Thinking Like Your Editor* by Susan Rabiner and Alfred Fortunato.

Mondale: Quoted in *The Rhetoric of Film* by John Harrington.

Sayles: *Thinking in Pictures: The Making of the Movie* Matewan by John Sayles.

Dickson: Washington Independent Writers conference, May 17–18, 2002, Washington, D.C., National Press Club taped roundtable on narrative nonfiction.

Chapter 5

Opening quote: *The Columbia World of Quotations (1996).*

Hirst: Quoted by Nathan Edwards on the Damien Hirst Website (http://www.geocities.com/SoHo/Museum/4686/hirsthome.html).

Dickson: Washington Independent Writers conference, May 17–18, 2002, Washington, D.C., National Press Club taped roundtable on narrative nonfiction.

Srodes: Ibid.

Junger: *The Perfect Storm* by Sebastian Junger.

Franklin: Quoted in "Tom Wolfe's Revenge" by Chris Harvey, *American Journalism Review,* October 16, 1994.

Stewart: *Follow the Story* by James B. Stewart.

Chapter 6

Opening quote: *The Columbia World of Quotations* (1996).

Sheed: *New York Review of Books,* October 27, 1988.

Galassi: Interview with Peter Rubie, fall 2002.

Spicer: Quoted in *How to Write and Sell True Crime* by Gary Provost.

Olsen: Quoted ibid.

Powers: Review of *Bush at War* by Bob Woodward, *New York Times Book Review,* December 15, 2002.

Fry: Quoted in "Tom Wolfe's Revenge" by Chris Harvey, *American Journalism Review,* October 16, 1994.

Woodward: Quoted ibid.

Hart: "Ethics of Narrative Nonfiction," roundtable, reported by *Editor & Publisher,* November 28, 1998, confirmed in an interview in fall 2002 with Rubie.

Gethers: Interview with Peter Rubie, fall 2002.

Seligman: *Salon.com,* February 29, 2000.

Cahill: "The Age of Creative Nonfiction," *nidus* Roundtable Discussion, 2001 (http://www.pitt.edu/~nidus/archives/fall2001/rt1.html).

Gutkind: Ibid.

Chapter 7

Opening quote 1: *The Columbia World of Quotations* (1996).

Opening quote 2: *Writing the Breakout Novel* by Donald Maass.

. . . the . . .

Chapter 8

Opening quote 1: *The Guardian* (London), June 21, 1990.
Opening quote 2:: *The Columbia World of Quotations* (1996).
Van Straaten: *Publishers Weekly,* November 19, 2001.
Warren: Q&A for Rubie, fall 2002.

Chapter 9

Opening quote: *The Guardian* (London), April 21, 2001.
Srodes: Washington Independent Writers conference, May 17–18, 2002, Washington, D.C., National Press Club taped roundtable on narrative nonfiction.
Cahill: "The Age of Creative Nonfiction," *nidus* Roundtable Discussion, 2001 (http://www.pitt.edu/~nidus/archives/fall2001/rt1.html).

A HIGHLY OPINIONATED AND TOTALLY SUBJECTIVE READING LIST

● ● ● ● ● ● ● ● ● ● ● ● ● ● ● ● ● ● ● ●

Okay, no one expects you to read all these books. However, if you're looking for a place to start to figure out what's good to read, and potential models to use for your book, this is a pretty decent place.

All the President's Men by Bob Woodward and Carl Bernstein
Allen Dulles: Master of Spies and *Franklin: The Essential Founding
    Father* by Jim Srodes
Angela's Ashes by Frank McCourt
The Arcanum by Janet Gleeson
Autobiography of a Face by Lucy Grealy
*Band of Brothers: E Company, 506th Regiment, 101st Airborne from
    Normandy to Hitler's Eagle's Nest* by Stephen E. Ambrose
Barbarians at the Gate by Bryan Burrough and John Helyar
The Best and the Brightest by David Halberstam
Black Hawk Down by Mark Bowden
Borrowed Finery by Paula Fox
A Bright and Shining Lie by Neil Sheehan

Cinderella & Company: Backstage at the Opera with Cecilia Bartoli by
    Manuela Hoelterhoff

A Civil Action by Jonathan Harr

Common Ground by J. Anthony Lukas

Communion by Whitley Strieber

Dead Certainties by Simon Schama

Den of Thieves by James B. Stewart

Dispatches by Michael Herr

The Diving Bell and the Butterfly: A Memoir of Life in Death by Jean-
    Dominique Bauby

Eleanor of Aquitaine: A Life by Alison Weir

The Executioner's Song by Norman Mailer

Fatal Vision by Joe McGinniss

Fermat's Enigma by Simon Singh

Fermat's Last Theorem by Amir D. Aczel

Fingerprints by Colin Beavan

The Founding Fish by John McPhee and *The John McPhee Reader*, edited
    by William Howarth

Greed and Glory on Wall Street by Ken Auletta

Heart So Hungry by Randall Silvis

A Heartbreaking Work of Staggering Genius by Dave Eggers

The Hot Zone by Richard Preston

House; The Soul of a New Machine; Among Schoolchildren by Tracy Kidder

In Cold Blood by Truman Capote

Indecent Exposure by David McClintick

The Informant: A True Story by Kurt Eichenwald

Into Thin Air by Jon Krakauer

John Adams by David McCullough

The Killer Angels by Michael Shaara

The Kiss by Kathryn Harrison

Kon-Tiki by Thor Heyerdahl

Last Man Down by Richard Picciotto

Longitude, by Dava Sobel

Low Life by Luc Sante

Lucky by Alice Sebold

Max Perkins: Editor of Genius by A. Scott Berg

Midnight in the Garden of Good and Evil by John Berendt

A Murder by Greg Fallis

Nickel and Dimed: On (Not) Getting By in America by Barbara Ehrenreich

No One Left Behind by Amy Yarsinske

Our Story: 77 Hours That Tested Our Friendship and Our Faith by Jeff
    Goodell (editor) and the Quecreek Miners

Paper Lion: Confessions of a Last-String Quarterback by George Plimpton

Paula by Isabelle Allende

The Perfect Storm by Sebastian Junger

The Professor and the Madman by Simon Winchester

The Rape of Nanking by Iris Chang

Riding the Iron Rooster by Paul Theroux

The Right Stuff by Tom Wolfe

Rivers of Blood, Years of Darkness by Robert Conot

Schindler's List by Thomas Keneally

Silent Spring by Rachel Carson

Sleepers by Lorenzo Carcaterra

Small Sacrifices by Anne Rule

South by Ernest Shackleton

Sputnik: The Shock of the Century by Paul Dickson

Spy: The Inside Story of How the FBI's Robert Hanssen Betrayed America
    by David Wise

A Trial by Jury by D. Graham Burnett

Under the Tuscan Sun by Frances Mayes

The Von Bulow Affair by William Wright

Walking the Bible by Bruce S. Feiler

A Year in Provence by Peter Mayle

INDEX

· · · · · · · · · · · · · · · · · · · ·

. . . the . . .